"SUNSET" COX

IRREPRESSIBLE DEMOCRAT

Yours Sincerely
S. S. Cox

"SUNSET" COX
Irrepressible Democrat

by DAVID LINDSEY
Associate Professor of History
Los Angeles State College
of Applied Arts and Sciences

DETROIT • WAYNE STATE UNIVERSITY PRESS • 1959

Library of Congress
Catalog Card Number
59–9324

Wayne State University Press
Detroit 2, Michigan

to *A. L. L. and D. S. L.*

FOREWORD

The job of Congressman in the American scheme of government is a large and exacting one. The Congressman is called upon to attend to countless details on behalf of his district and his home constituents. He must inform himself upon problems and matters of policy so that he can reach intelligent and wise decisions on the committees on which he serves. He must constantly weigh the demands of his constituents, the interests of the nation as a whole, and the leadings of his own conscience in the intricate process of formulating judgments and making decisions.

In order to perform these functions well, the Congressman must possess energy, vitality, intelligence, alertness, personal tact, and good humor. He must be willing to contend for what he believes to be the proper course; yet at the same time he must also be conscious of the needs and demands of others, which may require a modification of his views and actions in reaching a workable compromise in the best interests of the entire country. This requires infinite patience, tolerance, respect for others, fairness and self-restraint—a rare combination, but one usually found in the effective political leader.

Too little time, effort, and devotion have been given to those men of our country who have contributed to making it great. One of these men who gave of his time and devoted himself unselfishly to mankind was Samuel S. Cox, one of the earlier members of Congress. I am pleased to write a few words in commemoration of his life and his untiring efforts to keep the United States united and strong.

Samuel Sullivan Cox, better known as " Sunset " Cox, was a man of many talents. He was owner and editor of the Columbus (Ohio) *Statesman* in 1853 and 1854; was appointed Secretary of Legation to Peru in 1854; was author of several works and a constant contributor to the press and periodicals. During the crisis-laden winter of 1860-61, he worked strenuously to develop a formula that would hold the Union together.

As a Democrat, Cox was elected to the United States House of Representatives from the Columbus, Ohio district to the Thirty-fifth, Thirty-sixth, Thirty-seventh, and Thirty-eighth Congresses (March 4, 1857—March 3, 1865). Gerrymandered out of his position by a hostile Republican legislature in Ohio in 1865, he moved to New York City, was elected again to the House of Representatives in 1868 and served regularly (with but two brief breaks) until his death in 1889.

Samuel Sullivan Cox truly served his day and generation and devoted his life to the service of his country.

Sam Rayburn
Speaker, United States House of
Representatives

Washington, D. C.
January 1959

PREFACE

This book grew out of a curiosity about why mid-nineteenth century Americans took up arms against each other in the Civil War. My first concern was to discover why otherwise peaceful Americans, who for generations had settled their differences by discussion, accommodation, and compromise, resorted to violence in 1861. This concern led me to investigate the career of Samuel Sullivan Cox, a political leader, who sought by reason and persuasion to bring his fellow Americans to adjust their conflicts peacefully. Even during the Civil War and for the subsequent quarter century, his work as a practicing politician was directed toward a reasonable conciliation and adjustment of interests.

In the following pages, quotations from Cox and other nineteenth century sources retain the capitalization, spelling, and grammatical construction of the original material.

I extend here my warm thanks to my professors, friends, colleagues, and associates who gave aid in the preparation of this study. Their many kindnesses can be returned only in small measure by words of thanks. Especially, I thank the following University of Chicago professors: Avery O. Craven, whose verbal artistry and contagious enthusiasm have stimulated a generation of students and who gave me wise counsel and encouragement at every step of my way;

William T. Hutchinson, scholar and teacher, and Walter Johnson, friend and counselor, both of whom made many valuable critical comments; and Louis Gottschalk, who initiated me into the intricacies of historical research. My gratitude extends also to the University of Chicago for a fellowship, which enabled me to pursue my research, and to Baldwin-Wallace College for a year's relief from teaching duties.

Further, my friend and former student, Lee Templeton, who first brought " Sunset " Cox to my attention, Professor Homer C. Hockett, who helped in the early stages, and Professor Allan Nevins, whose reading of the manuscript and encouraging words were most helpful, are heartily thanked.

I acknowledge, too, my debt to the following persons, who were generous with their time in helping me with this study: Professor Harry Ridenour of Baldwin-Wallace College; Clark Williams and the late Professor Thomas Hoover of Ohio University; Norris Schneider, Mrs. Lydia Taylor, Mrs. James Bailey, Eleanore Baily Johnson, all of Zanesville, Ohio; Laurence Cox of Floral City, Florida; Mrs. Theodore S. Cox of Williamsburg, Virginia; the late Abram Garfield of Cleveland; Gilbert Grosvenor of Washington; and William Timbers of Darien, Connecticut.

Librarians and staff members of the following institutions cheerfully smoothed my path by making research materials readily available: the University of Chicago Library; the Manuscripts Division of the Library of Congress; the New York Public Library; the Baldwin-Wallace College Library, especially its ever-helpful librarian, Clyde Haselden; Cleveland Public Library; Oberlin College Library; Ohio State University Library; Ohio University Library; Zanesville Public Library; and Cooper Union Library. The following historical societies, their directors and staffs, also gave generous assistance: Ohio Historical Society, especially James Rodabaugh; Hayes Memorial Library, especially Watt P. Marchman; Historical and Philosophical Society of Ohio; New York Historical Society; Western Reserve Historical Society; Historical Society of Pennsylvania; and Wisconsin State Historical Society. The National Association of Letter Carriers through its national secretary, Jerome J. Keating, the Market Street Baptist Church of Zanesville, the Parke-Bernet Galleries, and the Carnegie Book Shop of New York gave aid on specific points.

Finally, to Director Harold A. Basilius and others of the Wayne State University Press, who have guided the manuscript through the editorial maze to final type, my sincere thanks.

D. L.

Claremont, California

CONTENTS

INTRODUCTION

On December 16, 1857, the national House of Representatives convened for the first time in its newly-finished hall in the south wing of the nation's Capitol. For the first time, too, it listened to the powerful voice of Samuel Sullivan Cox, the thirty-three-year-old representative from Ohio. Older members, expecting the customary platitudes of another maiden speech, settled back in their chairs. But not for long, for the gentleman from Ohio was saying things that no freshman member had any business saying. He was defying the President of the United States and the leaders of the party he had helped to elect.

A little more than thirty years later, on January 15, 1889, Samuel Sullivan Cox, now representing a New York City district and approaching the end of his long career, delivered in the same hall what was to be virtually his last political utterance. Once again congressmen were surprised to hear him seek to persuade his party on the same subject he had discussed over thirty years before—freedom of choice by the citizens of a territory of the United States. In the 1857 speech the question that Cox argued was one of crucial importance to the country. By 1889, however, the question had dwindled to relative insignificance.

What had happened in the meantime to reduce the importance of the territorial question in the eyes of the country is an incidental concern of this inquiry. The principal aim of this study is to trace the political career of Samuel Sullivan Cox in an effort to understand a representative nineteenth-century politician. Cox was a politician of prominence and importance in his day, but his figure and the importance of his work have been obscured in the constant reshuffling of historical evidence.

This study will examine Cox's career against the background of the changing American political scene from the middle of the nineteenth century until his death in 1889. It will inquire into the major political developments of the three-decade interval but will focus particular attention on the role played by Cox in American politics, the manner in which he wrestled with the leading issues of his age, the solutions that he offered, the means that he used to implement his solutions, the interests that he represented, and the successes and failures that he experienced in dealing with the problems of his day.

From his first election to Congress in 1856 until 1889, he was a nationally recognized leader of the Democratic party, serving almost continuously as a representative, first from Ohio and then from New York. During the period of his active political career, the United States underwent a series of rapid and remarkable political, economic, and social changes. The United States of the 1850's was still in its early adolescence. "Young America" was an apt description as well as a rallying cry. American boundaries since 1840 had leaped over plains, mountains, and deserts to the Pacific shore, and by 1860 the country encompassed thirty-four states and more than thirty-one million people. In the fifties, the physical resources of the country were just beginning to be tapped on a large scale while the vast mineral and timber areas were virtually untouched, and technology and invention were still new forces. The incipient industrial revolution had affected only the relatively small Northeastern corner of the country. Agriculture was master in the rest of the nation with commerce its handmaiden. Railroads, which had appeared a score of years earlier, were just beginning to tie the Midwestern prairies to the Atlantic seaboard.

The people were predominantly rural in residence, Protestant in religion, and Northern European in extraction, with the execption of some four million Negroes in the South. In the late forties and early fifties, a heavy influx of German and Catholic-Irish immigrants swelled the population of Eastern and Midwestern cities.

Politically, the nation was, as usual, in turmoil. The Polk Administration, after its blanket settlement of the tariff, banking, and internal improvement questions, was beginning to feel the pressures that arose from the very territory Polk had acquired. The Whig party, disintegrating under the shock generated by the political crisis of 1850, staggered through the 1852 presidential election, while the nativist issue sired the American party. More important was the appearance of the sectional Republican party in the mid-fifties, which insisted upon pushing the issue of slavery into politics as a moral question. The Democratic party, chafing under an ineffectual, jealous leadership, was ready to break into hostile factions. Indeed, in the late fifties the danger was more than apparent that democratic government itself might not survive the forcing of a moral issue that did not lend itself to political discussion and compromise.

By the late 1880's the picture had changed. Population had more than doubled. The number of states had increased to forty-two. The region between the Missouri River and the Pacific had attracted settlers in such substantial numbers that, in the census of 1890, an American frontier line was no longer recognized. National wealth had jumped from eleven billion dollars in 1855 to sixty-five billion dollars in 1890, while national income had grown from four billion to nine and a half billion dollars in the same period. Natural resources, especially iron, coal, oil, and timber, were being exploited at a breath-taking rate. Manufacturing had become a primary industry. The business man had taken economic leadership away from the merchant and the farmer. Railroads, only pigmies at mid-century, had become transcontinental giants, while huge industrial combinations posed new and trying problems for the country. Although the population still contained a majority of Protestant Northern Europeans, immigrants from Southern and Eastern Europe, mainly Catholic, were pouring in at the rate of half a million a year.

The political stage also presented an entirely different cast. Engendered by the moral reform drive of the fifties, the Republican party pushed for slavery restriction and extinction. The slavery issue evaporated in the Civil War explosion and was replaced by newer issues of currency, tariff, civil service reform, railroad regulation, and control of trusts. In managing the Civil War, the Republican party shed its armor of moral reform and enacted a sweeping economic program by providing a national banking system, a high protective tariff, large land grants to railroads, and a liberal immigration policy. Such a program was largely a political reflection of the country's economic transformation. Reaching westward to incorporate the economic interests of the rapidly industrializing Old Northwest, the Northeastern section, through its control of industry and capital, became economically dominant over both the South and the West. Along with the growth of large-scale business enterprise went a centralizing trend toward giving the national government supreme power in many fields, a trend accelerated by the Civil War. More and more, men were turning to the central government for aid in solving problems which the industrial revolution had thrust upon them and which they found themselves unable to solve alone. The Democratic party, after its severe decline during and immediately following the Civil War, had recovered much of its political muscle by the early eighties and was able to battle on practically even terms with the Republicans, who had monopolized the White House for a quarter of a century.

In the midst of these kaleidoscopic changes, Samuel Sullivan Cox played an active and brilliant part. As an opposition party leader, he performed a three-fold function: he served to check the extremes and excesses of the party in power, to keep it honest and effective, and to prevent its running rough-shod over helpless minorities; he offered an alternative course of political action, which, when failing of actual adoption, often forced the party in power to accept an agreeable compromise; and he aimed to prepare himself and his party to assume political power when the opportunity arrived, as it did in 1885 with Grover Cleveland's inauguration as President.

In the years preceding the Civil War, Cox tried to make men see that forcing the moral issue of slavery toward a political showdown would endanger the Union, and he sought to arrange adjustments that would keep the sections in peace, if not in full harmony. During the Civil War, his efforts were directed toward effecting a rapid conclusion of the war before war-born bitterness cut too deep and while conciliation of the sections within the Union might still be possible. He fought to preserve constitutional, democratic government against the menace of an all-absorbing central government under a power-laden executive that threatened not only the rights of states but the liberties of individual citizens as well. He strove to preserve the agricultural-commercial order of the mid-nineteenth century against the increasing radical inroads of industrialism.

In the years following the war he aimed to lessen sectional animosities and to restore the Southern states as quickly as possible to their proper place in the Union. While taking steps to rid the Democratic party of its pro-slavery stigma, he tried to restore its power by allying the commercial and laboring elements of the Northeast with the agricultural elements of the Midwest and the South. He opposed the Republican economic program which embodied high tariffs, federal grants to private corporations, and privileged banking. Instead, he urged freedom of trade, freedom of individual enterprise, as in banking and shipping, and a revival of the agricultural-commercial economic order of the pre-1860 days. Recognizing, but baffled by, the powerful forces of the new industrial age, he was willing, where necessary, to use the power of the national government to restrain the resulting abuses. He stood for hard money, based on gold and silver, and strenuously opposed efforts toward inflation through large issues of paper money. He called upon the United States to play a larger role in world affairs, especially in the Western Hemisphere in regard to Mexico, Cuba, and Panama. He supported reform in the civil service, enlargement of the census, the establishment of a United States Lifesaving Service, and aid to underprivileged groups, such as newly-arrived immigrants and underpaid, overworked letter carriers.

In an age not noted for high moral standards among politicians, he stood well above his fellows and was held in high esteem by his associates, Democrat and Republican alike.

This book is directed toward elucidating and understanding the career of a man who hitched his wagon to a sunset.

one

SUNRISE:
THE EARLY YEARS, 1824—1860

1

YEARS OF PREPARATION
1824–1857

FAMILY: A MODERATE BACKGROUND

The Cox heritage was American of the middle-states variety, a blending of diverse national, religious, and cultural elements. The father, Ezekiel T. Cox, had caught the " Ohio fever " following the War of 1812. Abandoning his job as state printer in New Jersey and lugging his Ramage printing press with him on the long trip across the mountains, he settled at Zanesville, then Ohio's second largest town. In a short time he had built a paper mill and was proprietor-editor of the *Muskingum Messenger*, soon to become the leading Jackson paper in the area.[1] Political rewards followed: he became clerk of the county court and of the state supreme court, state senator, and eventually United States marshal.[2]

The man who persuaded Cox to settle in Zanesville, Samuel Sullivan, had himself arrived there several years before from Delaware. Originally a migrant potter, who had switched allegiance from the Roman Catholic to the Baptist Church, he was now a successful ceramicist. In 1816 he was elected county judge, and later served as Ohio senator, as state treasurer, and as Zanesville postmaster. By 1822 Judge Sullivan had acquired Ezekiel Cox not only as clerk of his court but also as his son-in-law. On September 30, 1824, he acquired a grandson and namesake—Samuel Sullivan Cox.[3]

During Sam Cox's boyhood, Zanesville was rapidly emerging from frontier conditions into a stable community which promised to become a major center of industry and commerce. Although sixty miles up the Muskingum River from the Ohio, it considered itself a port, while its location at the junction of the National Road and Zane's Trace made it a busy trading center. Nevertheless, it was losing out in the commercial race since the Ohio Canal had been located in the Scioto Valley, forty miles to the west. Its people were mainly of middle-states origin, Pennsylvanians predominating, with a sprinkling of upland Virginians.[4]

Sam Cox regularly attended Sunday School at the Market Street Baptist Church, where the senior Cox served as deacon and trustee.[5] At the town academy Sam studied Greek and Latin under Professor Howe, who was the butt of some of his boyish pranks. Brown-haired and brown-eyed, Sam was an eager, quick, inquisitive, youngster, small in stature but precocious. By the age of seven, Cox had won the nickname of " Captain " and impressed his friends with his " marvelous " memory. One schoolmate later recalled that Cox " easily committed to memory the entire book of Romans, and . . . knew the old thirty-ninth volume of the Ohio laws by heart." With his grandfather serving as local postmaster and his uncle editing a Democratic newspaper, he easily acquired the knack of political debate and became ambitious for public office. At the age of eleven he was working with his father at the courthouse. At fourteen he was appointed deputy clerk of court and "could draw up any pleading without consulting Chitty." [6]

EDUCATION: AMONG THE YANKEES

At sixteen Samuel Cox entered Ohio University's preparatory school at Athens. The scanty records show that his studies included courses in geography, algebra, natural science, Greek, Latin, and moral philosophy.[7] Always interested in art, he drew a large mural of the Laocoön group flanked by two Greek gods on the wall of his dormitory room in West College Hall, now McGuffey Hall.[8] He began writing for the town weekly, "sometimes poetry and sometimes prose." His growing interest in politics was apparent in a letter he wrote home, asking his Democratic grandfather to "contribute to the youthful aspirations of a young Democrat like me" by sending "me Duff Green's newspaper . . . 'The Free Trader'. . . . Oh, but he is a scorcher, he lashes with no uncommon virulence." [9]

Cox expressed his intellectual independence in another note: "I would not care three straws for how I dressed, what I eat or drink, provided I could revel sufficiently in my own thoughts." [10] In the Athenian Literary Society, of which he was secretary and president at various times between 1841 and 1844, he found a training ground for his talent in public speaking and debate. Here with fellow students, like Robert Woodrow (uncle of future President Woodrow Wilson), he discussed such current questions as the annexation of Texas, temperance, slavery and abolition, woman suffrage, and free trade. In these student discussions he doubtless formulated many views which he later expressed

on the floor of Congress.[11]   Internal difficulties at Ohio
University under the administration of President William H.
McGuffey of *Reader* fame probably contributed to Cox's
decision to withdraw.   In 1844 he wrote to his father,
expressing his desire to attend an Eastern institution.

> I am resolved to get an education, and I don't want to do
> it half, if you only encourage me and assist me by your means.
> The education is for life . . . it is, too, the means of life; and
> these means will be great in proportion to the education. . . .
> Will you not give me the right encouragement? I know you
> will. Some fathers, I know, would glory in having their lazy,
> hanging-around, doing-nothing sons go to college, even should
> they go through as a drag and come out as asses.[12]

The father agreed to supply " the right encouragement,"
for in the spring of 1844 Cox transferred to Brown University. A short time after his arrival there he was writing the
perennial plea of the college student to parents: " The
expense here will cost me more than I anticipated. . . . The
money ($7.50) I now have will barely suffice to pay my
washerwoman and other expenses at the close of the term."
These years in Providence prepared him for his future public
life. He was active in his social fraternity, Delta Phi.[13] He
was fascinated with the political economy courses under the
noted Professor Francis Wayland, who later called Cox not
only " a pronounced political partisan . . . always on the
stump," but also " the most prominent member of his class,"
even before the end of his first year at Brown. Wayland
exercised a large influence on Cox, who later credited the
professor with providing " the secret of my doing so much
work." The secret, he said, lay in the process of thought
analysis: " We were trained to think analytically " so that
" in making a speech . . . I can see the end before I begin "
and in writing " I made a skeleton before I wrote a chapter."

Cox's later free trade ideas seem to have stemmed directly from Wayland's instruction.[14]

Speaking and debating came naturally to Cox. He was affected by the reform spirit of the age, embodied in movements for universal peace, woman's rights, prison reform, temperance, utopian socialism, greater public participation in politics, and the abolition of slavery. In his rhetoric class he delivered a speech on Fourierism that brought a rebuke from the professor on subject matter but praise on manner of delivery. Cox also joined the temperance crusade, recording that he had taken the pledge himself and had made numerous speeches on the subject. The imprisonment of the amazing Thomas Dorr, leader of a vociferous popular uprising in Rhode Island, aroused Cox to address a large protest meeting in the Providence streets. But for abolition he had no sympathy, and when Wendell Phillips spoke at Brown, he joined with other students in hissing Phillips and delivered an anti-abolitionist harangue himself.[15]

Not only did he develop an effective "free and easy, Western stump-speech manner," but his writing brought him college prizes and checks from *Knickerbocker Magazine*, which published some of his work.[16] He was never quite sure whether he liked or trusted New England Yankees, but apparently he concealed his doubts. A fellow student, James B. Angell, later president of the University of Michigan, noted Cox's "attractive social qualities," which made him " a great favorite in college." His natural bent for joking and good humor caused his classmates to remark that " he was cheerful, bubbling over with fun " and laughter " about all the time." But underneath lay a seriousness of purpose, a determination to succeed, and a capacity for hard work. After graduating with honors, he left Providence in the summer of 1846 and returned to Ohio.

TRAVEL: *A Buckeye Abroad*

Settling down to the study of law in Zanesville, Cox renewed his acquaintance with Julia Ann Buckingham, daughter of a prominent Zanesville merchant, whom he had met several years earlier on a stage-coach trip to the East. Eighteen months after their wedding in October 1849, he and his bride embarked upon a belated honeymoon tour of Europe.[17] They travelled through England, France, Germany, Switzerland to Rome, Naples, Venice, Sicily, Athens, Constantinople, and Smyrna, a journey which, for a Midwesterner of the mid-nineteenth century, was unusual, and Cox lost no time in capitalizing on it. His recorded impressions appeared in an entertaining volume, *A Buckeye Abroad*, published by G. P. Putnam in 1852. The book achieved considerable popularity, running through eight editions by 1860 and winning for Cox something of a name in the literary world.

The European excursion provided four advantages for Cox, now twenty-seven: (1) it broadened his horizons, giving him perspective to view events in his own country with perhaps less passion than many of his contemporaries; (2) it reinforced his confidence in his verbal ability to reach the public; (3) it gave him popular acclaim as a writer, which may have dictated his later decision to enter the newspaper business; and (4) it put his name before the people of Ohio, an advantage for a man with political ambitions.

THE LAW: AN INDIFFERENT ATTORNEY

The legal profession was the customary means of entry into politics, and Cox followed the familiar course. His acquaintance with the law was of long standing, going back to his early teen-years as deputy clerk of Muskingum County court. After his return from Brown he began his legal study in earnest and quickly won admission to the bar. Shortly after his European trip he moved to Cincinnati where he formed a law partnership with George E. Pugh, later United States senator from Ohio. Cincinnati at that time was teeming with promising young attorneys, such as Salmon P. Chase, George H. Pendleton, Rutherford B. Hayes, and Stanley Matthews.

Even while practicing law, Cox retained his interest in scholarly and literary pursuits. On August 3, 1852, he delivered an address on " The Scholar as the True Progressive and Conservative " to his old literary society at Ohio University. He cited Hugo Grotius and his work in international law as the prime example of the scholar as the true agent of progress and urged his student listeners toward this ideal, for, he said, " America must become the theatre of international thoughts." [18] The next year he negotiated with publisher George Putnam regarding a magazine article on President Franklin Pierce and a new edition of his own book.[19] After two years of rather desultory legal practice in which he showed little interest, Cox determined to launch into a more exciting, if less stable, enterprise.

JOURNALISM: FORTUNE IN A SUNSET

By January 1853 Cox had moved to Columbus and had taken up residence in " an unpretentious cottage " on Town Street between Sixth and Grant.[20] He purchased a part interest in the state's official Democratic organ, the *Ohio Statesman*. The co-owner was James H. Smith, son-in-law of the newspaper's founder, Samuel Medary, who had operated the enterprise since the days of Andrew Jackson. Cox's literary talent needed only the opportunity to express itself, and the opportunity was not long in coming. On May 19, 1853, the front page of the *Statesman* featured a story that captured the attention of its readers and gave editor Cox a personal label for the rest of his life. Under the title of " A Great Old Sunset," Cox exulted:

> What a stormful sunset was that of last night! We do not remember ever to have seen the like on the round globe. The scene opened in the west, with the whole horizon full of golden, impenetrating lustre, which colored the foliage and brightened every object with its own rich dyes. The colors grew deeper and richer, until the golden lustre was transformed into a storm-cloud, full of finest lightning, which leaped in dazzling zigzags all around and over the city. The wind rose with fury . . . and quaint trees made obeisance to its majesty . . . thunder roared grandly, and the fire-bells caught the excitement and rung with hasty chorus. . . . The west all at once brightened up in a long polished belt of azure, worthy of a Sicilian sky. Presently a cloud appeared in the azure belt, in the form of a castellated city. . . . The sun, wearied of the elemental commotion, sank behind the green plains of the west. . . . The rich flush of the unearthly light had passed and the rains ceased; then the solemn church bells pealed; the laughter of the children, out in the air, joyous after the storm, is heard . . . while the forked and purple weapon of the skies still darted illumination around the Starling College. . . . Candles are lighted. The piano strikes up. We feel that it is good to have a home—good to be on the earth where such revelations of beauty and power may be made. And as we cannot refrain from reminding our readers of everything wonderful in our city, we have begun and ended our feeble etching of a sunset which comes so rarely, that its glory should be committed to immortal type.[21]

The twenty-nine-year-old editor had captured in words an experience known to each of his readers. Thereafter he was known as " Sunset " Cox, a nickname coined in derision

by a rival editor.[22] But the catchy nickname, exactly fitting
his initials, proved to be an asset to a man bent on a career
in politics. Having by this time become a member of the
Democratic State Central Committee, Cox soon succeeded
to the chairmanship and plunged into the anxiety and turmoil
of Ohio politics.[23]

BUCKEYE POLITICS IN THE FIFTIES

The geographic origin of Ohio settlers, whether New
England, Pennsylvania, or upland South, tended to provide
differences in political orientation, but the variations and
exceptions were numerous. By 1850 European immigrants,
unknown in Ohio earlier, formed an appreciable part of the
state's 1,980,000 people. Although the immigrants were
unevenly distributed throughout Ohio, a third of them,
largely German, lived in Cincinnati, and the rest were
largely Irish who lived in the Lake Erie counties and along
the canal routes. By 1860 the population had grown to
2,239,000, including 112,000 foreign born and 39,000
Negroes.[25]

By mid-century, Ohio's economy had moved far from its
frontier beginnings. Its total property, valued in 1850 at
three-quarters of a billion dollars, had doubled in the following ten years, and Ohio became third among the states in
wealth as well as in population. Still primarily agricultural,
Ohio ranked first in the production of corn, second in wheat,
first in sheep, with cattle and hogs important. Cincinnati
was still a " porkopolis." With a surplus of farm products
there was a need for outlets larger than those offered by the
National Road, the Ohio River, and the Ohio and Erie
canals. Railroads, which were fanning out across the state,
were designed to meet this need and to tie the state more

11

closely to the East. Industry had already made a beginning with iron and coal production in the Southeast, while agriculture had centered at Cincinnati. By 1850 Ohio was the most mature part of the older Middle West.[26]

Mid-century Ohioans held a number of basic beliefs, labelled by Professor Ralph Gabriel as the belief in progress, the free individual, fundamental moral law, and a sense of mission.[27] Progress called for a greater exertion of human energy to make the world better. The free individual meant private economic initiative and popular participation in politics. But all activity had to conform to God's moral law and to the United States Constitution. Since American institutions were the best possible, naturally their benefits should be extended beyond national borders, for progress demanded American expansion. Although the Jeffersonian egalitarian tradition was widely accepted, exceptions existed. The Negro, as the Ohio Constitutional Convention of 1851 decreed, was not entitled to suffrage or to full civil rights. Finally, a distinctly Western attitude arose, glorifying the West as a section with interests of its own in better transportation, in increased manufactures, in larger foreign markets, and in the fulfillment of its own destiny. Although the West thought of itself as distinct from the East and the South, it retained the Jacksonian belief in the inviolability of the Union.[28]

Economic, social, and cultural forces throughout the forties engendered sectional animosities that created trouble in the following decade. Western and Southern groups had pushed expansion to the Pacific and the adoption of the Walker Tariff of 1846 had modified protection. But Westerners felt that *they* particularly had been sold out when Polk failed to acquire all of Oregon, vetoed river and harbor improvements in the Great Lakes area, and stymied adoption of a homestead bill. A rift was beginning in the Democratic party that would disrupt the Union by 1861.

The slavery issue, which had but a few years earlier gained respectability in political circles, was now seized upon by some Westerners to vent their dissatisfaction over sectional disappointments. They responded with the Wilmot Proviso, which aimed at barring slavery from territory acquired from Mexico. They also formed the Free Soil party, which urged the end of slavery in all territories and which in 1848 won considerable support from many former Democrats. The Compromise of 1850, by admitting California as a free state, upset the balance of free and slave states in the Senate, the very effect that the South had feared for years. A shift in location of political power was clearly in the making. Although the Whig party controlled the White House at mid-century, the next few years saw its final disintegration.

In the fluidity and turmoil of Ohio politics the Whigs generally included such groups as the larger farmers, incipient manufacturers, bankers, and canal and railroad promoters who hoped for government aid. Their greatest strength lay in the northern and eastern parts of the state. Fun-loving Thomas Corwin, gentlemanly Thomas Ewing, and " bluff " Benjamin F. Wade provided their leadership. Among the Democrats, small farmers, merchants, artisans, laborers on the canals and railroads, recent German and Irish immigrants, and free traders were the major components.

By the late forties the new Free Soil party in Ohio, having drained off discontented Democrats like Jacob Brinkerhoff and antislavery Whigs like Joshua Giddings, combined with the regular Democrats to send political newcomer Salmon P. Chase to the Senate in 1849. In 1850 a Democratic resurgence was under way while the Whigs were slipping back. The Compromise of 1850 further undermined the

Whigs, who failed in 1850 to win either the governorship or a majority of the delegates to the state constitutional convention.[29]

Despite these gains, the Democratic organization encountered internal difficulties. Antislavery radicals, calling themselves " Free Democrats," refused to support the regular gubernatorial nominee in 1851. But their leader, Chase, was soon wooing the Democratic party, hoping to convert it into a full-fledged antislavery combination and to insure his own re-election to the Senate. He was rebuffed by the Democrats, who were suffering factional friction, due mainly to conflicting personalities and rivalry over patronage. Samuel Medary of the " Young America "-Douglas wing of the party was feuding with ex-Senator William (" Fog Horn ") Allen, whose presidential aspirations Medary successfully blocked in 1852. Although Democrat Franklin Pierce carried Ohio in the 1852 presidential contest, his margin was a slim 17,000 votes. The Democratic State Convention of January 1853 was expected to determine whether party wounds could be healed.

THE OHIO DEMOCRATS

It was at this juncture that Cox entered the political picture. He had taken over the *Ohio Statesman*, the official state Democratic organ, from Medary in the interest of party harmony. As a member of the State Central Committee, he had his first close contact with party politics, and at the January convention, he witnessed a compromise, shrewdly calculated to give each faction a prize. The Medary platform, calling for stricter state banking laws, was adopted, but the nomination for governor went to the Allen-backed candidate, William Medill. As a newcomer to party councils without enemies in either camp, Cox was assigned the task of managing Medill's campaign. The gratifying result of his efforts was a Democratic victory by an 11,000-vote majority.[30]

This triumph brought him new prestige in the party and an offer from President Pierce of the secretaryship of the London legation.[31] He declined the offer, preferring the Ohio stump to the English drawing room. When he was confirmed as permanent chairman of the state committee in January 1854, he faced another intra-party row over the selection of a candidate for Chase's Senate seat. Allen, Medary, Pugh, and George Manypenny, newly appointed commissioner of Indian Affairs, all aspired. For two months the battle raged. Due to Cox's political finesse, the choice finally settled on George Pugh, his former law partner.[32]

The year 1854 brought more trouble to the reigning Democratic party in Ohio. Douglas's Kansas-Nebraska bill, providing popular choice of slavery in the new territories, caused further division of the Democrats and raised an opposition party that soon controlled the state. Cox, enthusiastic over the popular sovereignty idea, wrote Douglas, to whom he had already received " a passing introduction." Cox declared: " I have kept up the fight for you. . . . You have made cords of friends here. . . . We can today whip the Whigs and Abolitionists clean out." [33] This was an over-optimistic appraisal of the situation, as events proved. Chase's shrewd " Appeal of the Independent Democrats " aroused old-line Whigs and antislavery men against the repeal of the Missouri Compromise.[34] There were anti-Nebraska protest meetings throughout the state. The Democrats, bewildered at first, lined up slowly in support of the Douglas measure when the *Ohio Statesman*, the Cleveland

Plain Dealer, and the Cincinnati *Enquirer* stressed the democratic principle of popular sovereignty.

The opposition formed swiftly. A statewide convention at Columbus in July brought together Free Democrats, Whigs, Abolitionists, and disgruntled party men of various stripes. Here was an opportunity to express disappointments, frustrations, and resentments which had been simmering since the days of Polk. Resolutions opposed further increase of slave territory and denounced as " inoperative and void " that part of the Kansas-Nebraska Act which repealed the Missouri Compromise's slavery restrictions.[35] A political revolution was under way even while the Ohio revolutionists argued over calling themselves the " People's Movement," " Anti-Nebraska Movement," " Fusionists," or " Republicans."

The Democrats, discounting the strength of the opposition, were troubled by the strong nativist agitation directed mainly against Irish and German Catholics. With the appearance of the Know-Nothing party, the discontented, whether nativists, Whigs, anti-Nebraska men, or special reformers, were offered a rallying point against the Democrats, who generally attracted the foreign groups.[36]

The combination of internal dissension, anti-Nebraska protest, and nativism spelled Democratic disaster at the polls in 1854. The fusionists captured all of Ohio's twenty-one congressional seats. Ohio Democrats staggered under the shock of this political avalanche. Cox, reappraising his own political fortunes, accepted a second Pierce offer of a diplomatic post—this time as secretary of the legation in Peru. He left Ohio early in 1855, but a fever contracted at Panama forced his return to the United States.[37] While in Washington, he met national Democratic leaders, attended many dinners, and wrote a guest editorial for the administration paper denouncing the Know-Nothings.[38] Back in Ohio in the fall he campaigned vainly for Medill's re-election against the Republican candidate, Chase. With the Republicans firmly in control of the state government, Cox resumed his law practice in Columbus, retaining a small financial interest in the *Statesman*.[39]

COX GOES TO CONGRESS

Having reformed their lines, Ohio Democrats grew more optimistic that the next year would bring success. Several factors worked in their favor. In the Republican ranks, economic conservatives found antislavery radicals uncomfortable associates. The Republican legislature, seeking to please both wings of the party, passed laws exempting banks from taxation, called for repeal of the fugitive slave law, adopted personal liberty laws designed to obstruct recovery of runaway slaves, and re-elected Ben Wade to the Senate.[40] On the other hand, many Know-Nothings were beginning to shed their Republican allegiance.

The Democrats presented an outward appearance of unity, but vacillated between Douglas and Buchanan for the presidential nomination. Medary, in boosting Douglas, called ex-governor Medill " an old clucking hen " for threatening " a day of retribution " for the Ohio Democrats who opposed Buchanan.[41] But after the latter was nominated at Cincinnati on a popular sovereignty platform, the party closed ranks and worked energetically for Buchanan's election. Bitterness marked the campaign oratory in 1856. Democrats were blamed for many things: the disorders of Kansas, which newspapers were rapidly distorting into a " civil war "; the attack by Congressman James P. Brooks, which sent Senator Charles Summer sprawling unconscious on the Senate floor;

and the Southern sympathies of the " doughface " Democratic candidate. In reply, Democrats denounced Republicans as abolition fanatics, disunionists, and proponents of Negro equality.[42] Although Republican John C. Fremont carried Ohio in the election, Buchanan triumphed in the nation at large with only 45 per cent of the popular vote, while Fremont carried all but five of the non-slave states.

In Ohio's congressional contest Democrats regained some of the ground lost two years before. The Twelfth District in mid-state, which consisted of a farming region in Licking, Franklin, and Pickaway counties with Columbus at its center, saw " Sunset " Cox as Democratic candidate.[43] Campaigning on a popular sovereignty platform, Cox attacked his opponent, incumbent Samuel Galloway, for the latter's support of a bill to revive the Missouri Compromise line. He sought Know-Nothing support, on the one hand, by indicating that his position on slavery was the same as theirs. On the other hand, he appealed to the German population by inviting leading Germans from Cincinnati to speak in Columbus.[44]

Passions mounted during the campaign. *Uncle Tom's Cabin*, now dramatized, drew fire from the Democratic press. Declared the *Ohio Statesman*: " To see Uncle Tom performed, the most pious rush to the most disreputable holes, nicknamed theatres. . . ." Fremont meetings were called " nigger meetings." Pugh, Medary, and Congressman Clement L. Vallandigham stumped for " Union, no North, no South, no East, no West. Let the people of each state and territory govern themselves." [45] Cox's opponent charged Cox with favoring Negro equality, citing a passage from *A Buckeye Abroad* as indicative of this view. The election vote was close, but Cox squeaked through to victory with 9,800 ballots to Galloway's 8,500.[46] In all, the Democrats recovered eight of Ohio's twenty-one seats lost in 1854.

2

A FLEDGLING CONGRESSMAN,
1857–1860

KANSAS: PRINCIPLE, PATRONAGE, PARTY
HARMONY

During the 1850's the American people were more preoccupied with politics than with almost any other activity. Even with the 1856 election over, politics were not " adjourned." Local and state party conventions and rallies were held in endless succession. Not all states held elections at the same time. Congressional elections occurred in some states in October or November of the even-numbered years, while other states held them in spring or summer of the odd-numbered years. Added to these were the county, municipal, and other local elections which came at various times during the year. Thus political agitation and discussion were virtually endless. Following the 1856 elections the question of admitting Kansas to the Union as a free or as a slave state attracted the attention of most Americans. Under the provisions of Douglas's Kansas-Nebraska Act the decision was to be made by the Kansas settlers themselves.

The incoming Buchanan Administration realized the difficulties involved in the Kansas issue. Since 1854 the Republicans had been working to bar slavery from the territories of the United States. The struggle on the plains of Kansas had been going on throughout 1856. Free state men were armed with Yankee rifles known familiarly as " Beecher's Bibles "; " border ruffians " raided from Missouri; and John Brown of Ossawatomie murdered Southern settlers. The nation waited to see whether Douglas's scheme for popular sovereignty would result in a new free state or a slave state. President Buchanan approached the Kansas question with characteristic caution. Pondering the implications in the question for his own party, he promised in his inaugural address that the will of the majority would prevail and be respected.

Two days later the Supreme Court delivered the decision that Negro Dred Scott, because he was a slave, had no standing in court. Furthermore, since slaves were property and since the Fifth Amendment of the Constitution protected property from congressional interference, Congress had no power to bar slavery from the territories. This decision obviously knocked the props from under the Republican party whose platform had called for Congress to ban slavery in the territories. It also weakened Douglas's popular sovereignty doctrine, for now the Supreme Court probably would void a territory's prohibition of holding property in the form of slaves. But Douglas argued that the two views could be reconciled. Whatever the final outcome in regard to slavery, Buchanan hoped that Kansas might yet be saved as a state in the Democratic column. He sent Robert J. Walker to Kansas as governor in the hope of calming and organizing the territory, preparatory to statehood. The new governor found conditions chaotic. Free-state men refused to participate in the election of a constitutional convention, which met in the fall and drafted the Lecompton constitution, insuring the protection of slave property in Kansas.

In regard to Kansas, Cox continued to uphold the popular sovereignty doctrine believing it would work out fairly in practice. He spent the first half of 1857 in winding up the affairs of his Columbus law office which he had maintained even while editing the *Statesman*. He thought the persistent agitation of the slavery issue was deplorable, for it kept men's passions aroused and made a reasonable, equitable settlement more difficult. In September he went East to deliver the commencement address at Brown University. Here in New England, where the agitation against slavery was strongest, Cox seized the opportunity to plead for restraint. The Brown seniors were told that the country needed less nervous hurry and more deliberation, " earnestness without extravagance, imagination without wild romance, talent . . . without vehemence and rashness." [1] He inserted a word of praise for the national Democratic Administration and commended the work of former Secretary of State William L. Marcy.[2]

Back in Ohio Cox campaigned vigorously for gubernatorial candidate Henry B. Payne against the incumbent Chase. The revelation of a half-million dollar shortage of state funds under the Republican state treasurer, coupled with a feeling that popular sovereignty was making Kansas a free state anyway, shifted many voters back into the Democratic ranks. Chase won re-election by only a slim margin. The Democrats gained control of the legislature and quickly repealed most of the " personal liberty " laws, which had made enforcement of the federal fugitive slave law almost impossible.[3]

As the opening session of the new Congress approached, the country staggered under the shock of the economic panic of 1857. Even as Cox spoke in Providence, stock market prices were plummeting. By mid-October all but one of the New York banks had suspended specie payment. Money went into hiding. Factories closed their gates. Bankruptcies, suspensions, price-cutting, and unemployment followed. The country was swept into the whirlpool of economic depression.

At this time men turned to religion for consolation. A wave of religious revivals, daily prayer meetings and evangelism swept the country. In the North the feeling against the sin of slavery mounted. As Cox and other congressmen left for Washington, economic distress and religious outbursts in their home districts added to the already growing tensions in the political arena. These factors made it difficult for Congress to reach an agreement on complex and heated political issues.

When the Thirty-fifth Congress convened in December 1857, President Buchanan tossed a political football into the lap of the reluctant legislators, urging in his annual message the admission of Kansas under the Lecompton constitution which permitted slavery. This constitution was scheduled for a plebiscite in Kansas late in December, but the proposition was so worded that, whichever way the vote went, slavery was assured as legal in Kansas under constitutional guarantee.[4] On December 9, Senator Douglas announced his opposition, declaring that the Lecompton " fraud " was contrary to the proper working of true " popular sovereignty." Several Ohioans wrote to Cox urging him to take the same stand on the President's message.[5]

On the following Sunday, Congressman Cox visited Douglas and laid before him a speech which the latter approved. Three days later, on the first day that the House of Representatives met in its newly-completed hall at the south end of the Capitol, Cox secured the floor. His speech opened with praise for the President's efforts to effect a

peaceful settlement of the Kansas issue, but he warned that
"there will be no peace from this admission of Kansas under
the Lecompton constitution. Expediency is a dangerous doctrine, when in collision with principles." Here was a freshman member of Congress challenging his own Administration. Older members sat up and listened. "Conscience,
honor, pledges, and constituency, all compel me" to demand
"submission of the whole constitution to the whole people."
James Hughes of Indiana and John Quitman of Mississippi
tried to interrupt, but Speaker James Orr ruled that Cox could
continue. He did—giving high praise to Douglas "who
framed the act of Kansas and Nebraska" and whose view
"is more binding as to its true intent and meaning" than
any other man's. "I now propose to nail against the door
at the threshold of this Congress my theses." He then proceeded to tick off in debating fashion his major points of
argument with supporting material for each. Urging that
the right of self-government "means the will of the majority,
legally expressed," Cox condemned the Lecompton procedure
as undemocratic in not permitting any real choice. He
opposed admission of Kansas by such a scheme, "even
though the constitution might have all the excellences of
Plato's Ideal, More's Utopia, and Harrington's Oceana."
He echoed Douglas: "It is no question of African slavery,
no maudlin sentimentality about the black race; but it is the
right of the white man that is attempted to be filched from
him by a pack of land-hucksters and political jobbers. . . ."
In conclusion, "though trembling like an aspen," [6] Cox
pointed to the retrogression of the Republican party in Ohio
after its initial success of 1854 and pleaded with Southerners
not "to resuscitate the waning fortunes of a sectional party"
which would place "the northern Democracy in the wrong
where it can be reproached and insulted." His final words

were defiant: " The events of the next month may alter " the question, " but for myself nothing can change my determination to stand by the principle of Democracy." [7]

Reactions to Cox's speech were fairly uniform in the North. That he had stated the views of his Democratic constituents appeared to be beyond question. The Democratic *Ohio Statesman* made this clear: " We take the earliest occasion to commend . . . Mr. Cox. . . . The people at home will applaud." A few days later, after reprinting the speech in full, the same editor commented: " Instead of Mr. Cox's speech being calculated to give aid and comfort to Black Republicanism in the Northwest, the policy he advocated will extinguish that faction in less than a twelve month." [8] Favorable notices appeared in the New York *Times*, the New York *Tribune*, and the New York *Herald*, while the Philadelphia *Press* said, " Mr. Cox begins his career at the right time. . . . His argument is unanswerable." From New York an invitation reached him to address a Tammany Hall meeting. Unable to appear, the Ohio representative sent his regrets and added a plea for " that according harmony in which we all may join." [9]

In his home district in Ohio, the Republican *Journal* conceded that Cox's initial performance was " a profound sensation." After some hesitation the editor declared that " Mr. Cox's denunciation of the Kansas Constitution swindle is terrific—fiercer than we have seen in any Republican paper." The *Journal* was perhaps closer to popular feeling in the Northwest when it objected to Cox's statement of indifference to slavery in Kansas. " The people of the Northwest do care whether Kansas shall be free or slave." The editorial added that Cox's position was weakened by the " moral effect " of his indifference.[10]

But support came to Cox from home. The Ohio legislature

under Democratic control passed a set of anti-Lecompton resolutions in January 1858. A month later some twelve hundred Democrats at a district meeting in Columbus registered " our hearty approval " for " the manly and uncompromising opposition of our Representative to the Lecompton Constitution," who spoke as the " voice of the Democracy of Franklin County." [11]

In Washington, however, trouble was brewing and pressures mounting. The referendum in Kansas on December 21 carried the Lecompton constitution " with slavery " by a vote of 6,143 to 569. Free-state men, who had refrained from voting, cried " fraud " and arranged a new plebiscite, which, early in January, rejected the Lecompton constitution by 10,266 votes to 162. The plebiscite strengthened the position of the anti-Lecomptonites in Congress. Governor Walker, too, gave his support, having returned from Kansas to resign, in protest against the Lecompton scheme, and to warn the President against it.

While Douglas fought the Administration on Kansas in the Senate, some twenty-four anti-Lecompton Democratic members of the House, mostly from the Northwest, conferred in January to consider their position. A delegation of three, including Cox, was sent to the White House to press for compromise, but Buchanan insisted on Lecompton as the test of party loyalty.[12] Cox continued in opposition, sending his reassurance to a state-wide anti-Lecompton meeting in Columbus and asserting that those who would read Western anti-Lecompton Democrats out of the party " might as well *try to read the hickories out of the Western woods*." [13] Early in February debate grew so heated in the House that in one all-night session on Kansas when Galusha A. Grow, a Pennsylvania Republican, crossed over to the Democratic side of the House, fire-eater Lawrence M. Keitt of South

Carolina ordered him back to his own side. When Grow
defied him, Keitt lunged at Grow, saying: "I will choke
you for that." In the general melee, Northerners and
Southerners, "the belligerent members," Cox noted, "came
trooping down the aisles of the House" with "fierce clutch
and glaring eye." Before order was restored, there had been
much pushing and punching, and one member lost his wig.[14]

The Administration began to crack down on Cox and
other anti-Lecomptonites as it did on Douglas. Cox wrote
in vain for the appointment of his friends to federal offices.[15]
The postmaster at Columbus, Thomas Miller, Cox's close
friend and loyal supporter, was fired early in March to be
replaced by pro-Lecomptonite Samuel Medary.[16] Cox later
complained that he had been forced "to wander for four
years throughout the Administration of President Buchanan
. . . without influence to help a single friend." [17]

In April 1858 after Senate and House had passed different
bills on the admission of Kansas, a conference committee
brought out the compromise English bill. By it, the usual
offer of public lands for educational purposes was to be
made to Kansas. If Kansas voted to accept this offer, it
would be admitted under Lecompton, but rejection would
delay admission. Here was an adroit compromise measure,
allowing the Administration a strategic retreat from its
former rigid insistence on Lecompton and permitting face-
saving by Southern members who had violently opposed
resubmission of the Lecompton "fraud."

The English bill, the new test of party loyalty, placed anti-
Lecomptonites in a position of seeming self-contradiction.
By indirection it provided what they had been urging—a fair
vote in Kansas; therefore, to reject it would be to defeat
their own ends. But to accept it would appear to contradict
what they had been saying for months in regard to the

Lecompton constitution. The bill was misinterpreted in the hinterland as a bribe to get Kansas to accept Lecompton. Ohio Democrats shared this view and urged Cox to oppose the bill.[18] At the same time he received messages through intermediaries from such Cabinet members as Treasury Secretary Howell Cobb and Postmaster-General Aaron V. Brown, implying that favors might be forthcoming in return for his support of the English bill.[19] Cox conferred with Douglas who found himself in a similar dilemma. Professor Roy F. Nichols in his book, *The Disruption of American Democracy*, seems to be certain that Douglas was ready to accept the English bill when he became convinced that the best course to secure its adoption was to oppose it, since only then would Southern support come forward. Cox, on the other hand, assured by Governor Walker that a new vote in Kansas would reject Lecompton, decided that attaining the objective was more important than apparent consistency. He therefore voted for the English measure " even though this bill may not, in every respect, conform to my best judgment." [20] With thirteen anti-Lecompton Democrats, including Cox, supporting it, the English bill passed the House and was adopted shortly thereafter by the Senate.

In shifting from bitter denunciation of the Lecompton constitution in December to support of the English bill in April, Cox's motives were mixed. To a considerable degree, he was convinced that acceptance of the English compromise would promote the real goal he sought. But personal ambition, hope of patronage plums, and concern for party harmony—all doubtless played a part in encouraging his shift. Two weeks after the English bill passed, he wrote President Buchanan requesting a post office printing contract for the *Ohio Statesman*. Though rebuffed, Cox later pressed Buchanan for Miller's " reinstatement " as Columbus post-

27

master, a request that the Administration granted in December, after Medary had gone to Kansas as governor.[21] Cox could claim vindication, however, on practical grounds when the people of Kansas in the summer of 1858 voted to reject the offer of immediate admission under the Lecompton constitution.[22] Whatever his motives or justification, his action was seized upon as Republican campaign material. The *Journal*, which had earlier praised him for opposing Lecompton and even talked of throwing Republican support his way, now labeled him as " Ichabod " and declared: " His epitaph is written. . . . Cox is dead." [23] Actually, the Kansas issue was only the beginning of his lengthy career.

THE TARIFF: A WESTERN VIEW

The Democratic platform of 1856 had called for economy in government. Official presidential messages, endorsed by congressional leaders, urged cutting governmental expenditures to prevent the Republicans from demanding a raise in tariff duties to make up for the potential deficit. But talking economy and actually reducing expenditures were two different matters. Demands for money and appropriations poured in from all sides. The planned military expedition against the Mormons in Utah required supplies and equipment as well as men. Various claims-agents appeared to present their clients' demands for government reimbursement. The Post Office Department was annually running a deficit of $3,500,000. Congressional committees presented bills to raise postal rates, to abolish franking privileges, and to reduce subsidies on steamship mail-carrying contracts. Although ocean mail subsidies were ultimately defeated, the bill to reduce Post Office expenditures and increase its revenue was lost. The Sundry Civil Appropriations bill, launched as an economy measure, had $2,000,000 added to it before it passed. The cause of economy made little headway.

In these financial matters, Cox took the position of his party. He favored economy, but on specific questions he often supported expenditures, especially when they were to the advantage of his state or district. His sentiments on the tariff, expressed in a speech in June 1858, presented the viewpoint of the agricultural interest of the West. Advising the West to guard its interests, Cox said " The true glory of this nation . . . is her new states, made up of simple men of simple habits." He deplored " all these expenditures for the benefit" of the East, and he pointed to the " power arising in the West which will . . . after the next census " have " on this floor, one hundred and twenty-five members out of two hundred and forty-one." Those states with a common interest in agriculture and commerce " will have a preponderance." The Northwest alone could outnumber New York and New England. " It can afford to wait. The lines of empire are on the face of the cradled Hercules." He rejected current talk of raising the tariff. Recognizing the effects of the previous year's panic on government revenue, he urged that the " economy which the people are now practicing in their own troubles " be adopted by " our Government and its rulers " who are " far in advance of the people in the vices, and far behind them in the virtues of republican life," the " simplicity " of the people " having but little reflection either in the social life or the political legislation of this metropolis." [24]

Here, Cox echoed the Jeffersonian belief in the virtues of the simple, agrarian life, of government frugality, and of non-interference by the government in the economy through a tariff. He also expressed confidence that the future belonged to the West, knowing that his words would find a warm response among his farmer-constituents.

KEEPING HOME FENCES IN REPAIR

Cox naturally sought to please his constituents by giving voice to the resentments of the West and of his own district. Regarding internal improvements at national expense, claims and private relief bills and post roads and post offices, he performed his routine congressional duties with skill and imagination. He often argued that his section was not getting its fair share of federal expenditures. In June 1858, objecting to a river-harbor bill, he declared that it was " got up from a sectional point of view " which " has not properly cared for " the needs of the West. The Atlantic coast, he complained, received more than it deserved for improvements, " while . . . the needs of the West are defeated." [25]

He urged the building of a new post office in Columbus and got his bill reported out favorably by the Committee on Post Offices and Post Roads in May 1858. Arguing that Columbus, as a state capitol serving some 40,000 people, deserved a better post office than a shop wedged dangerously between a bakery and a coffee-grinding establishment, he pointed out that while Ohio paid $6,000,000 a year in federal taxes it received only $601,000 in federal expenditures. " Is it not fair and just that a State so liberal and ready to do her part toward the federal revenue should receive some consideration? " [26] The House felt otherwise, and the bill was lost. In 1860 Cox was again fighting for a new Columbus post office.

As chairman of the Committee on Revolutionary Claims, he presented private relief bills which benefitted claimants of Virginia military lands and Canadian refugee lands located in his district.[27] When Francis Blair charged that Cox's constituent, George Manypenny, former commissioner of Indian Affairs, had sold rifles to Indians along the Santa Fe Trail, Cox went to great lengths to refute the charges and to show that Manypenny, now editor of Cox's old newspaper, actually performed his duties as commissioner ably and honestly.[28] Cox also worked for the establishment of post roads favorable to central Ohio. For this he received the praise of the Columbus *Gazette*.[29] In addition he did what little he could to satisfy his constituents' demands for federal jobs.[30] One faithful Democratic constituent wrote in gratitude: ". . . we have a representative of whom we should feel proud." [31]

At the end of the congressional session, Democratic leaders could boast little in the way of solid accomplishment. Economy had failed. The only constructive measure to pass, the English bill, had seriously divided the party. The Democrats found themselves in a rapidly weakening position. Their need now was to recover sufficient party strength to win the 1858 elections.

CAMPAIGN AND RE-ELECTION, 1858

On his return to Columbus Cox began vigorous campaigning for re-election to Congress. On July 3 he spoke at a Licking County rally. Three weeks later the Democratic State Convention adopted resolutions which endorsed the English bill as a settlement of the Kansas issue and which sustained Democratic congressmen who voted for the measure.[32] The next week Cox appeared before his district convention to receive its plaudits and renomination " by acclamation." [33] Loyal Democrats pitched in with financial contributions and verbal encouragement.[34]

The campaign was a bitter one. Republicans charged that

Cox's shift on Kansas was dictated by an Administration bribe. He was accused of shifting from being a prohibitionist to being a tippler. Another accusation, resurrected from the previous campaign, was that Cox favored Negro equality.[35] It is little wonder that he later complained of

> . . . a campaign for its unprovoked fierceness, its base and baseless charges of personal corruption, its conceit, its ignorance, its imprudence, its poltroonery, its billingsgate, its brutality, its moneyed corruption, its fanatical folly, its unflagging slang, its drunken saturnalia, and its unblushing libels and pious hypocrisy! The people were ashamed and indignant at the audacious falsehood and brazen clamor from the little penny-a-liners and pettifoggers who echoed the libels.[36]

While over in Illinois Douglas fought for his political life against attacks by Abraham Lincoln, Republicans, and Buchanan Democrats, Cox in Ohio also fought for political survival. In the summer of 1858 farmers in the Licking and Scioto valleys found their wheat crop ruined by a widespread attack of wheat weevils. Cox's father had developed a strain of weevil-resistant wheat, and Cox, seeking to ingratiate himself with his constituents, sent small sacks of weevil-proof wheat to the farmer-voters in his district. The Republicans emptied these sacks of the good seed and refilled them with weevil-infested wheat, chaff, and scrapings from barn floors. At Republican rallies, these sacks, bearing Cox's name, were displayed, and their adulterated contents poured out on the platform, while Republican orators, one of whom was Tom Corwin, denounced Cox for supporting " weevil and the English bill." Taking his cue from the Illinois senatorial race, Cox managed to stage a series of debates in the Ohio capital district. At Newark on August 29, he debated with his rival, exposed the trickery of his opponents, and coined the Democratic rallying cries," Down with Weevil and up with Democracy" and "Squatter Sovereignty and Good Crops."[37]

The election returns gave Cox a majority of 647 and an absolute increase of 1,000 votes over his 1856 total. His victory was the more remarkable, considering that only one other of the eight Ohio congressmen who had voted for the English bill survived the election.[38] After a bumper wheat harvest the following year, Cox, with a glow of satisfaction, boasted, " If my anti-weevil wheat has proved the salvation of your grain harvests, so have my anti-Lecompton votes proved the salvation of Kansas."[39]

Having squeaked through the 1858 elections in spite of the fire of "the Buchanan Old Lines," who condemned his opposition to Lecompton, and of the "Douglas-Young Americans," who denounced his support of the English bill, Cox accounted it "a marvel" due only to "my youthful and unsophisticated sincerity."[40] He kept in mind, however, the need to improve his relations with both wings of the party. The next year he asked Douglas for copies of the latter's popular sovereignty article (which had been published in *Harper's Monthly*) in order to distribute them in Ohio. At his invitation, Douglas spoke on the popular sovereignty theme at both Columbus and Newark in Cox's district.[41] With Democratic state chairman, George Manypenny, Cox ushered Douglas around even while he kept dissentient Democrats at arm's length. Later, two dissentients wrote complainingly to Douglas that "the Thomas Miller–S. S. Cox clique" were "too much interested in spoils and money, perhaps too close to the Buchanan administration" and "two more unscrupulous knaves and charlatans it has never been my lot to encounter."[42]

In 1859 Cox encountered other difficulties closer to home. When his father, fulfilling his duties as United States Mar-

shal at Zanesville, arrested a fugitive slave, the Baptist
Church, of which he was trustee, expelled him for following
" human laws in conflict with the divine law." [43] Meanwhile when Cox's friend, Postmaster Miller, co-owner of
the *Ohio Statesman*, was again in danger of removal, Cox
wrote two letters to President Buchanan, defending his friend
and expressing his hope that together " we shall cultivate a
spirit of harmony." [44] Buchanan, however, remained cold
to the overtures. " You and I are still antipodes," he replied,
but he agreed not to remove Miller. In spite of this, agitation for Miller's removal continued, and as late as July 1860
Cox was asking Lewis Cass to intercede with Buchanan to
save his friend.[45]

Although Cox won re-election in 1858, the year was an
unhappy one for the Democratic party, involving the loss of
eighteen congressional seats. Unless this loss could be offset
by proportionate gains in the Southern congressional elections
the following year, the next House of Representatives would
fall under Republican control.

DEMOCRATIC IMPERIALISM: *" La Joven America "*

Traditional Democratic foreign policy favored territorial
expansion, and the Buchanan Administration followed the
party line. Twice during his pre-war congressional career
" Sunset " Cox made speeches in which he waved the flag
of " manifest destiny." He used the time-worn rationaliza-
tions of self-defense, inevitable growth, and the sharing of
American benefits with other peoples.[46]

In his first " manifest destiny" speech in January 1859,
Cox praised Buchanan for his efforts to purchase Cuba.
" Self-preservation," Cox told the House," forbids us to be
indifferent." The island, of little use to Spain, " is of in-

calculable advantage" to us. "The law of growth and destiny" decreed that weaker, disorganized lands should be absorbed by the stronger nations. Cuba as a part of the United States would end those "harsh protective and indefensible" features of the tariff regarding sugar. His "district alone has paid $500,000" in the past ten years as a "tributary to the few sugar planters in the South!" If purchase of Cuba failed, he "would favor its seizure in case of foreign war, or of European intervention." Here was a belated echo of the Ostend Manifesto.

Speaking of other regions he asserted that, although the United States should have kept all of Mexico in 1848, the present policy of "good neighborhood" required that we recognize the Juarez government. "The law of American progress" demanded agreements with Juarez to secure "a foothold in the northern Mexican States, which can be made permanent without war." The Monroe Doctrine had to be upheld against all British and French threats of intervention. He said that in Central America our interests demanded the abrogation of the Clayton-Bulwer Treaty, for we could not allow ourselves to be shut out of the trade there, since this region "will give us coffee, indigo, and cocoa" and "in return they will take our flour, pork, machinery, fabrics, and a thousand other articles." As to possible slave states in Central America, he told "southern gentlemen" that the Constitution guaranteed "equality of rights" but "the moment you claim equilibrium of States, that moment your honor is compromised and your loyalty to the Constitution is questioned." His speech closed with a plea for "perpetual growth and unsevered Union." [47]

A year later Cox elaborated the same theme. He now urged immediate ratification of the McLane-Ocampo Treaty which promised an American railway concession and military occupation in the Tehuantepec Isthmus in exchange for American protection for all of Mexico. This, he added, would make " Mexico as useful a dependency upon us as ever India was upon England." Free trade with Mexico would mean higher prices for the Ohio farmer as well as for the " planter of cotton on the Gulf," the " iron interest of the Middle States," and " the manufacturing interest of New England." Mexico would send us coffee and sugar. Furthermore, under the " law of necessity," we ought to " save our neighbor's house when its burning would imperil our safety." About the continuing struggle within the United States, he said " an active outgoing policy would divert attention from internal dissensions." Referring to the Madrid newspaper reports which denounced " the impetuosity of ' *La Joven America*,' " Cox concluded, " call it what you will, manifest destiny, territorial expansion, star of empire, *La Joven America*, and even filibusterism—it is here. . . . The finger of Providence points to our nation as the guiding star of progress." [48]

By ringing the tocsin of the " Young America " movement, so popular earlier in the decade, Cox no doubt hoped to divert attention from troublesome domestic matters, as the Republican *Ohio State Journal* charged on March 22nd. The *Journal* declared that Cox, in preparation for the 1860 campaign, was speaking for Douglas who hoped to win the presidential nomination.

NEEDLING THE REPUBLICANS: GIDDINGS, SHERMAN, CORWIN

In domestic affairs, Cox took great delight in showing up Republican inconsistencies, especially when he found Republican members in the House contradicting each other.

His efforts in this direction were intended to influence Ohio state politics rather than to solve national problems. Three prominent Ohio Republicans—Joshua Giddings, John Sherman, Thomas Corwin—all came within range of his fire.

In January 1859 when Giddings declared that he wanted to see Cox " driven from under the bush " regarding his stand on the slave trade, Cox retorted that Giddings " knows better than any other man, that the Democratic party " stands upon " the doctrine that Congress should not interfere in relation to slavery." He hoped Giddings would be nominated for governor of Ohio. Let Giddings " come to Central Ohio . . . with his theories on personal liberty, and we will give him to ponder on the philosophy of Aristides, who said that he yielded to the popular will, even when it drove him into exile. . . ." Cox then accused Giddings of having advocated Negro equality, and asked, " Is the gentleman in favor of allowing Negroes of Ohio to vote? " The question was loaded with political dynamite, for Ohio had consistently voted down Negro suffrage. Giddings dodged with an answer that Negroes were on the same plane as Democrats. Cox persisted: " Answer the question, sir. The gentleman talked about my hiding under the bush. Let him come out if he dare from his covert." When Giddings evaded again, Cox crowed, " I will not press the gentleman further. He never could get nominated for the governorship if he answered my question categorically; and I am anxious that he should be nominated. . . ." [49]

During the succeeding gubernatorial campaign, Giddings was not the candidate. Some 30,000 copies of Cox's speech, printed under the title " Father Giddings dodges under the bush with his colored friend," were distributed as Democratic campaign literature in Ohio. The Republicans elected William Dennison in spite of Cox's efforts to expose the dangers of Republicanism.[50]

Meanwhile, in the second session of the Thirty-fifth Congress, the Democrats failed to produce any constructive legislation or to heal party wounds. Even with control of both houses they were unable to reach any agreement or to reduce the hatreds caused by the earlier Kansas fracas. A weak Pacific railroad subsidy bill passed the Senate but was ignored by the House. A homestead bill passed the House but failed in the Senate. The bill to donate land to agricultural colleges met a presidential veto. Once again river and harbor appropriations disappointed Western members. Southern attacks on Douglas grew bitter. The willingness to compromise, which had made legislation possible earlier, was no longer in evidence. With the party rift growing wider, Democratic success in 1860 was dubious.[51]

Events in the fall of 1859 did not lessen sectional, political, and personal animosities. Rather they heaped more fuel on the fire. Douglas's article in the September *Harper's Monthly* explaining his popular sovereignty views more clearly, lost him much of the support that remained for him in the South. John Brown's raid at Harper's Ferry in October aroused the country. In the North, radicals applauded Brown as a saint carrying out God's will, while conservatives disapproved, pointing out the relation between Brown's attack and the talk of " irrepressible conflict " and " higher law." But many in the North thought that, while Brown's objective in freeing the slaves was good, his method was poorly chosen. Little wonder that " John Brown's body " became the symbol of marching Northern armies during the Civil War. In the South alarm was widespread. Brown's attack highlighted the possibility of a slave insurrection, which Southerners had been fearing as the worst kind of calamity for their section.

Edmund Ruffin distributed the pikes, used by Brown men throughout the South, to symbolize the dangers that the people faced at the hands of Northern abolitionists. The Brown raid, more than any other event, served to arouse the common people of the South, who owned few or no slaves, to a pitch of feeling that made them willing to support extreme measures, even disunion, in order to escape the violence of Northern attacks.[52]

In such an atmosphere the new Congress assembled in December 1859, with the Republicans holding 109 seats, the Democrats 101, and the American-Whigs 27. The Republican caucus named John Sherman of Ohio for speaker, the Democrats, Thomas S. Bocock of Virginia. Neither could command a majority, and the ensuing deadlock stretched the bitter debate over the next two months. When, early in the debate, John Sherman's fitness was called into question because he had endorsed Hinton R. Helper's *Impending Crisis*, Tom Corwin defended Sherman and his party in general, asserting that Republicans favored faithful execution of the fugitive slave law.

This brought a quick response from Cox, who declared that Corwin, whose views did not differ from those of the Democrats, had joined the Republican party in order to break down Republican " sectionalism and destroy its distinctive features." Corwin's support of the fugitive slave law, Cox held, did not reflect the views of the Republican party in Ohio. " I want the country to understand " the Republican party's " lawless and orderless character." To this end, he described the Oberlin-Wellington rescue of a fugitive slave and the subsequent parade through the streets of Cleveland, with Giddings leading and Oberlin College students singing the *Marseillaise* in French. He denounced Giddings again for an earlier speech which heralded the day " when the slaves shall rise in the South . . . when masters shall turn pale and tremble, when their dwellings shall smoke." This, Cox said, was " where the seed was sown of which the insurrection at Harper's Ferry was the inevitable consequence."

Turning on John Sherman, Cox asked whether Sherman believed in the constitutionality of the fugitive slave act, as advocated by Corwin. Sherman refused to answer. Cox then accused him of evasion, stating that he wished " only to expose the inconsistent, heterogeneous elements which make up this mosaic, called republicanism in Ohio."

Moving on to Corwin's relations with Governor Chase, he told how Chase had approved the " individual sovereignty " doctrine of Wendell Phillips, which encouraged defiance of federal authority. He cited a meeting in Columbus between Corwin and Chase, when " you had a most affectionate hug before the people of Ohio." Then he charged Corwin with giving implied approval to Chase's lawless doctrine while at the same time arguing to uphold the fugitive slave law in Ohio. This, he said, was self-contradiction. " The time for the Republican party to have denounced these dangerous doctrines was not after the Harper's Ferry affair " but " when Governor Seward said there was a ' higher law ' than the Constitution which required the extermination of slavery," and when " Giddings made his speech here in favor of servile insurrection. . . ." The people of Ohio, " outside of the Western Reserve, are not in favor of insurrection and dissolution. I think that the Reserve ought to be cut off and slid over to Canada. . . ." We " would be glad to exchange " the Reserve " for Cuba and cheap sugar and molasses." [53] This speech, along with the one of 1858, was printed in the *Ohio Statesman* on December 28, 1859, and used by the Democrats in the Ohio campaign of 1860.

In the speakership struggle of 1859-1860 Cox voted for Bocock for the first twelve ballots, then shifted for the next twenty-seven ballots to various men such as William English, John McClernand, and George Pendleton. On December 28 he announced he would support any anti-Lecompton Democrat. He rejected the thought of a split between Northern and Southern Democrats, declaring hopefully that all differences could be peacefully settled in the coming 1860 convention. On the final balloting, he switched to William Smith, an old-line Whig of North Carolina. On February 1 William Pennington was chosen.[54] For his switch Cox was condemned by fellow-Congressman Robert Hatton of Tennessee, and a duel between the two almost resulted.[55] In self-defense Cox published a series of letters in the *Statesman*.

Meanwhile, state conventions were choosing delegates for the Democratic convention, scheduled to meet on April 23 in Charleston, South Carolina. Douglas was lining up a long string of delegates, who, without exception, came from Northern states. Southern delegates were either instructed or expected to oppose him. The Alabama convention in January ominously directed its delegates to insist that the Democratic platform include a plank calling for federal protection of slavery in the territories. If the nominating convention failed to include this plank, the Alabamans were instructed to withdraw at once. The outlook was not promising, but many still hoped that experienced politicians would manage to keep the Democrats united. The crucial question was whether the party that had held national power almost continuously for over half a century could set aside sectional and personal antagonisms in order to preserve the party and, with it, the Union. The Charleston convention was expected to give the answer.

CRISIS OF 1860

It was in the spirit of hopeful moderation that Cox went to Charleston, South Carolina, in April 1860, as a delegate to the Democratic National Convention. Four years earlier Charleston had been chosen as the 1860 convention city. No worse selection could have been made. Meeting in any other city, the party might have saved itself from disruption. But at Charleston, crowded living quarters for the delegates, inadequate facilities for deliberations in the South Carolina Institute Hall, and oppressively hot, damp weather all conspired against party harmony.[56]

Northwest Democrats clearly realized that their political survival depended on nominating Douglas and adopting a moderate platform. Douglas alone, of all the Democratic aspirants, was capable of winning their section against the rising tide of Republicanism there. Since only by capturing some Northern states could a Democrat carry the election, it was both only reasonable and smart party strategy to select a candidate who could make a strong appeal in the North. It was the Southern extremists who were neither in a reasonable mood nor concerned with smart party strategy. Willingness to compromise, so apparent four years earlier, was now absent. " Fire-eaters," like William L. Yancey, seemed determined to break the party and the Union.

Southern demands for federal protection of slavery in the territories were rejected. Cox's former law partner, Senator George E. Pugh, declared " Gentlemen of the South, you mistake us. . . . We will not do it." This brought on the Southern bolt. The subsequent conventions at Baltimore and

Richmond named Douglas as the Northern Democratic candidate and John C. Breckinridge as the bolters' nominee. The fatal breach in the Democratic party had now become real: the one remaining political bond between North and South had snapped. Politics, following the earlier trend of the churches and other institutions, had become sectionalized.

The Democratic party-split filtered down to the state level. The Ohio State Convention in July broke up into Douglas and Breckinridge factions. In the Twelfth Congressional District, however, Democrats managed to hang together. Cox was renominated with " grateful acknowledgment for his eminent services " by " a most enthusiastic and unanimous district convention," notwithstanding a group of dissentient " *soi disant* Democrats " who " tried to get up a cloud over my personal voting for the English bill." [57] During the campaign, Congressman John Sherman attacked Cox for inconsistency in the speakership struggle of the last Congress. Replying in kind, Cox upbraided Sherman for failure to support Oregon's admission. Douglas visited Columbus in September and urged the voters to re-elect Cox, whose vote on the English bill Douglas attributed to " an honest difference of opinion." [58] In October Cox won over former Congressman Samuel Galloway, although his majority was slightly smaller than two years before.[59]

Meanwhile, Douglas, supported by Northern Democrats, threw himself into a man-killing campaign. Nothing like it had been seen before in American politics. The Republicans had nominated Abraham Lincoln on a platform that opposed slavery in the territories, advocated government aid for a Pacific railroad, and demanded a protective tariff and a homestead law. The protective tariff and the candidate were expected to pull Pennsylvania and Illinois respectively into the Republican column. The outcome should have been easily predictable. Lincoln carried the North and the Pacific Coast; Breckinridge the lower South; John Bell of the Constitutional Union party the upper South; Douglas took only Missouri and part of New Jersey's vote. Lincoln's popular vote of 1,866,452 constituted only 40 per cent of the total, compared to Douglas's 29 per cent, or 1,376,957 votes. But, no matter how the returns were analyzed nor what post-mortems were held, the nation would have a Republican President beginning next March 4. The question still to be answered was whether the Southerners would carry out their oft-repeated threat of withdrawal in the face of a " Black Republican " victory.

Certainly all was not lost for the Democrats. They had shown surprising resilience in the congressional elections and, if party lines held, they could still command a majority in the next House of Representatives.

Lincoln's election resulted in threatening moves toward secession, which alarmed those Ohioans who had voted for Douglas and even some who had voted for Lincoln. As November passed, a conciliatory spirit seemed to gain ground.[60] When Congress convened on December 3, Cox joined with George H. Pendleton and Clement L. Vallandigham in an effort to check the Southern move toward secession. Plans were soon under way to develop a formula, in the fashion of the compromise of 1850, acceptable to Southerners and Republicans alike. The Committee of Thirteen under John J. Crittenden in the Senate and the Committee of Thirty-three under Tom Corwin in the House tried to find the appropriate formula. Southern disappointment that no Democrat from the West had been appointed to the House committee was expressed by a Florida representative: " I would have been glad to have seen my friends from Ohio, Vallandigham and Cox . . . who have stood by the South " on this committee. By late December the failure of the compromise committees was evident. No acceptable measure had been produced. South Carolina had already voted to secede, and other Deep South states were moving closer to the fateful step. On December 18 the entire Ohio congressional delegation considered a Cox-sponsored resolution which called on the Ohio legislature " to abrogate all laws in conflict with the Constitution for the return of fugitives from justice." This was voted down.[61]

Men of moderation still hoped, however. As the old year waned, a new Committee of Fourteen was formed with Crittenden as chairman and Cox as secretary. This group deliberated and on January 4, 1861 presented a plan modifying the original Crittenden compromise by making it virtually impossible to acquire new territory. It defined more clearly the possible boundaries of future slave states south of the proposed extension of the Missouri Compromise line and provided that fugitives must be surrendered on demand.[62] This proposal was pronounced acceptable by Douglas, border state leaders, the President, and August Belmont and other leading New York businessmen. By making it difficult to add new territory, the proposal erased Lincoln's objection to the original Crittenden plan. Republicans were urged to support it. But when submitted to the House, it was blocked from consideration by Republican votes.[63]

On the last day of 1860 Cox wrote home from Washington that he hoped the border states would stay in the Union. He declared that South Carolina's position was indefensible and that cotton would have to be shipped up the Mississippi and then east to New York, thus bringing a great boom to cities like Memphis and Cincinnati.[64]

Six days later he addressed the House with a powerful plea for preserving the Union at all costs, despite the already announced withdrawal of four Southern states. He was

" appalled at the colossal strides of revolution. . . . South Carolina has been singing her Marseillaise, . . . it but echoes the abolitionism of the North. . . . Extremes north have aided extremes south in the work to disintegration." He denied the right of secession. The South should not withdraw because " progress itself " demanded that the Union hold together. " Let there be *sacrifice* and *compromise*. These words are of honorable import. The one gave us Calvary, the other the Constitution. Nothing worth having was ever won without them." The Republican regime would not be the dangerous threat the South feared: " Mr. Lincoln in the White House will not be the rail splitter out of it. Abraham in faith may offer up his ' irrepressible ' offspring. He will be conservative to the total oblivion of the radical. The one will ' conflict ' with the other." Moderate Republicans " will drown the Giddings crew." Cox concluded with a plea for unity: " Clouds are about us! There is lightning in their frown! Cannot we direct it harmlessly to earth? The prayer of the people I speak for in such meekness, rises in strength that our States continue to be one." [65] But the tragedy Cox sought to avert moved on inexorably.

two

STORM
THE WAR YEARS, 1861–1865

3

LEADER OF THE LOYAL OPPOSITION
IN WAR TIME

The story of Samuel Sullivan Cox in the war years, 1861-1865, is the story of a moderate man in a time of extremes and violence. He viewed with horror the swift coming of the war in 1861, and, as a reasonable man, skilled in the political art of accommodation, he did his utmost to avert it. However, the press of events and the radicalism of extremists on both sides of the Mason-Dixon line were too much to hold in check. " But it is ever thus," he said. " History shows it. Extreme men drag moderate men with them." [1]

With the advent of war Cox assumed leadership of the loyal opposition in Congress. He supported armed efforts to bring the Southern states back into the Union, and at the same time he sought to temper force with moderation and generosity toward the South. At home he defended civil liberties as guaranteed by the Constitution against war-born manhandling. As the war leaders moved further away from the war's original objective of restoring the Union, he endeavored to slow the " revolutionary " changes and to preserve all that he considered good in the " old Union."

At the beginning of 1861, despite South Carolina's already announced withdrawal, people generally hoped that a timely compromise would save the Union. There were " Union meetings " in Northern towns, which passed resolutions offering every degree of concession. On January 31 Samuel Medary, Quaker and former Kansas governor, alarmed at the disintegration of the Union, founded in Columbus the *Crisis*, a weekly, with the aim of re-establishing unity by " fraternal feeling and discussion " on the basis of states rights. The paper's circulation grew rapidly in its first few weeks. At the Ohio Democratic State Convention, which met in Columbus, members urged acceptance of the Crittenden compromise or any other plan that would save the Union. They used almost the exact words of Cox's speech of January 5.[2]

Republican opinion was divided on the subject of compromise. At one extreme Horace Greeley and the Ashtabula *Sentinel* (voicing Giddings's views) wished to let the seceders " go in peace." [3] Still other Republicans denounced secession but refused to make any concession that would mean the loss of Republican supremacy and the spoils of last November's victory.[4] Between the extremes, a great many Republicans stood willing to compromise and looked for leadership to William H. Seward, John Sherman, Thomas Corwin, and Thomas Ewing.[5]

Northern Democrats generally favored a compromise settlement, although over what compromise and over what course of action to follow, if compromise failed, they were sharply divided.[6] In January 1861, a majority of Northerners probably would have supported any reasonable accommodation had a referendum been held at that time.[7] Northwestern Democrats were especially disturbed as they saw commercial ties, social and personal bonds, and political affiliations with the South breaking. Democratic leaders like Douglas, Cox, and George Pendleton, while not ruling out war as an ultimate measure, worked with skill and vigor to win adoption of compromise measures. On January 3 Douglas delivered a powerful peace-at-almost-any-cost speech in the Senate.[8] Cox spoke in a similar vein in the House.

Events gained momentum in the first few months of 1861: the Confederacy was organized at Montgomery; the Washington Peace Conference failed; and on March 4 Buchanan wearily passed on his burdens to Lincoln. Cox's hopes rose when Lincoln gave the South assurance—" The Government will not assail you. You can have no conflict without yourselves being the aggressors." Nevertheless, apprehension hung over the inauguration, as Cox noted: " For the first time in the history of the Republic a Chief Magistrate is installed under the protection of artillery charged with grape and cannister." [9]

Emotions had been stirred too high for reasonable men to reverse the tide. Events moved too rapidly. Cox felt his personal helplessness to be a tragedy. He later described it:

> When this war appeared as a speck on the horizon, I pleaded and voted for every compromise. . . . I preferred the bonds of Love to the armor of Force. I found in the Sermon on the Mount a wisdom beyond that of Presidents or priests. . . . I hold that . . . it was wisest to agree to any compromise . . . which would have averted these calamities.[10]

While extremists, North and South, called for action, Lincoln moved cautiously. Federal forts, customs houses, and post offices in the South were taken over by state authorities until only Fort Pickens at Pensacola and Fort Sumter at Charleston remained in Union hands. Bearing in mind the sad fate of Buchanan's *Star of the West* relief expedition to Sumter, Lincoln and his cabinet searched for possible courses of action and weighed the dangers involved. At length in early April he determined to supply Sumter and publicly announced the non-aggressive character of the expedition. The announcement touched off the bombardment of the fort in the Charleston harbor. The long-awaited, dreaded war had finally come.[11]

With the firing on Fort Sumter, the suspense broke. Tensions had risen so high in the North that even the relatively calm Thomas Ewing exclaimed: " I want to see the issue accepted and fought out." Northerners were relieved to know that now action would replace uncertainty and endless words. Mingled with relief, however, was a sense of shame and sadness that Americans had failed to settle their differences by the democratic process of free discussion and adjustment rather than by gunfire and bayonet. Later, Cox said in retrospect:

> Could not this Union have been made permanent by a timely settlement, instead of being cemented by fraternal blood and military rule? By an equitable adjustment of the territory this was possible. . . . The Crittenden proposition . . . the radicals denounced. . . . They were determined to prevent a settlement. . . . Those who sought to counteract the schemes of secession were themselves checkmated by extreme men of the Republican party. . . . One leading fact will always stand stark and bold, namely, that with the aid of a handful of secessionists *per se* the whole body of Republicans were—as Andrew Johnson later . . . [said]—" acting out their policy." In the light of subsequent envents, that policy was developed. It was the destruction of salvery. . . . Whether a great war with its infinite and harmful consequences, was the proper means to such an end,

is not for the writer . . . to determine. . . . The general belief at this time, 1885, is that the war has given us, in a new order, full compensation for its cost in means and life. Whether this be a correct estimate or not, the historians and philosophers of the future can better judge.[12]

WAR'S PURPOSE: RESTORE THE UNION, 1861-1862

While the appeal to arms drove four more states out of the Union, Lincoln's call for volunteers in mid-April brought an enthusiastic response in the North. In the initial outburst of martial enthusiasm some Northern Democrats gave their whole-hearted support to the Administration's decision for war; other Northern Democrats questioned the rightness, wisdom, and the expediency of coercing the seceded states. While remaining a distinct party during the war, the Northern Democrats varied in opinion from outright Southern sympathy through indifference to virtual full support of the war. Some Northern Democratic papers like the *Crisis* clung to their earlier opposition, while others like the *Cincinnati Enquirer* and the Columbus *Ohio Statesman* gave lukewarm support.[13]

Sometimes referred to as the " Peace Democracy," at other times called stronger, less complimentary names like " Sesechmen," Butternuts, and Copperheads, Northern Democrats were taunted for their views. They believed that the war had been caused in part by Northern extremists; they denied the right of secession; but they questioned the constitutional right of the federal government to use force against the South. They proposed a national convention to adjust differences, drew a careful distinction between the national government and the national Administration, and sought to protect the former against the arbitrary assaults of the latter. Spokesman of the rabid wing was Clement L. Vallandigham who had been elected to Congress three times. He openly asserted his opposition and coined the slogan, " The Union as it was, the Constitution as it is! " [14] Often aligned with Vallandigham were Ohio's retiring Senator George E. Pugh, Congressman George H. Pendleton, Samuel Medary, editor of the *Crisis,* and former Senator William (" Foghorn ") Allen.[15]

Cox had been closely associated with these men (as Pugh's one-time law partner, a fellow congressman with Pendleton and Vallandigham, and a newspaper partner with Medary's son-in-law), but he made up his mind independently that secession was impossible and that the use of force, although a calamity, was necessary under the circumstances. He maintained, however, that force should be used for as short a time as possible and should be accompanied by continuous, persistent, vigorous efforts to arrange a settlement that would re-establish the old Union. Early in March 1861, homeward bound from Lincoln's inauguration, Cox spoke to his fellow congressman, William S. Holman of Indiana, who later recalled that they both then knew " war was inevitable," yet for them, " there was no hesitation. . . . The Union must be maintained at every hazard." Each would " cordially " sustain the Administration of President Lincoln " in every measure deemed necessary and proper to uphold the Federal authority in all the states of the Union." [16]

In general, Cox followed the Democratic line with regard to the war, but he gauged the demands of the situation better and gave more vigorous support to the war than the Medary-Vallandigham group.[17] Perhaps his close friendship with his fellow Brown alumnus, John Hay, gave him a clearer insight into the problems that Lincoln faced. Perhaps he was more fully convinced than this group that to reunite the Union, war was necessary.

At any rate, he supported the war while simultaneously urging measures for peace. Paradoxical as this seemed to some of his contemporaries, it was a reasonable, logical, humane effort to terminate a dispute between fellow Americans by the most satisfactory of political means, compromise, followed by a restoration of America's pre-war society. This constantly recurring theme permeated his activity during the war years as well as in the reconstruction era. Regretting the changes being made in the old order, he opposed the " second American Revolution " and tried to prevent changes from coming too rapidly and too radically.[18]

In late April 1861 Stephen Douglas, acknowledged leader of the Northwest Democrats, announced his support of the Administration's war policy. On May 1 he declared: " There can be no neutrals in this war; only patriots or traitors." [19] Following this pronouncement Democratic papers like the Chicago *Times* and Democratic leaders like William A. Richardson of Illinois shifted from opposition to support of the war.[20] By July even Vallandigham announced that he was ready to vote for whatever men and money might be needed " to defend the Federal Government." [21] The later elevation of Democrats like George B. McClellan to important army commands no doubt helped effect the change in Democratic opinion.

With Douglas's death on June 3, the Democrats lost their most dynamic leader. " Who can take his place? " Cox lamented as the party foundered for want of a program and a leader. Various Democrats attempted to fill the gap. Of these, although Vallandigham became most conspicuous, Cox was closest to Douglas's position and he substantially inherited the Douglas mantle. In many ways Cox was like Douglas—small in size, powerful in voice, bursting with vitality, skilled in parliamentary maneuvering, always active, pondering new ideas, forceful as a stump speaker, and immensely popular. Both men believed in the supremacy of the Union and the Constitution, popular sovereignty, and states rights, its kindred doctrine in matters not clearly within the power of the central government; but, above all, they recognized the necessity of compromise as the essence of the political process. Thus, their position concerning war was one of critical support or of loyal opposition. During the war years, Cox served as minority leader in the House, a job that Douglas, had he lived, would have held in the Senate.

When the special session of Congress convened on July 4, 1861, Cox received the complimentary Democratic vote for Speaker of the House. Willing to support a war to restore the Union, he wanted no more of war than was necessary to that end. Nor did he want a war used for other purposes, such as strengthening the Republican party, punishing the Southern states, or freeing the slaves. " I will vote," he declared early in the session, " what is required to enable the Executive to sustain the Government—not to subjugate the South. . . . I distrust power wherever it is delegated. Its tendency is always to aggrandize itself." Cox voted enthusiastically for the Johnson-Crittenden resolutions that stated the war was being fought " to defend the supremacy of the Constitution . . . to preserve the Union . . . [and] as soon as these objects are accomplished the war ought to cease." [22]

Following through with a resolution of his own, he asserted his aim to end the present " difficulties by rational methods " and proposed that a Northern commission composed of Martin Van Buren, Millard Fillmore, Franklin Pierce and others should meet with an equally eminent Southern commission " on the first Monday of September next " to work out a settlement. Although voted down

85-41, this resolution clearly expressed Cox's position on the war—war as necessary, a reasonable compromise settlement as soon as possible.[23]

Cox had no use for Democrats who joined with the Republican party. In his official eulogy of Douglas on July 9, he called the latter " a statesman, who, foreseeing and warning, tried his utmost to avert the dangers which are now so hard to repress." He urged his fellow congressmen to heed Douglas's final words " to his children and his country: ' Love and uphold the Constitution of the United States.' I speak it reverently when I say that this was his religion." [24] The Democratic party in the North, Cox said, should still seek to " repress " those dangers Douglas foresaw and should maintain a separate, distinct organization, keep a watchful eye on the Lincoln Administration, and be ready for the day when Democrats would return to power. Of his own political activity in the fall of 1861, Cox wrote a fellow representative: " I have been busy . . . making my Dist.—all right as usual. . . . Dem by increased majorities— although the meanest combination of bastard Dems united with this new party to defeat us." [25] At the same time in a note to Senator Andrew Johnson, Cox suggested that his 1859 attack on Joshua Giddings might be of use to Johnson in his fight against " some extreme Fire-Eater of the South." [26]

Even while supporting vigorous prosecution of the war, Cox tried to encourage Southern Unionists by calling for fair treatment of Confederates, a quick exchange of war prisoners, a readiness to consider proposals to end the war by negotiation through conciliation and adjustment of interests. Consequently, he opposed efforts at change, such as emancipation of slaves and raising of the tariff. These, he said, were measures of revolution, not of restoration of the Union as intended by the Johnson-Crittenden resolutions.

Using traditional appeals, he resorted to that ancient refuge of the minority—states rights under the Constitution. The Administration, he held, must be constantly watched and called to a halt when it exceeded its constitutional authority. Eternal vigilance must be exercised to preserve personal liberties and constitutional guarantees. Radical congressional leaders must not be allowed to impose their wills on a reluctant people. As a representative of the rural agricultural West, he protested against New England abolitionists and Pennsylvania protectionists and sought to defend agricultural interests and to revive the flagging Democratic party, based on a loose affiliation of the agricultural West and the commercial Northeast.

In the fall of 1861, Democrats generally suffered defeat and discouragement. Mobs in Ohio destroyed Democratic newspaper offices and broke up Democratic rallies. These outbursts of violence brought the Democratic leaders to the realization that the best way to oppose the Administration was to appeal to the Constitution, which guaranteed individual liberties—a strategy used by antislavery leaders a quarter of a century earlier in the battle over the " gag " rule in Congress. The charge that the Republicans fashioned the war simply to destroy the Democratic party came to be repeated and elaborated by Democrats in their appeals to the voters throughout the war.[27]

When Congress reconvened in December, Cox began to goad the Republican leadership. Employing the traditional methods of political opposition, he offered dilatory motions and motions to amend; he insisted on roll calls and satirized Republican inconsistencies. As minority leader in the House he often won his point by taking full advantage of any chink in the opposition's armor. At other times, he used rational persuasion to accomplish his purpose.

The exchange of war prisoners especially concerned Cox, since one of his brothers was serving in the Union army. If the uprising were construed strictly as a rebellion, captured Confederate soldiers and sailors would logically be considered traitors subject to the death penalty. The practical difficulty that blocked execution of this legally correct view was the large number of prisoners captured by both sides. President Lincoln, by proclaiming a blockade of Confederate ports, had given at least partial legal recognition to the belligerent status of the Confederacy. In spite of this, the North, early in the war, threatened to treat Confederate privateersmen as pirates, subject to the death penalty upon capture. In response, the Confederate government announced that it would retaliate in kind against Northern prisoners if the Union threat were carried out. Cox argued that fellow Americans should avoid measures of such extreme cruelty to each other, even in war. If speedy restoration of the Union were to be achieved and friendly feeling re-established, harsh treatment of prisoners could not be tolerated.

Early in January 1862, Cox offered a resolution in the House to obtain information from the President regarding the arrangements for prisoner exchange.[28] When no answer came, Cox, pressed by some New Yorkers to intercede, called on Lincoln at the White House. Their first conference was unproductive, but Cox was invited to call again. He did, and later reported on the interview:

> " Mr. President, you are endeavoring to put down this insurgent force by force." " Yes." " You desire to keep alive the patriotic sentiment?" " Yes." " The Irish are a martial race. The Sixty-ninth [New York regiment] are Irish. . . . Will you discourage them?" " No." " Will not this threat of retaliation and hanging rob the service of some of its best soldiers, and detract from its gallantry and *esprit*?" " Yes." " Well, then,

Mr. President, if much good and no harm results from relieving our Union officers in durance, South, why not exercise your prerogative? " " Ah, there it is," said the President, " you will have me recognize these pirates as belligerents. Remember that the fight on land is one thing, but on an unstable element like the sea, where men are isolated and helpless, is another."

This was, then, the sum of the reasoning against the exchange of prisoners. It had in it no element of humanity or international law. The writer then put one more question: " What is the difference between firing a shot at yonder flag (pointing out the White House window to the flag flying from one of the forts on the Virginia hills from Ball's Cross Roads, where you can almost see the ' stars and bars,' and firing a shot at the same sacred emblem from under the same ' star and bar' bunting upon the mobile element? Are not both shots intended to take the life of the Union? Where is the difference in intent and conduct? Does the difference consist in yonder red banks and another from the blue sea? " The President quizzically pondered a moment over the *ad absurdum*, and then admitted there was no substantial difference. He promised relief. It came. Secretary Seward ordered an exchange of the so-called pirates as prisoners of war.[29]

Cox counted the early exchange of prisoners as one of his personal achievements in mitigating the harsh effects of war. An official exchange agreement with the Confederacy was finally concluded in the summer of 1862.[30]

Using humor and ridicule as a weapon, Cox, in January 1862, delivered a major speech that proved to be one of the most entertaining congressional performances of the session.[31] Several House members, notably John A. Gurley of Cincinnati, had denounced General George B. McClellan for failing to make any military progress. In reply Cox launched an attack on Gurley for working hand in glove with Secretary of War Edwin M. Stanton for McClellan's dismissal.

Commenting on Congressmen as military critics, Cox gave a rousing description of the precipitous retreat in which " Congressmen won the battle of Bull Run against our own soldiers. . . ." He then pointed to Gurley:

> . . . my colleague after a fatiguing race to Centreville, and having passed that point with the speed of Gilpin . . . was careening along like the devil . . . until luckily he met . . . a herd of stampeded cattle, who were from my own beloved district—Texas cattle, sir, wintered in the Scioto valley, and selected by their drover for the stampeding propensity . . . when, seizing upon the extreme rear of a noble bull, he was bourne from the field, holding with vigorous prehension to the tail of the animal! . . . This was Bull Run indeed!

Amidst much guffawing, the Speaker's call for order went unheeded. One member confessed: " I laughed; but for my life's sake, I could not help it." Cox went on from the " unique performance of my constituent and my colleague " to urge Gurley, a minister of the gospel, to have a little faith in McClellan.

He then enumerated McClellan's accomplishments. He related how McClellan had saved Washington, " held Beauregard and his army in a vise," retained Maryland, won Virginia's eastern shore, and whipped an army of 100,000 undisciplined men into an effective fighting force. McClellan deserved praise rather than censure for his generaliship:

> I would prefer that the war should be carried on and ended by bloodless tactics rather than by bloody carnage. . . . I would leave as little hate as possible as the legacy of this conflict. . . . General McClellan is not making this a war of vengeance, but a war for the restoration of the Union. . . . We shall see the Union element in the South dilating and emerging from its despondence.

It was evident that Cox hoped for a speedy end of the war.

As to proposed confiscation and emancipation, if such legislation should pass, " the North will rise to drive the free blacks from their soil and no good will accrue to the black or the white." Emancipation " will paralyze the efforts of the army." It " would be an act of fraud on the soldiers," converting the war into an antislavery crusade, thereby making it " a gigantic swindle upon the people." Not Congress but the state legislatures should decide the slavery issue. In the face of this " persistent and unreasoning fanaticism," Cox condemned " that dangerous and horrible malversation of our congressional office, which would usurp the power of the States over their own institutions." [32] This powerful speech, printed and later used as Democratic campaign material, turned men's thoughts to the nature of the war, the nature of the Union, and the complications that would arise from radical persistence in extreme measures like emancipation.

Letters in the next few months praised Cox for his damning ridicule of abolitionist Gurley and for his staunch defense of General McClellan. " Your speech on Gurley has been copied more or less by every paper in the Northwest," wrote one constituent. Another thought the speech had invigorated " dull and desponding " Democrats and urged Cox to " give Abolitionism the devil." One correspondent hoped that Cox would " get Ben Wade tied to the tail of a Jackass and then kick him to death. I mean Wade, not the Jackass." Ex-Congressman William H. English wrote from Indiana: " Would to God there were more like you in the House," while Cincinnati journalist Murat Halstead thanked Cox for " a hearty laugh at the expense of Col. Gurley who will probably never more relish ox-tail soup." [33]

By spring 1862, Cox, " busy watching the devilish machinations of these Abolitionists here," wrote optimistically to ex-President Franklin Pierce, " I think we have them beaten in the House." [34] In April he was paired against the bill, which passed, for compensated emancipation in the District of Columbia.[35]

As the tempo of the fighting increased, with Union armies pushing down the Mississippi Valley and pressing Lee's forces on the peninsula, so too the temper of politics rose. Radical Thaddeus Stevens in the House continued to press for confiscation of Confederate property and emancipation. Earlier, in August 1861, Congress had enacted a confiscation act providing for seizure of all property used for " insurrectionary purposes," a phrase left perhaps intentionally vague. Now a far more sweeping measure, the second confiscation act, was introduced and ultimately passed. It proposed the confiscation of the property of all " enemies," slaves of all persons supporting the rebellion to be " forever free of their servitude." [36]

Cox denounced this proposal in a lengthy speech on June 3. Recalling the Johnson-Crittenden resolutions, he urged the President to " reassure . . . the public mind " as to the purpose of the war. Then, playing on Northern fears of Negroes flooding the North, he boldly asked: " Is there a member here who dare say that Ohio troops will fight successfully or fight at all, if the result shall be the . . . movement of the black race by the millions northward to their own State? " Pressing his point home, he said, " I would protest against this ambiguous policy " of professing a war to preserve the Union but actually fighting a war to abolish slavery. As for the cause of the war, he argued: " Slavery is the occasion, but not the cause . . . but slavery agitation, North and South, is the cause." War guilt should be shared by both " secession and abolition." Republicans were condemned for working " to free the Negroes, regardless of Constitutional limitations and consequences."

Republicans, Cox charged, were changing their attitude on the nature of the war. Where first they had asserted that it was not a civil war, now they were contending that the laws of war between nations should apply and should make confiscation possible. Granting, however, that confiscation and emancipation were Constitutional and in accord with the law of nations, Cox based his opposition on " more conclusive reasoning." The question was " the preservation of the people and society of the North." Northern states would not receive freed slaves, even though many " will be freed incidentally by the war." Indiana and Illinois, the President's own state, already forbade entrance of Negroes. Then, in explanation, Cox offered: " I do not speak these things out of any unkindness to the negro." Rather, " I speak as their friend when I oppose such immigration . . . of the free negroes."

Emancipation would benefit, therefore, neither North nor South. The effect in the North would " detract from the prosperity of the community." Returning soldiers would find Negroes in their former jobs and rates of pay down by 50 per cent. On the other side, with the South's labor system destroyed, " the markets of the South will be closed " and " our prices of corn, wheat, beef, pork, etc., will be reduced. . . ." Thus emancipation would mean " loss to the South and damage to the North . . . and no gain to either." Cox's answer to the problem was to " leave to the States their own institutions " where the Constitution left them and " keep your faith in the Crittenden resolutions." [37]

At home in Ohio Cox's views on emancipation and speedy restoration of the Union won approval from at least one segment of public opinion. Letters from constituents and others praised his work. One wished that Cox were President " instead of that old Rail Splitter and Union Splitter." Murat Halstead urged Cox to lead in forming a new party separate from Republicans and Democrats to " administer the government so as to let the people alone as much as possible and permit the progress of the natural order of things." [38]

Ohio Republican legislators, resenting Cox's obstructionist attacks on the Lincoln Administration, proceeded to redistrict the state under the new federal reapportionment act that cut Ohio's congressional representation from twenty-one to nineteen. Cox's district was redrawn to make his re-election virtually impossible. George Converse wrote from Columbus: " Every Democrat will vote against any bill that will not save the capital district." The final gerrymander lines set by Republican leaders aimed primarily at removing both Cox and Vallandigham from Congress. " This deed of infamy," wrote a Cox supporter, " out-Herods Herod. . . . It is a shame and a disgrace." [39] It was small solace to Cox that Democrats in Ohio's legislature gave him their complimentary vote for Wade's seat in the Senate.[40]

Reporting the change, the *Ohio State Journal* of April 18, 1862 predicted that " Sam Cox . . . an admirable fool killer " would be buried " 1500 fathoms deep " in the coming elections. The new district had in 1861 given a Republican margin of 2,200 votes out of a total of 18,000.[41] Although resenting this legislative scheme for his retirement, Cox wryly referred to himself as a " prospective constituent of . . . [Samuel] Shellabarger . . . in the new district," which the legislature " has made for my especial contemplation." [42]

Before leaving Washington, he served as secretary of a group of thirty-five congressmen, who, under the lead of John Crittenden, issued a statement declaring that the Constitution and the Union must be preserved; that the army should not fight for any party purpose; and that the war's purpose should remain as stated in the Johnson-Crittenden resolutions of 1861.[43] This was the platform on which Cox stood for re-election.

August and September 1862 found him campaigning vigorously in his new district. He was condemned by the opposition paper for canvassing while his opponent, former Congressman Samuel Shellabarger, enlisted to help defend Cincinnati. Cox scoffed at this " squirrel campaign " and pointed out that he himself was assisting Colonel H. B. Carrington in securing army enlistments as well as campaigning for the restoration of the Union under the Constitution.[44] Hoping to reinforce his campaign emphasis on speedy reunion of the warring sections, he invited Crittenden to visit him at home and " give me a speech in this hour of trial." [45] Possibly because the fighting was raging near the Kentuckian's home, Crittenden declined with thanks but expressed his hope for Cox's election to prevent perversion " of this holy war for the . . . union into a mere anti-slavery party war." [46]

Many influences added up to Republican defeat in October 1862—waning enthusiasm for the stalemated war and the threatened military draft; fear that Lincoln's Emancipation Proclamation had changed the war into a crusade to free the Negroes who threatened to flood the North; and resentment against the arbitrary imprisonment of many newspaper editors, among them Congressman Edson B. Olds, John H. Kees, and Archibald MacGregor. These imprisonments underlined Democratic charges of despotic disregard of civil liberties.[47] As a result, Democrats captured fourteen of Ohio's nineteen congressional seats. Cox beat the odds stacked against him in the gerrymander, a 1,600-vote edge in his home county enabling him to win. Evidently, more than half the voters of his district approved his advocacy of armed force tempered with offers of conciliation but no emancipation. Shortly after the election, a newspaper correspondent quoted Cox as rejoicing " more over the defeat of Vallandigham than of any other candidate for Congress." [48] While Republicans cast about for explanations of their defeat, Cox led the Democrats back to Congress, confident that the people had just spoken in favor of his party.[49]

CRITICAL OPPOSITION: DEFENSE OF CIVIL LIBERTY, 1862-1863

One of the most ticklish problems in any civil war is the dilemma in which a government is pressed to respect civil liberties while it is prosecuting a war. In constitutional theory, government is expected to operate under the restraints of law. Where to draw the line between the government's power to defend itself and the individual's right to freedom of speech and action is at best a complex matter. Very often during the Civil War, exercise of war powers clashed head-on with exercise of individual liberties as guaranteed by the Constitution. To compound the difficulty, certain practices, branded as " disloyal," were often intertwined with agitation designed merely to embarrass the Lincoln Administration and to gain partisan advantage.

Notably in Ohio and New York, Democrats used the appeal to the rights of free speech, press, and assembly to agitate for the end of the Republican rule and for a negotiated end of hostilities with the Union preserved. Some observers charged the Democrats with self-contradiction. Others interpreted the Democrats' stand as sympathy for the Confederate cause. A conspiracies act and a treason act providing punishment for disloyal activity were not well enforced. President Lincoln, proceeding on his own initiative, suspended *habeas corpus* in specified areas and directed summary arrest of suspected persons. In September 1862 he proclaimed that, for the duration of the war, individuals engaging in disloyal activities would be subject to martial law and trial by military commission. Under this directive the War Department jailed thousands of offenders without civil trial. Democratic success in the elections of 1862 sprang partly from popular reaction against this policy of arbitrary arrest.[50]

Cox, outraged by the Republican charge of disloyalty against Northern Democrats, turned the charge against the Radicals. It was not Democrats " who urged the ' Wayward sisters ' to depart in peace," he said. " Were they Democrats," he asked,

> . . . who hounded on the war, and then bought Southern negroes to fight the battles in which they would not risk their own lives? . . . How many abolitionists . . . were hiding from the draft, or paying . . . substitutes? It was such craven creatures as these, who charged Northern Democrats with secession sympathy. . . . By what irony of events was it that these creatures— who were at times more disloyal to a constitutional Union than the most violent secessionists—who wormed themselves and their plots into national affairs, and prolonged the war in which they had no part, except to incite the conflict and fan the flames of passion? [51]

This view, though violently partisan, nevertheless contained a kernel of truth.

As the short session of Congress began in December 1862, Cox offered resolutions in the House condemning military arrests " as unwarranted by the Constitution " and " as a usurpation of power never given up by a people to their rulers." [52] Although these resolutions failed, Cox announced he would "keep on probing" this "most vital" question of personal freedom because the "Republicans are very much disposed to shirk" it.[53] On Thaddeus Stevens's bill authorizing the President to suspend *habeas corpus* and giving immunity from indictment to officers making military arrests, Cox joined twenty-five fellow congressmen in signing a formal protest.[54] This protest he forwarded to Lincoln with a letter asking why Edson Olds was not released from prison.[55]

In a mid-December speech on "The Meaning of the Elections of 1862" Cox blamed the Administration for the radical rule that had resulted in a divided Union, a national debt of $2,500,000,000, a tariff paying "millions into the pockets of capitalists from consumers," the destruction of "the rights of personal liberty," and the deaths of "at least 150,000 of the best youth of the country." Urging moderation, he maintained that the people in the recent elections had issued a new Ten Commandments:

> Thou shalt have no other source of power before you.
>
> Thou shalt not take unto thee any graven image of ebony. . . .
>
> Thou shalt not take the name of Liberty in vain; for thou shalt not be held guiltless for such sacrilege upon personal and constitutional freedom.
>
> Remember the election days of November . . . to keep them holy. . . .
>
> Honor the Constitution and the Union, if you would have your days long in the land.
>
> Thou shalt not kill—in vengenance and in vain.
>
> Thou shalt not degrade the white race by such intermixtures as emancipation will bring.
>
> Thou shalt not steal, nor suffer the money of the people to be stolen by the army of jobbers and contractors.
>
> Thou shalt not bear false witness against thy neighbors, charging them falsely with disloyalty.

> Thou shalt not covet they neighbor's servants . . . nor tax the
> people for their deliverance.

While these commandments were received with much laughter, Cox feared they would be ignored because " too many of the other side have lost their sense of responsibility by losing their offices."

The real purpose of the war, " so long hinted at," was at last revealed in the Emancipation Proclamation. The abolition of slavery " by Federal legislation and Executive proclamation " Cox promised to oppose as unconstitutional unless enacted by the states. He argued that the Administration would have to resort to a conservative policy " to adjust the causes of strife and bridge over this abyss, below which is surging the torrent of blood." The President would have to return to that key to political achievement found in " this once-honored word—COMPROMISE." " Force may subdue rebellion," Cox argued, " but other means must reconcile the people North and South," and the Union might yet be reunited " in the spirit of Christian brotherhood." [56]

During 1863 Democrats in Congress steadily opposed action by the Administration. Cox once again used old themes with new variations: New England's responsibility for the war, the unconstitutionality of emancipation, and the arbitrary despotism of the President.[57] He used exaggeration and distortion to check what he considered extreme action.

In February, he and his cohorts won modification of a Stevens-sponsored indemnity bill. Although the power to suspend *habeas corpus* was granted the President, military officers were required to give the names of those arrested to the federal judges of the districts in which the arrests were made. If the local grand jury did not indict within a specified time, the judge was to discharge such persons upon their taking an oath of allegiance.[58] Such tactics won Cox the grudging admiration of fellow Congressman James A. Garfield, who called him one of the " hardest Congressional opponents and critics that any Republican could hope to meet." [59]

Outside Congress, Cox's speech of January 13, 1863, before the Democratic Union Association of New York, attracted public attention and sharp criticism. Speaking on " Puritanism in Politics," he denounced the " arrogant, selfish, narrow and Puritan policy" of abolition which " has made the Union, for the present, impossible." War had come because " puritanism introduced the moral elements involved in slavery into politics." Condemning " republicanism that sustains emancipation " and abolitionism, he contended, " They are two separate links of the same Bologna made out of the same canine original " seeking to " undermine the structure of our society." Hailing the 1862 elections as evidence of a changed public opinion, he concluded: " The Democracy will . . . fight . . . for the restoration of THE UNION AS IT WAS, but the supremacy of THE CONSTITUTION AS IT IS " in the " healing spirit of mutual confidence and conciliation." [60]

When a new conscription bill was pushed toward a vote in the House at the end of February, Cox's efforts to amend proved futile. He finally took the floor to defend Democratic loyalty and to plead for a return to the original purpose of the conflict, citing the Johnson-Crittenden resolutions again. Accordingly, Democrats were striving to make the war " short and successful." To that end, the " present mission of the Democratic party " had to be " criticism upon the administration," yet the party had to remain " fearlessly vigilant against the encroachments of power." " We are for this Union by war " while war was necessary; " we are for this

Union by peace whenever peace is honorable and possible. We are opposed to any war for the abolition of slavery. . . . We are opposed to any peace that will mutilate the Republic." The proposed conscription bill would " mutilate the Republic " by depriving the states of their constitutional power over their own militia. As a result the national government would become " an irresponsible despotism." His own position, Cox felt, had been undermined in the past year. He had in good faith recruited soldiers by urging men to defend their Union only to discover that the war was now being fought to abolish slavery. This Cox called " base treachery and falsehood " to those who had joined the army to preserve the Union. Because of this shift in basic purpose, he declared he could " not trust the present Chief Magistrate." [61]

Recognizing extreme peace Democrats as a " large element in our party," he wanted it understood that " we in Ohio of the dominant kind in our party " wanted peace only with a restored Union. He urged editor Manton Marble of the widely-read New York *World* to express this view by " tabooing the Breckinridge element." Such tactics, he thought, would enable Democrats and moderates to control " this House in its next organization " in December 1863. Encouraging reports reached him from Albany: New York's governor, Horatio Seymour, had conferred with Vallandigham and Daniel W. Voorhees, an Indiana Peace Democrat, and had " modified their view " on peace at any price.[62]

The campaign for governor in Ohio had already begun when in January 1863 ex-Congressman Vallandigham announced his availability. Campaign material was soon at hand with the destruction of Sam Medary's *Crisis* office in Columbus by a mob of soldiers from nearby Camp Chase on March 6.[63] Democrats saw signs of statewide victory when the local spring elections swung in their favor.[64]

In mid-April General Ambrose E. Burnside, now commander of the Department of the Ohio, issued General Order No. 38 authorizing arrest of those " in the habit of declaring sympathies for the enemy." [65] On May 1, at an all-day mass meeting in Mt. Vernon, Ohio, Vallandigham, Cox, and George H. Pendleton denounced the Administration policy of suppressing civil liberties. Four days later Vallandigham, arrested at midnight in the bedroom of his Dayton home, was taken before a military commission.[66]

At the hearing, Vallandigham denied the commission's jurisdiction and called only one defense witness, Samuel Cox, who had hastened to Cincinnati the day after Vallandigham's arrest. On the stand Cox testified that Vallandigham's only reference to Burnside was that " he [Vallandigham] was not there [at Mt. Vernon] by the favor of Abraham Lincoln, David Todd, or General Ambrose E. Burnside." Cox declared further that he would have noticed any epithets applied to Burnside " because Burnside was an old personal friend of mine." Cox added that Vallandigham had spoken vehemently about the " President and his minion " but " I understood his condemnation of the war to be launched at the perversion from the original purpose." [67]

Vallandigham was convicted and sentenced to banishment. Indignant Democrats howled. Protest meetings gathered in Albany, New York, and Philadelphia.[68] Cox himself viewed Vallandigham's arrest as the " illegal compulsion of an arbitrary and tyrannical power." [69] The action by the military commission was strictly unconstitutional and illegal, Cox maintained. The President had not suspended the writ of *habeas corpus* in Ohio, and the War Department had not given Vallandigham's name to the federal district court, as required by act of Congress. The President's claim to authority implicit in his war powers, would, if recognized, make the President a " purely despotic " dictator, Cox said. The civil courts were still open in Ohio. If Vallandigham had done wrong, let them try him. While his own views differed from Vallandigham's, Cox argued that Vallandigham was entitled to exercise his right to free speech.[70] Although the Supreme Court refused to review Vallandigham's case, it reached a conclusion in the *Milligan* decision two years later that showed the law to be clearly on Cox's side.

But many of his constituents disapproved Cox's words. For example, the *Ohio State Journal* of June 22, 1863 referred to " little Sammy Cox " as a " demagogue," while on September 8 the Philothronean Literary Society of Westerville, Ohio, expelled him from honorary membership. Concerned over his own freedom, he rigged up at his bedside in his Columbus home a rope connected to a bell to warn his Democratic friends, " who were averse to a repetition of the Vallandigham outrage." [71] Such concern, however, did not deter him from forthright expression of his views, for in an address at Cooper Union in the fall he urged the people to maintain their civil liberty against " all the minions of power." [72]

In June 1863 the Democratic State Convention at Columbus nominated Vallandigham for governor. Cox was disappointed that McClellan was not named. In spite of having several thousand friends shake his hand so vigorously he had to have it bandaged,[73] he was able to compose a long letter to President Lincoln, pointing out that while " my position . . . on the war . . . has not been exactly that of my late colleague," nevertheless, Vallandigham had the " right to comment freely on all the acts of the Administration." He hoped that Lincoln would observe " the rules of fair play " and prove himself " magnanimous " by allowing Vallandigham's return.[74]

Although chosen by the convention as a member of the committee to carry a protest to the White House, Cox did not go to Washington. Instead, in mid-June, he addressed the Illinois Democratic State Convention at Springfield and shortly thereafter spoke to an audience of " twenty-thousand " in Milwaukee.[75] After a quick trip to New York, he continued his agitation for Vallandigham's return. In a letter to Secretary of State William H. Seward, who passed it on to Lincoln, he expressed his " faith in your sagacity " and hoped for a " reconsideration " of the case.[76] Later while stumping northern Ohio, he found himself trailed by a military agent. And when Burnside ordered suppression of the outspoken New York *World*, Cox had to make a " private agreement " to secure his copy as " waste paper " discarded by the Columbus post office.[77]

Vallandigham's defeat in the fall election crushed Democratic hopes for the year. Most Democratic papers agreed that the nomination had been a mistake since Vallandigham did not truly represent the view of the majority of Democrats on the war.[78] Cox thought that the out-of-state troops cast the decisive votes.

FOREIGN AFFAIRS

The chief concern of American foreign policy during the war was to prevent foreign intervention and aid to the Confederacy. As a member of the House Foreign Affairs Committee during the war years, Cox not only revealed an active interest in the shaping of American foreign policy but insisted that Congress should share in the making of that policy. At various times he offered resolutions calling on the President to submit to the House diplomatic correspondence with other nations: with Spain regarding Santo Domingo; with England, France, and Spain regarding the blockade of the Confederacy; and with all foreign powers regarding maritime rights from 1853 to 1861.[79]

Although in November 1861 Cox at first applauded the Navy's seizure of the British ship *Trent* and its Confederate commissioner-passengers, James M. Mason and John Slidell, sober second thought led him to a different conclusion. At the height of the *Trent* excitement, acting for his committee, he reported a bill for the relief of the owners of the British ship *Perthshire*, which had been seized by the United States. This action on his part took considerable courage in the face of mail from home which urged that the United States not " humble herself " before " the Lion's growls." [80] In support of the relief bill Cox contended that, despite our position regarding the *Trent*, we should make amends for the wrongful seizure of the *Perthshire*. The House agreed and ultimately voted payment.[81]

The House Foreign Affairs Committee turned over the *Trent* matter to Cox for presentation to the House. He was quick to see the reversal of the traditional positions of the United States and England regarding neutral rights on the high seas in wartime. By December 17, 1861, when he made his speech to the House, he was convinced that the United States should accede to England's demand for the release of the Confederate commissioners, since only by doing so would the American doctrine of freedom of the seas be upheld. Both Cox and Crittenden of the Foreign Affairs Committee attended a dinner at Secretary Seward's home when Seward announced the government's decision to release Mason and Slidell.[82]

Cox thought the *Trent* affair offered " the opportunity of giving an impulse to liberal maritime law." In a letter to ex-President Pierce, he stated that while " I almost regret I am in public life now," here is a " public question . . . in which I may take pleasure " and which provides " a chance to vindicate your administration." [83] England and France, he thought, would now be in a mood to give sympathetic consideration to the question of neutral rights at sea. In March 1862, therefore, he introduced a series of resolutions proposing to revive negotiations for American adherence to the Declaration of the 1856 Paris Congress on maritime rights. In return, European nations were to accept the conditions laid down at that time by the United States for the protection of private property at sea. The United States had previously rejected the Declaration of Paris on the ground that it did not give adequate protection in time of war to private property in international commerce. Elaborating on the importance of commerce, Cox insisted that " a vessel is the floating territory " of a nation, hence it is entitled to free movement at sea unless carrying contraband to a belligerent. He argued that if contraband had been defined more specifically, " the *Trent* difficulty would never have occurred." The release of Mason and Slidell, was " of little moment," he asserted, " if it be the occasion for a settlement of the law in favor of neutral rights." [84] In spite of strong feeling against our accession to British demands, Cox's constituents generally approved his course.[85]

Congress adopted his resolutions of March 1862, and shortly thereafter Secretary Seward opened negotiations with England on the subject, only to encounter an evasive response. For Seward, with whom Cox was on intimate terms, and for Seward's conduct of foreign affairs throughout the war, Cox had high praise, recording that the Secretary acted " in a spirit of moderation and patriotism " and " with an ability not surpassed in the diplomacy of any time." [86]

Early in 1861 Cox had assumed the job of counsel for many clients who were pressing claims against the government of New Granada (later called Colombia) for damages resulting from a riot in Panama City on April 15, 1856. His correspondence contains numerous letters regarding negotiations on this matter.[87] His clients included the Panama Railroad Company of which his friend, David Hoadly, was president, the Pacific Steamship Company, and forty-eight individual claimants. The corporation claims totaled more than $396,000, while individual claims amounted to about $225,-000.[88] The New Granada government, in a convention with the United States signed September 10, 1857, had acknowledged liability and agreed to have the claims submitted to an arbitration commission.

The commision began hearings on June 10, 1861. Cox filed his clients' claims and supporting briefs during the remainder of 1861 and the early months of 1862.[89] For a time the hearings were suspended and not resumed until late in 1865 when Cox appeared again as counsel.[90] The decisions, rendered in 1862, 1865, and 1866, brought awards of slightly over $25,000 and $5,000 to the Panama Railroad Company and the Pacific Mail Steamship Company respectively, while individual clients received amounts totaling $99,000.[91] How much Cox was paid for his legal services in these cases does not appear in the records. John Hay once observed that Cox had made a sizable fortune in claims cases. A 20 per cent fee would have brought him about $26,000. Perhaps he was looking toward future cases when, in March 1864, he secured House passage of a bill to authorize a convention with Ecuador for the settlement of neutral claims.[92]

Whether his efforts as a claims agent were responsible or not, Cox developed an active interest in Latin American affairs. In February 1863 he suggested that the United States should dismiss the minister of the deposed Colombian government.[93] In objecting to a later proposal to merge all missions to Central American nations into one mission, Cox asserted the importance of Central America to the United States, considering the Panama Isthmus, the Panama Railroad, the claims against Nicaragua, the Nicaragua canal proposal, and the possibility of expansion by Maximilian's Mexican government southward. " If there was ever a time," he added, " when we should have American diplomats in all these states, it is now " since Central America " is the connecting link between our eastern and . . . our Pacific States." [94]

Throughout the war, he reiterated his long-held view that it was the constitutional right of Congress to formulate and declare foreign policy. In support of this, he traced precedents through American history. A House resolution to enforce the Monroe Doctrine against French intervention in Mexico had been disregarded by the State Department, which intimated that the House had no right to instruct the executive in foreign relations. But Cox, with Henry Winter Davis, Foreign Affairs chairman, protested that it was the duty of the executive to respect foreign policy as formulated by Congress. He urged further that the House should maintain its independence and " not cringe before the executive power." [95]

DEFEAT IN 1864 AND REMOVAL
TO NEW YORK

MINORITY FLOOR LEADER: FOR THE
OLD UNION

By mid-1863 Cox sought support for his plan to gain working control of the new House for the Democrats and to win the speakership for himself. The growing rift between conservative and radical Republicans provided a favorable opportunity. Rumor had it that some Republicans might try a coup to nullify the effects of the Democratic success of 1862.[1] In August, assured of support from Ohio and border state delegations, Cox asked Charles Lannan, librarian of the House, to act " discreetly at the proper time to aid me." [2] In November he declined an invitation to attend the Gettysburg National Cemetery dedication in order to visit New York, where he won editor Manton Marble's support for his speakership candidacy.[3] By the end of November he was gloating: " I shall be the caucus nominee and shall combine as much of the Conservative vote as any one." [4]

When the new Congress met on December 7, 1863, he was generally acknowledged the outstanding House Democrat, but his plan failed. Nominated for Speaker, he received 42 votes to 101 for Schuyler Colfax, the successful candidate. The result left Cox minority floor leader and a member of the key Rules Committee.[5] As minority leader, he gave the Republican majority many anxious moments as well as plenty of laughs throughout the session.[6] He told John Hay, Lincoln's secretary, with whom he dined often, that " it was delightful to be in the minority," but that he was tiring of Washington and would go to Europe after McClellan's hoped-for success in the 1864 election.[7] Much of his opposition, which was in a jocular vein, was designed to place the majority in a ludicrous or contradictory position and to embarrass the Administration.[8]

Attacking the Administration's conduct of the war, Cox early in the session demanded more rapid exchange of prisoners and greater economy in departmental expenditures. His effort to secure repeal of the 1863 conscription act failed by a narrow margin but gave him an opportunity to condemn such " an unrepublican system of raising troops." [9]

In January 1864 he denounced confiscation as an "utter failure " since it " only stimulates rebellion " and " destroys the last remnant of Union feeling . . . in the South " by using " the weapons of revenge and despair." Confiscation, he asserted, was unconstitutional, amounting to an attainder and involving " posthumous punishment " of " unborn children." He praised the President for insisting that previous confiscation bills be in line with the obvious meaning of the Constitution. Here he pointed to Thaddeus Stevens who " must stand by the Administration " or " I charge him with being a traitor or a secessionist if he now desert Mr. Lincoln. . . ." [10]

Cox's bantering covered a deep seriousness of purpose. He opposed the revival of the grade of lieutenant-general for Ulysses S. Grant, and persuaded the House to adopt his resolution " that the rebellion . . . is hereby abolished." [11] George S. Boutwell, Massachusetts representative, later recalled how Cox had shrewdly blocked a move by Thaddeus Stevens to secure federal reimbursement for Pennsylvania's part in the Gettysburg campaign.[12]

Later in the session when Alexander Long of Ohio suggested in the House that the war be ended by a recognition of the independence of the Confederacy, Speaker Colfax came down from the chair to move Long's expulsion from the House. This " extraordinary spectacle " aroused Cox to an extemporaneous but careful explanation of the Democratic position. Long, Cox observed, spoke only for himself, not for the Democratic party, which disavowed all talk of recognizing the Confederacy. Then turning the accusation around, Cox listed prominent Republicans who earlier had expressed similar sentiments and who therefore deserved as much censure as Long. These Republicans were Congressman James Garfield, recently a supporter of a candidate who urged letting the South go, Senator Ben Wade, editor Horace Greeley, and even Abraham Lincoln who in 1848 had talked of the " people's right to rise up and shake off the existing Government." As to his own position, Cox asserted that he

> . . . would blast the power of the rebels by the strong hand of war. . . . The Republicans would blast the Constitution . . . and by destroying the Constitution you do not put an end to this war nor suppress the rebellion. . . . I will say this, THAT UNDER NO CIRCUMSTANCE CONCEIVABLE BY THE HUMAN MIND WOULD I EVER VIOLATE THAT CONSTITUTION FOR ANY PURPOSE.

In conclusion, he said that Northern Democrats opposed any

recognition of the Confederacy; they were "for the old Union, one and indivisible." [13]

Cox received praise from various quarters for his stand in the matter of Long's right to speak his mind. From Boston a correspondent wrote, lauding him for "your fearless and patriotic stand in opposition to the mad, furious, and destructive course of the ultra abolitionists. . . ." A native Georgian, living in Akron, Ohio, thanked him for his loyal "devotion to principle." [14]

Speaking for constitutional, democratic government in the United States, Cox called for a return to the "old Union." He protested regularly against the high-handed, arbitrary actions of the dominant Republican party, which menaced not only civil liberties but threatened the foundations of the democratic system in America.[15] His opponents tried to belittle him by referring to him as "that cunning and deceitful demagogue" who was "raising a side issue." [16] But the issue Cox raised was a central one in the war. He pointed out frequently that the triumph of Stevens and his cohorts would bring on a revolution affecting almost every aspect of American life. Although his opponents finally won and proceeded without regard for the Constitution, had Cox not spoken out, the political debacle that followed the war and almost destroyed democratic government might have been even worse.

Meanwhile, in Ohio, Democratic extremists made Cox's position more difficult. The extremists had not modified their position following Vallandigham's defeat in October 1863. Some even hinted at violence through secret societies, such as the Knights of the Golden Circle. Others laid plans to gain control of the Democratic national organization in 1864. In one case, violence actually occurred when a mob blocked the drafting of a group of men in Holmes county,

Ohio.[17] However, when the Methodist Church conference at Lancaster, Ohio, adopted resolutions of support for the Administration, Dr. Edson Olds led a walkout of "peace Methodists." [18]

CAMPAIGN AND ELECTION OF 1864

Although internally divided, the Democrats looked forward hopefully to the 1864 presidential election. The extreme Vallandigham peace wing was held in check by war-supporting Democrats like Cox. As the war reached a stalemate, with Sherman checked at Kenesaw Mountain and with Grant "hurrying so many into death" before Richmond in June, dissatisfaction with Lincoln's Administration grew. Extreme radical Republicans nominated John C. Fremont for President at a Cleveland meeting in May, while Horace Greeley prodded Lincoln to end the war quickly. Even after his own nomination, Lincoln despaired to the point of writing at the end of August: "It seems exceedingly probable that this Administration will not be re-elected." [19]

Chances for Democratic success, therefore, seemed bright, if Democrats could choose the right candidate and avoid the smear of disloyalty. In early May, Cox, encouraged by his constituents, was working for McClellan as the strongest possible candidate.[20] In mid-July, after a quick trip to New York City and Saratoga, Cox returned to repair political fences in central Ohio. He was bitter against the "peace ultras" who "have been knifing me all they could." His homecoming speech was aimed at "giving McClellan life" and blasting the peace men.[21] In another political tirade, he called Lincoln "this executive trifler; this retailer of smutty stories; this tyrant over men's thoughts, presses, letters, persons, and lives," whom Cox hoped "the people in November will damn to an immortality of infamy." [22] After a conciliatory conference at Yellow Springs, Ohio, with peace advocates, Washington McLean of the Cincinnati *Enquirer* and George Pugh, he took a brief vacation in Montreal to rest for the coming campaign.

By August 21, with the Democratic National Convention but a week away, he was in Chicago with his father-in-law, Alvah Buckingham, prominent commission merchant and grain elevator operator,[23] who lived on Michigan Avenue, not far from the Wigwam. A colonel in Sherman's army wrote " confidentially " urging that the Chicago convention adopt a " Union war platform " and nominate Grant or McClellan. He added that " every one of " his fellow officers " would vote for him [McClellan] as a candidate." [24]

When the convention met at the Chicago Wigwam on August 29, Western delegates generally favored a peace platform and a peace candidate. Eastern men and some Westerners, like Cox, wanted a war candidate. The choice fell on McClellan, whose nomination Cox seconded. To pacify the peace element, George Pendleton was given second place on the ticket. The platform spoke of the war as a failure and urged immediate peaceable restoration of the Union.[25] McClellan's personal magnetism was counted on to win many voters, while the restoration platform and the vice-presidential nominee were expected to keep peace Democrats in line. Early in September McClellan's letter of acceptance emphasized the war's original objective, restoration of the Union, but rejected the peace-at-any-price doctrine. If elected, he would discard the Republican objectives of emancipation and punishment of the South. He would prosecute the war for a speedy restoration of the Union with a generous recognition of Southern rights within that Union. Most of the active Democratic leaders, with the exception of the

Vallandigham-Long group, spoke in favor of this proposition during the ensuing campaign.[26]

But Sherman's capture of Atlanta gave new strength to the Republican Administration. The plans of dissident politicians to replace Lincoln were frustrated, and Fremont withdrew from the race. Anti-Lincoln radicals were appeased by the retirement of Montgomery Blair from the cabinet. The Republicans entered the final weeks of the campaign in a strong position.[27]

Back in Columbus Cox found that McClellan's acceptance letter had raised some " tall cussing " by Medary as well as by Vallandigham, who had now returned from exile. However, Cox wrote Marble that McClellan's letter might " save the State . . . but don't count big on Ohio." As for himself, prospects looked bleak. There was a 5,000-vote Republican majority in 1863 in his district. He felt " like a lamb " being led to slaughter and considered turning down the congressional nomination.[28] But by September, he couldn't resist the lure of the political arena and accepted the nomination, hoping that with " a fair response from my friends in the Army—I can get through."

Meanwhile, Medary's *Crisis* refused support. Vallandigham Democrats shied away. On October 11, 1864, the *Ohio State Journal* called Cox " this little dodger " and told its readers to " repudiate him forever." For his campaign, Cox spent $2,000 of his own savings before sending his brother East with an appeal for assistance. From New York August Belmont, Democratic national committeeman, sent literature for Cox to distribute.[29] It was little wonder Cox felt " I am making my fight all alone." Finally at the eleventh hour New York Democratic lawyer Samuel L. M. Barlow sent $599, but Cox thought it came too late to help. When he tried to rally support among soldier-voters at Camp

Thomas near Columbus, he was "driven three or four times" away at bayonet point.[30] His ballots were not accepted when soldiers attempted to vote for him.

On October 12 and 13, the *Ohio State Journal* published the Ohio election results which showed McClellan behind Lincoln by 60,000 votes. The Unionists swept seventeen of the state's nineteen seats in the House. In Cox's district the vote stood 9,587 for Cox, 12,756 for his opponent, Samuel Shellabarger. For the first time in his career "Sunset" Cox had lost an election.

"This is a sad blow to your friends," wrote Barlow from New York, "but it cannot have surprised you very much. The District was too strongly against you, and I have no doubt the administration made special efforts to defeat your return." [31] The *Journal* of October 13 gloated: "The sun has verily set upon our friend of the pensive hour. So goodnight, Mr. Cox." The one consolation was that the Democratic deficit, which in 1863 was over 5,000 votes in the district, had been cut to about 3,000 votes in 1864.[32]

LAME-DUCK CONGRESSMAN, 1864-1865

Cox returned to Washington for what appeared to be his last days in Congress. He was disappointed over the election outcome and discouraged over the continuance of the war. But he retained his lively wit in congressional debate, and his willingness to see the war through was shown in December when he helped to raise volunteers in his home district.[33] In January 1865 he praised Greeley's efforts to secure peace and introduced resolutions calling on the President to receive or send commissioners to secure the end of hostilities. After the Blair mission to Richmond and the subsequent Hampton Roads conference had failed, Cox offered a resolution declaring that the President, in seeking to negotiate, " is entitled to the gratitude of a suffering and distracted country " and the encouragement to continue such efforts. He hoped that " the President is not broken . . . by the fierce onslaughts of his radical adherents " who supported the war for " revengeful purposes " to gratify " resentments and hates." In practical demonstration of his anti-war feeling, Cox voted on February 25 against the last conscription bill of the war.[34]

During the session, a proposal was made that cabinet members appear in the House one day a week for questioning. In a long, humorous speech delivered on January 26, 1865, Cox opposed the measure as an infraction of the Constitution. It would, he said, give undue influence to the executive whose powers had already grown too large. English parliamentary practice, he went on to say, was not adaptable to the American Congress. The separation of the branches of the government, provided by the Founding Fathers, should be retained. In a hilarious flight, he imagined the potential absurdities if the change were made. He pictured Secretary of War Stanton appearing in the House:

> The thundering Stanton comes! . . . Upon his brow the very feature of Mars, to threaten and command. Room for the war minister! . . . What to him is the civil list of George III? . . . Millions hang upon his smile. . . . What to him are the satrapies of the Indies? Whole hecatombs of greenbacks daily are sacrificed by his order. . . . Around him throng millions of tons of forage, guns, wagons, horses, and mules. . . . Before him fall, as before an oriental throne, the prostrate House. . . . He is flanked by my military colleagues [Messrs. Garfield and Schenck], and the House is ready for the questions! . . . My colleague [Mr. Garfield] . . . asks . . . whether the blowing out of the bulkhead of the Dutch Gap canal by General Butler has seriously affected the backbone of the rebellion. . . . How many vertebrae are demolished? . . . The gentleman from

Illinois [Mr. Washburn] would call up the head of the Treasury, and ask whether it would be best to tax the whiskey drank in the last century, with a view to assist Legislatures of the States to a patriotic choice of Senators . . . and if so, what amount should be levied on the spirits of '76? . . . But the gentleman from Vermont [Mr. Morrill], ever alive to the interests of New England, would inquire triumphantly of Mr. Fessenden whether the tariff should not be amended so as to increase the duty on dyestuffs and paper, so that, on a future issue of $17,000,000,000 of greenbacks, the tariff would be prohibitory, the prices raised, and a satisfactory deficiency produced in our revenues? . . . Or whether raising the price of dyestuffs and paper the value of the greenbacks may not be made equal to the cost of manufacture? . . . A Democratic member, . . . rising solemnly, would inquire of the War Department what protection, in case of foreign war, is afforded by the manning of Forts Warren and Lafayette by their present loyal force; if so, how many are there at this time, how long have they been there, and with what prospect of relief? . . . The gentleman from Indiana [Mr. Holman], the most useful member of this House . . . with what crushing results could he inquire of Mr. Stanton, what effect our Democratic efforts here to increase the pay of the soldiers have had on the recent elections. And if not, why not? . . . The gentleman from Iowa [Mr. Grinnell] should ask the Navy Department . . . whether or not the Argonautical expedition of Admiral Jason would have any effect on the gold market or the price of wool? . . .

Cox declared himself utterly opposed " to that truckling subserviency to the power of the Executive which will dethrone the people and make them fit tools for the corruption of an evil day." [35] This speech brought a request for a copy from President Lincoln, who wrote that he " sought it for the humor said to be in it; but while it meets my expectation in that respect, it has a far higher merit." [36]

Cox himself drafted and introduced another change proposed by the Rules Committee to divide the House Ways and

Means Committee into three committees to handle financial matters. The Ways and Means Committee, already over-loaded with business, was to retain its primary function of considering tax bills, but a new Committee on Appropriations would consider executive department estimates and appropriations, while a new Committee on National Banks and Currency would deal with matters in those fields. This division of labor, Cox felt, would be advantageous all around. The House agreed and adopted the necessary measures to make this change effective at the beginning of the next session.[37]

THE NEGRO QUESTION, EMANCIPATION, RECONSTRUCTION

Perhaps the thorniest question connected with the war was raised by the Emancipation Proclamation in 1862: what should be done about the Negro? Obviously, the war would not have been fought had there not been four million slaves in the South. Possibly the war might have ended sooner had not the emancipation question been raised. Restoration of the Union would have been simplified and reconstruction far less vindicative if the problem of the Southern Negro had not become intertwined with the political, economic, and social questions of the day.

Legally, the President alone could not effect permanent emancipation, as Lincoln himself admitted. Could a constitutional amendment be legally adopted when eleven states were " out of their proper relation to the Union? " Could it actually be adopted in the face of opposition from the border states and from the North? Or, more immediately to the point, granting adoption of the abolition amendment, how would four million freed Negroes in the South fare while making the transition to social and economic freedom? What provision could be made to ease the transition and to obtain Southern acceptance? Would compensation of former owners help? But social and economic implications aside, would freeing the slaves further the immediate objective of the war—restoration of the Union?

On the basis of a negative answer to this last question, Cox rested his opposition to emancipation. He revealed a thorough grasp of the constitutional, social, and economic aspects of the problem. His views were carefully thought through, consistently developed, and generally reflected those of his state and his section.

Ohio had not gone quite so far in regard to the Negro as Indiana and Illinois, both of which barred Negro immigration. But Ohioans had long feared that the state might be overwhelmed by an influx of freed Negroes coming up from the South.[38] Speaking for his constituents, Cox expressed the fear that so much congressional attention to bills and resolutions concerning the Negro served only to arouse America's passions.[39] The abolitionists, on the other hand, argued that if Negroes were freed, they could help in the fight to defeat the South by serving in the Union forces. A bill to provide for the raising of Negro troops was debated in January 1863. Cox vehemently denounced the scheme. Pointing out that Negro soldiers if captured by the Confederates would not be treated as prisoners of war, he labeled the bill as unfair to the Negro. Besides, " the people of the border states," would not consent to this plan. He concluded once again that the purpose of the war was being perverted; the Union soldiers had been deceived, for " they never went into a crusade for abolition." [40]

Toward the end of the war, the bill to establish a Freedmen's Bureau aroused Cox to declare that this was simply a counterpart of confiscation. He pronounced the bill " sweep-ing and revolutionary " in its effects since " it begins a policy for this Federal Government of limited and express powers, so latitudinarian that the whole system is changed " into a centralized, unitary government, operating " by edict and bayonet, by sham election and juggling proclamation." The real question was " the old order with Democracy to admin-ister it, or continued revolution with destructives to guide it; the old Union with as much local sovereignty as may be saved from the abrasion of war, or a new abolition and military unity of territory, with debt, tyranny, and fanaticism as its trinity." [41] Despite Cox's opposition, the Freedmen's Bureau was established and later became a storm center of political contention.

Regarding reconstruction of the South, Cox presented his views in a speech in May 1864. The chief defects in Lincoln's plan for reconstruction were that emancipation had to be accepted and that governments established by one-tenth of the voters were not truly representative. The Democrats, he said, believed in conciliation and in the " gentleness and effectiveness " of the Sermon on the Mount as well as in " the normal supremacy of the States over their domestic affairs." If slavery must go, " let it die . . . by the voluntary action of the States." The Southern states were still in existence as states and so entitled to their rights " if secession is a nullity, and if the Constitution is not impaired," as the opposition held. The Wade-Davis bill failed to recognize this principle and overlooked the need for generous forgive-ness if harmony between the sections was to be restored. Without these two essentials any plan was doomed to fail and would not receive his support. Again, he called for " the restoration of the old Union " on the principle of " common consent to the common government." " THE SOMETHING

SACRED in our political system is the written Federal Constitution, and the system of State Governments . . . the reserved rights of the states, and . . . the reservation of sovereignty in the people." The way to peace was to " restore the Union through compromise " not by " military governors for rebellious provinces." [42]

When a constitutional amendment to abolish slavery was proposed in Congress and passed the Senate in the spring of 1864, Cox helped block its passage in the House. But by the following January, when the House began reconsideration of the amendment, Cox's views had apparently been modified. Although still holding that restoration of the Union was more important than abolition of slavery, he was now convinced that abolition was inevitable. For the sake of political peace, he said, it seemed best to " eliminate the slavery question out of our politics." On a visit to New York in December 1864, he discussed the question at length with leading Democrats, Samuel Barlow, Samuel J. Tilden, and Manton Marble " around a table at Delmonico's." [43] " I look upon it as a question of party policy," he later wrote Marble. " We must not give the *ne plus ultras* [the extreme Peace Democrats] . . . a chance to rule out the really dominant and salutary influences on our side." If Democrats voted against abolition, "where will it place us? " " Why not strengthen ourselves for the future, by throwing off the proslavery odium? " Democrats must " get rid of the element [of slavery] which ever keeps us in a minority and on the defensive."

As reports reached Washington that Southerners were freeing their slaves for use in the army, it was clear that the end of slavery would not be a bar to negotiations for a restored Union. So on January 21, 1865, as Cox recorded later, " I fully intended . . . to cast my vote for the amendment." [44] He had explained his position at length several weeks earlier. Conceding the power to amend the Constitution to abolish slavery, which some colleagues like Pendleton still denied, Cox preferred to leave the question " to the States individually." He had urged a policy of nonintervention by the government in the slave question ever since " I first came to this Congress." Slavery " is to me the most repugnant of all human institutions," but the principle of " self-government " by the states over their own affairs was " even more precious than the end of human bondage," for, if the federal government could interfere in this matter, then federal interference could be expected in all domestic matters. Most important of all, however, was the Union. If peace with Union could be achieved " by the abolition of slavery, I would vote for it." But if abolition " is an obstacle in the way of restoring the Union," as Cox felt it was at the moment (with the Blair mission in Richmond), then he would vote against it. [45]

However, with the amendment scheduled for a vote in the House on January 31, he decided to vote for it. But he changed his mind again, when, on reaching the House that day he learned that Confederate commissioners were actually at General Grant's headquarters ready to negotiate to end the war. Feeling now that the proposed amendment might " prove an insurmountable obstacle " to negotiations, Cox cast his vote against the amendment, despite the fact that he had brought with him a prepared speech announcing his intention to vote for it. [46] The following day he expressed regret over his vote: " I did want to vote for that [Thirteenth] Amendment."

But it was a relief to him to have the slavery question out of politics. [47] Later, when William H. Seward explained that it was " Mr. Cox . . . to whom personally, more than any other member, is due the passage of the constitutional amendment abolishing African slavery," he was referring obviously not to Cox's vote but to Cox's work in convincing other Democrats in the House that the Constitution could be amended in this regard.[48] Some eight Democrats refrained from voting, no doubt because of Cox's pleas. This number would have been able to prevent the necessary two-thirds approval, since the amendment passed by a vote of 119 yeas to 56 nays.

Before the lame duck session of Congress ended on March 3, 1865, Cox took care of a number of rountine matters and had the pleasure of seeing the House adopt his measure that created the Appropriations Committee and the Banking and Currency Committee to handle part of the work formerly in the hands of the Ways and Means Committee. He now concluded his first period of service as Regent of the Smithsonian Institution on behalf of the House, a post he had held with great interest since 1861.[49] After a visit to Grant's headquarters near Petersburg in mid-March 1865, he packed his bags. His own political future was uncertain, but he thought the Democrats should turn now to issues like the tariff. "Commerce and agriculture will, as soon as the excitements of war are over, . . . begin to grow so audibly that even the adders of politics will hear." [50]

REMOVAL TO NEW YORK CITY

With the war at an end, Cox decided to move to New York City. The factors that went into this decision are not entirely clear. With his defeat in the 1864 election and with the odds stacked against him by gerrymander of his Ohio district, he may have thought his political life finished, although he does appear to have been tired of it at the moment. Or, facing a dark future in Ohio politics, he may have been seeking "a more dependably Democratic district," as one recent writer has said.[51] A contemporary New Yorker gave support to this view when he wrote: "One of the best things Tammany Hall ever did was to offer to nominate Cox . . . if he would come to that city to reside."[52] Already Cox had made important connections in New York. He had spoken often before Democratic rallies there and counted among his friends such Democratic leaders as Samuel Barlow, August Belmont, Erastus Corning, and Manton Marble. It is possible that both family ties and his desire to improve his financial position entered into the decision. At any rate, when his father-in-law, Alvah Buckingham, bought the house at 13 East Twelfth Street in New York, Cox and his wife took up residence there, along with her sister, Elizabeth, and Elizabeth's husband, John A. Hardenburgh, a merchant and director of the Irving Savings Bank.[53] Cox also opened a law office at 132 Broadway in partnership with Charlton T. Lewis.[54]

Reviewing his congressional career, in the dedication of his book, *Eight Years in Congress*, which Appleton published in 1865, Cox told his Ohio constituents:

> I represented you truly, when I warned and worked from 1856 to 1860 against the passionate zealotry of North and South; when I denounced, in and out of Congress, the bad fallacy and worse conduct of the secessionists; when I voted to avert the impending war by every measure of adjustment; and when, after war came, by my votes for men and money, I aided the administration in maintaining the Federal authority over the insurgent states. Sustained by you, I supported every measure which was constitutional and expedient to crush the rebellion. In the perusal of these pages, no one will find any aid, by speech or vote, given to those who raised the standard of revolt.

Here, in his valedictory to Ohio, spoke the man of moderation who had fought against the tide of violence and civil war and who was now pushed aside to make way for even more extreme measures than the war had seen.

three

CLOUDS:

YEARS OF DESPAIR, 1865-1877

5

RETURN TO POLITICS,
1865–1872

In New York, Cox lived in a substantial, brown-stone-front house on Twelfth Street in the then currently fashionable section just east of Fifth Avenue. He had high hopes of improving his position financially as well as politically. His law partner, Charlton T. Lewis, characterized by James G. Blaine as a " man of brilliant attainments and one of the most accomplished graduates of Yale," [1] was an established leader of the New York bar. Professional success for Cox seemed assured. Clients included merchants, bankers, and shipping firms.[2]

He kept in close touch with both political leaders and political events. After Lincoln's assassination and President Andrew Johnson's proclamations of 1865, the Southern states attempted to re-establish their governments. It was in this return of the ex-Confederate states to the Union that Cox saw a chance to revive the Democratic party.

Radical Republican leaders, too, saw the possibility of Democratic revival and viewed it as a distinct danger. Johnson's plan of reconstruction was very similar to that of Lincoln. During the summer and fall of 1865 the ex-Confederate states adopted new constitutions, abolished slavery, organized new governments, and elected state and federal officials.

When Congress met in December 1865, Southern representatives-elect presented themselves. Had moderate counsels prevailed, these men would have been seated, the new Southern state governments would have been recognized, and reconstruction in a legal sense would have been effected. But Radical leaders, resenting Johnson's exercise of executive power and the appearance of prominent Confederate officers as congressmen-elect, refused to accept the situation. Thaddeus Stevens made no secret of his partisan intention to keep the Southern states out of the Union until Republican power could be consolidated, for, he asserted, " on the continued ascendancy of that party depends the safety of this great nation." Congress proceeded to repudiate the President's work. Years of wrangling, revolution, and punishment for the South ensued. " The Union was rent in twain," wrote Cox. " What neither secession nor war . . . could do was now done by act of Congress and radical hate. . . . Here began the second contest to save the Union; a contest no less pregnant with the fate of American institutions, and no less bitterly fought. . . . It took almost a quarter of a century to silence the guns of Moultrie and Sumter! " [3]

As differences between Johnson and Congress grew in the winter of 1865-1866, Cox gradually moved to support the Administration. He was convinced that the Radical Republicans posed as much danger to the country as the pre-war abolitionists had. In many cases they were the same individuals. In February 1866, Cox addressed a Baptist meeting in Washington, declaring that " New England is the Pea in the National Shoe," and two days later he spoke in defense of Johnson's reconstruction views.[4]

Cox's legal business necessitated frequent trips to Washington. His correspondence reveals his efforts on behalf of clients to secure oil leases, collect bills from the government, influence legislation, and collect further claims against the Colombian government.[5] But his heart remained in politics. When a friend wrote, " If Sam was here now we would put him through with a big majority," he was tempted to return to Columbus.[6]

As fall approached, he sniffed the air like an old fire-horse, his eye fixed on the nomination for Congress in a New York district. Manton Marble of the New York *World* gave him encouragement. The Sixth Congressional District representative, Republican Henry J. Raymond of the *Times*, had fallen out with the Radical leaders of his party over reconstruction policy. Cox could not conceal his desire for Raymond's seat. Realizing that the Johnson Administration tended to favor Raymond, Cox, on a trip to Washington, talked with cabinet members Henry Stanbery and Hugh McCulloch in an effort to check New York Customs House patronage of Raymond. Cox also tried to persuade President Johnson to accept the proposed civil rights amendment as a matter of political expediency, but " there's no budge in him. . . . It didn't change him," he wrote.[7] Although failing to secure the congressional nomination, Cox remained on good terms with Johnson and secured several federal appointments for friends as well as one for his father who became the federal pension agent at Columbus.[8]

Cox found political prospects in New York discouraging. A trip to Ohio to attend his mother-in-law's funeral in Sep-

tember made him question " whether it is worthwhile for
me . . . to come back to New York. I have had such ill
luck in all but making money!" When his former constituents of the " rough and hearty Democracy" gave him
a rousing welcome and when a former constituent named
his son " Samuel Cox Bell," he confessed, " it almost makes
me desire to return to Columbus." [9]

Back in New York in November, however, some of his
old buoyancy reappeared for a time. Scanning Democratic
prospects for 1868, Cox hoped that Grant woud accept the
Democratic nomination for President. As for George Pendleton, whose name was advanced by the Cincinnati *Enquirer*,
" he will not do," Cox asserted. Horatio Seymour, he observed, " will likely be the New York man." [10] When in
December it was rumored that Cox was to be appointed
minister to Austria by Johnson, Cox asked his friend Marble
to use his influence to secure the appointment. But the rumor
was soon denied. Cox lamented that " this life " was " nearly
a failure with me." He was also depressed by the death of
his brother Thomas (who died in Nashville while still a
Union army officer in 1866), the death of his mother-in-law,
and the serious illness of another brother, his father-in-law,
and his sister-in-law. " It is nearly breaking my old plucky
spirit," he wrote.[11]

But the year 1868 opened more hopefully for him. His
nomination to the Austrian mission was made. Despite heavy
odds, he hoped for Senate approval, simply on the grounds
that the Republicans would like to have him " sent out of
the country in this election year." [12] Although his appointment was not confirmed, Cox stayed on in Washington for
a few weeks, seeking White House approval of pensions for
some New York veterans.[13]

Meanwhile, the Radicals had taken over Capitol Hill.

They rebuffed the President's reconstruction arrangements and overrode his vetoes of the Freedmen's Bureau and Civil Rights Bills. A National Union convention at Philadelphia in August 1866 tried to rally forces to check the Radical revolution. Johnson's desperate " swing around the circle " failed to hold the Radicals down. As Professor Howard K. Beale has clearly shown, the industrial forces allied with the Radicals, fearing loss of control in Washington, were able to obscure the real issues in the campaign of 1866 by the " claptrap " of patriotic slogans and war shibboleths. An overwhelming vote gave the Radicals virtually complete control of Congress.[14] The result was imposition of military rule on the South, adoption of the Fourteenth Amendment designed to provide the Negro votes necessary to retention of Republican political power, and the Tenure of Office Act, followed by efforts to make the President a congressional errand boy.

Here was revolution in the making. As Cox phrased it, " Revenge was sweet, but political ascendency and the power it confers was sweeter." [15] He scoffed at the Radical theory that permitted the Southern states to act as states in ratifying the Thirteenth Amendment but refused to let them act as states in electing representatives to Congress. " The sole object " of the Radicals, he wrote, " was to secure permanent ascendency of the Republican party . . . to be effected by the aid of the colored voters." [15]

Johnson, resisting Radical congressional encroachment on executive powers, attempted to dismiss Secretary of War Stanton, a move that backfired and led to his impeachment in March 1868. Cox was shocked by Johnson's trial, which he attended during his frequent visits to Washington. He was impressed by the array of defense attorneys, including Attorney-General Henry Stanbery (Cox's friend of Zanesville days), Jeremiah S. Black, former attorney-general, and William M. Evarts, a leader of the New York bar. " No such assemblage of legal talent . . . no such gravity of criminal charge," wrote Cox, had ever been seen in the " history of the Republic." [16]

He feared that Republican leaders were determined to oust Johnson because he " had failed to keep step with " them " on the road of extreme radicalism." During the impeachment trial those senators who favored acquittal conferred regularly at Reverdy Johnson's house with representatives of the President. Toward the end of the trial Cox was called from New York to attend one of these conferences. He was asked to talk with Senator John B. Henderson of Missouri, a fellow Douglas-Democrat in the pre-war days. He found Henderson agitated by a demand from his Missouri constituents that he vote for the President's conviction. But Henderson announced that he would vote " not guilty " the next day and at his request, Cox wrote a reply to this effect. Cox was delighted to carry this news to the White House, where " he found the President gloomy." Soon, however, Johnson's spirits revived and " a festivity was improvised on the good news," and, as Cox recorded it, " the morning dawned with roseate hues " bringing " vindication of a President, than whom no man was ever more villepended without justifiable cause." [17]

ELECTION OF 1868

By 1868 the radical Republicans had moved far toward solidifying their control of the national government. The drastic reconstruction program, emphasizing Negro suffrage, was being forced upon an unwilling South to insure future Republican control, which in turn would insure the permanence of the war-born economic measures—a high protective tariff, a national banking system, land grants and money subsidies to railroad builders, and a liberal immigration policy to supply labor for Northern industries.[18] The Democrats, on the other hand, badly split during the war, labored under taint of disloyalty and disqualification of the party's Southern leaders. Their best strategy lay in checking the most stringent of Radical reconstruction measures in order to restore quickly the Southern states, whose large Democratic strength might again operate in national elections.

In the North, although factions in the Democratic ranks often disagreed, there were many elements to which the Democratic party might appeal. Merchants, who suffered from the high tariff policy, workingmen out of jobs, Irish and German immigrants, men opposed to Negro suffrage and to military rule of the South, men shocked by Radical attacks upon the President and the Supreme Court, farmers whose prosperity declined once the war ended—all these might vote the Democratic ticket if politically courted. Friction, however, continued between the former peace wing and the war wing of the party. While Eastern Democrats hoped to concentrate on Radical violations of the Constitution, many Western Democrats now urged adoption of " Gentleman George " Pendleton's " Ohio Idea " of having the federal government issue $2,000,000,000 in greenbacks to pay off the national debt, keep farm prices high, and eliminate interest payments on government bonds. But most Eastern Democrats could not swallow this inflationary proposal.

As the Democratic National Convention approached, Pendleton, Governor Horatio Seymour of New York, and Thomas A. Hendricks of Indiana appeared as the leading contenders, with Chief Justice Salmon P. Chase also in high

favor. Cox privately expressed himself in favor of Chase.[19]
It was hoped that conservative Republicans, such as William
H. Seward, Hugh McCulloch, and Thomas Ewing, might
aid the Chase movement.[20] Chase's chances improved as the
convention neared. The New York *Herald* of June 24, 1868
came out in his favor, declaring that, as Lincoln's Secretary
of the Treasury, he had given " bread and cash " in contrast
to Republican candidate Grant's " blood and carnage." The
New York delegation, which included Cox, Governor Seymour, Samuel J. Tilden, national chairman August Belmont,
A. Oakey Hall, and William M. Tweed, were on the whole,
contending for Chase.[21] On July 4, 1868, when the convention opened, Pendleton held a commanding lead. Just
as the New York delegation was ready to open a drive to
stampede the convention for Chase, Ohio leaders switched
to Seymour.[22] The embarrassed New York delegation could
scarcely oppose its own governor. Seymour, despite his protests from the chair, was nominated with Frank P. Blair, Jr.,
of Missouri as his running mate.[23]

Since the popular Grant was the Republican standard-
bearer, the Democratic campaign was unrewarding. But the
year 1868 proved to be the beginning of a new political
career for Cox. Before the end of July he abandoned his
law practice and got " a little boost " from Manton Marble
to send him to Congress.[24] In October he was nominated as
the Democratic candidate for Congress in the Sixth Congressional District of New York. General George McClellan
wrote: " I congratulate New York City on your renomination, and . . . the Democratic party that you are going back
to your old place as leader in the House." [25]

The campaign was marked by strong support for Cox
from the regular Democratic Tammany organization, from
Marble's *World*, and unexpectedly from the New York

Post,[26] which urged Cox's election on the grounds that he stood for tariff reform. On the other side, Greeley's *Tribune* condemned Cox as " a brilliant little carpet-bagger from Ohio " and warned its readers that, if Cox were elected he would " be the leader of the Democratic party in the House." [27] When the election was over Seymour had lost to Grant by a 300,000-vote majority nationally, though he carried New York. Republican control of the South had paid off. In New York's Sixth District, 12,362 ballots were counted for Cox to 9,682 for his Republican opponent, George Starr.[28]

The district which had elected Cox lay on the lower west side of Manhattan, bounded by Houston Street on the south and West 25th Street on the north, 14th Street and Sixth Avenue on the east and the North River on the west.[29] The area was a conglomeration of busy docks, shipping firms' headquarters, warehouses, offices, tenements, and brownstone-front houses, occupied by stevedores, dockworkers, draymen, and office employees. The working class inhabitants totalled 123,000 of Manhattan's population of 942,292. Over 34,000 were foreign born, mainly Irish and German, while a large portion of those labeled " native " by the Census Bureau were probably first-generation Americans.[30]

With the election over, the strain of campaigning began to tell on Cox's small and not too robust physique. At the close of the canvass he suffered a hemorrhage and was put to bed "under morphine and politics." With symptoms of " lung trouble " appearing, he was advised to take a trip abroad for his health. By the end of November he and his wife were preparing to depart with a " trunk full of maps and books to study up Palestine and the Orient." [31]

Their trip lasted from December 1868 to September 1869. Months of rest on the French Riviera helped him recover from the attack of tuberculosis. But even abroad, Congressman-elect Cox could not forget American politics. He sent Secretary of the Treasury Hugh McCulloch congratulations on his proposed contraction of greenbacks and asked for a copy of economist David A. Wells's revenue report. Learning that a special session of Congress was called for March 4, 1869, Cox worried that his New York constituents might object to the absence of their representative. He wrote Marble asking that the reasons for his stay in France be explained in the *World*. After March 4 the " rampant doings " of Congress disturbed him. Wondering " if [Speaker James G.] Blaine put me on a committee," he remarked, " I suppose not. I shall have to play the guerilla." [32]

RETURN TO CONGRESS, 1869-1870

Cox's return to the United States in 1869 coincided with the climax of the infamous Jay Gould-Jim Fisk " gold conspiracy " that culminated in the " Black Friday " debacle. His re-entry into politics coincided with the rise of " Grantism " in the national government and " Tweedism " in New York. The prosecution of the Civil War with its shoddy contracts and vast bond sales had fostered indifference about the methods by which wealth was obtained. In the late 1860's a large group of men, enriched by the war, sought further means to increase their fortunes. The low moral tone of business spread into other fields. Contemporaries commented on the " steady demoralization of the bar," the debased nature of the press, and corruption in courts and legislatures.[33]

In the national government, Radical control of Congress had already opened the doors to plunderers seeking vast land grants, to lobbyists working for subsidies and tariff favors for their corporations, and to general adventurers.[34] The reconstruction program, plus flag-waving and boasts of patriotism, made an effective cover for the pursuit of private gain. The Grant Administration simply carried on what had already begun.

In New York, Tammany, long the power in local politics, had fallen under the control of " Boss " William M. Tweed's political machine, a machine with gears which meshed smoothly in each precinct, ward, and district under a batallion of lieutenants and " ward-heelers." Through its control of city patronage, courts, contracts, and taxation, and by direct favors to voters, especially to newly-arrived immigrants who would vote the " straight ticket," the Tweed machine won elections with monotonous regularity. In fact, Democratic majorities of almost any given size could be produced in the city, as the Republicans charged had been done in the 1868 elections.[35]

Cox received Tammany support, as did any Democrat who hoped to be elected in Democratic New York City. How close the relationship was, however, is impossible to determine. Cox, as well as other eminent Democrats, such as Samuel J. Tilden, Abram S. Hewitt, Charles O'Conor, and George B. McClellan, appeared on the same platform with Tweed. Although Republican charges of corrupt election methods in 1868 were directed at many Tammany districts in lower Manhattan, they were not leveled at the wards comprising Cox's district.[36]

When Congress reassembled in December 1869, Cox took up where he had left off four years before. During the special session in March, Congressman Fernando Wood had drawn a good seat for Cox down front, and Speaker Blaine had appointed him to committees, thus obviating Cox's fears of being " a guerilla." [37] As he looked about him, he missed many of the old leaders, notably Thaddeus Stevens and Schuyler Colfax. Others, however, like Fernando Wood, Robert C. Schenck, James A. Garfield, William B. Allison, Daniel W. Vorhees, and Henry L. Dawes were familiar. His Democratic colleagues expected him to give leadership to the wobbly ranks of the minority. Appointment to the important committees on Rules, Banking and Currency, and Foreign Affairs indicated something of his standing. He was also reappointed regent of the Smithsonian Institution.[38]

As an opposition party member, he resorted to the tactics he had used to such good effect during the Lincoln Administration—argument, delay, ridicule, witty retorts, dilatory motions, and demands for roll calls. At one point, in order to get a bill passed, he went out of his way to make a strong contrary statement, which brought Republican support for the bill as an almost automatic response.[39] More often, however, he thought, " There is only one way for a Dem. in opposition—that is, to charge the other side . . . with making all the mischief and failing in any remedy." [40] If this failed to block measures completely, it did perhaps keep the Republicans from more extreme steps.

Early in the session Cox plunged into the tariff controversy. High tariff duties, ranging from 30 to 500 per cent *ad valorem*, sometimes in addition to specific duties, had been passed partly as a wartime measure and partly as a sop to manufacturers to balance high internal revenue excises levied on practically all manufactured products. By 1868 most internal taxes had been repealed, but tariff rates still stood at high wartime levels. Any suggestion to reduce customs duties was denounced by manufacturers as a British plot to destroy American industry. These manufacturers spoke through the wool and iron lobbies, through congressmen like William D. ("Pig Iron") Kelley of Philadelphia, and through journalists like Horace Greeley.[41]

David A. Wells, special commissioner to study revenue problems, made a series of reports recommending that the tariff, at least on raw materials, be reduced in the interest of lower manufacturing costs and lower consumer prices.[42] Manufactured goods continued to rise in price during the post-war years. The tariff, if not "the mother of trusts," was certainly an effective wet nurse. Some Western farmers were beginning to oppose a high protective tariff which did not include farm products but increased the prices of the articles they had to buy. Some consumers, who were pinched by higher prices, as well as shippers and importers, whose volume of trade was cut, joined in the opposition. For these opposition groups Cox proved an effective spokesman in Congress. He advocated a lower tariff which would stimulate foreign trade, lower prices of manufactures in America, and bring general economic well-being. He spoke partly in terms of a return to the old order of commerce and agriculture, and partly, perhaps more than he realized, in terms of the future need of foreign markets for American goods.

The Cox fight for tariff reduction pursued many tacks. On petition days he presented petition after petition from constituents and others urging elimination or lowering of duties on coal, steel, books, cigars, salt, lead, provisions, tobacco, coffee, tea, and sugar. He introduced one bill calling for the elimination of specific duties, thus leaving only the *ad valorem* duties; he introduced another to end the duty on coal and thereby "obtain cheaper fuel, light, steam and iron." He recalled that the 1864 tariff bill committee, on which he had served with Justin S. Morrill and William P. Fessenden, had agreed that high tariff rates were temporary and were to be reduced in the future when internal taxes were lowered.[43]

His great tariff speech in this session came on March 28, 1870, when he made a full-scale analysis of the protective system, its effects, and its remedy. The speech, filling ten pages of the *Congressional Globe*, contained a clear analysis in addition to the usual entertaining phrases and political bombast. He argued that the current high tariff forced the mass of the people " to contribute to the protected classes " through " the most . . . remorseless form of public robbery " ever practiced. The argument that American wages were higher because of the tariff was mere " buncombe," and, even if true, would apply only to that 7 per cent of Americans engaged in protected industries. The great minds of the age —Adam Smith, Richard Cobden, John Stuart Mill, Francis Wayland, Wendell Phillips, Henry Ward Beecher—had all seen the light of free trade. England had prospered since adopting free trade. How could Republican leaders, " so gushing with sympathy for blacks and humanity," close their eyes to the languishing state of American commerce and the " suffering paupers " among American industrial workers? Could they not see the " interdependence of nations " ?

With his flair for satire, he declared that that arch-protectionist, " Pig Iron " Kelley, carrying protection to its logical extreme, wished to pass a law eliminating the sun since it competed with American industry:

> He [Kelley] would close all windows, skylights, outside and inside shutters, curtains, blinds . . . openings, chinks, clefts, fissures, whereby the sun had entered into the prejudice of the meritorious manufacturers of candles, waxlights, lamps, candlesticks, street lamps, snuffers, extinguishers, and the producers of matches, oil tallow, rosin, and alcohol. . . . [Kelley would speak] for these manufacturers against the " sunbeam ",

as a free trader, destructive of American industry. . . . He must care for the producer of petroleum; he must stop this external competition from daylight! . . . He would say, What right has this uppish, solar foreigner to rival the coal-gas of Pennsylvania. . . . When he appears, is not the market for brass candlesticks and gas burners disturbed? . . . Is he not a secret enemy, bought by foreign gold? . . . He destroys the tallow business. That is a blow at agriculture, at hogs, oxen and sheep! . . . It is a foul blow at meadow, meat, wool, hides, manure. . . . He destroys the oil market! He plugs the gushing oil wells! He thus interferes with transportation, throws out of work workmen innumerable, and reduces wages. . . . He invades Alaska (and ruins the seal business). . . . Even the 4,000,000 seals practicing the Mormon doctrine will forget the gentleman's vote on Utah, and extend him their thanks with their flippers! . . . Why not build an opaque roof ribbed with steel over the land, regardless of expense, . . . that every coal-bank and mine may furnish coal for an American-made gas-retort.

Here was the protective tariff reduced to an absurdity. Could not Kelley see that where " God had provided different countries with different soil, climate, and raw materials " to produce different things, " *Providence teaches us freedom of exchange?* " Even Kelley illustrated " the dependence we bear on one another." Kelley was " a neat man " getting his silk handkerchiefs from Italy and his perfume from Cashmere, " a gay man " getting his diamonds from Holland, " a fast man " getting his sherry from Spain, " a smoking man " getting his cigars from Cuba, and " a family man " getting his coffee from Java. How could he speak of " isolation and seclusion " ?

The protective system raised prices on everything " from a flat-iron to a ten-penny nail; from a telegraph wire to a hoop skirt," thus enriching the iron and steel makers. " The farmer, mechanic, and laborer " really needed protection against "the privileged classes here, acting through their willing agent, the Republican party." The "system of duties and bounties" which made $100 worth of steel cost $207 in the United States was creating an aristocracy of wealth that shook the very foundations of democracy.

Cox's remedy was to lower the tariff and remove as many duties as possible. Let industry produce efficiently and cheaply under the stimulating competition of outside producers. As he saw it, Eastern laborers, Western farmers, and Southern planters were aligned against the industrialists of the East. The parties, he hoped, were now entering a clearcut contest on economic issues. "The Republican party represents the moneyed and privileged classes; the owner of Government bonds; the owners of the national banks; the manufacturer and the iron master." The Democratic party wished to lower taxation, reduce expenditures, and emancipate industry "by a policy of free trade." [44] Cox's analysis of economic interests was shrewd, even though his hope for a corresponding political alignment proved futile.

While the tariff debate continued through the spring of 1870, the "free for all scramble" of contending interests and "the barren and debasing work of lobbying" went on.[45] Cox continued his protest against "the new order of things since the war." He presented amendment after amendment to reduce the duty on iron ore from $9 to $4 a ton and to cut the tariffs on raw wool, cotton and woolen cloth, silk, manila hemp, nails, iron, wire cloth, and printing machines. He succeeded in getting a reduction of the iron duty to $7 a ton, as well as reductions on tea, coffee, and wine. Coal and salt were placed on the free list, but rates on steel rails, nickel, marble, and some other articles were raised.[46] When the bill received the President's signature, Cox would well agree with the editor of the *Nation* that "the high tariff men . . . actually killed " any real reform that might stimulate American commerce.[47]

Closely related to the tariff were the other questions of government finance in which he, as a member of the Banking and Currency Committee, took an active interest. The two most pressing problems concerned the refunding of the $2,500,000,000 national debt and the nature and quantity of the currency. At various times during 1870, he not only opposed any further issue of greenbacks but urged that " the irredeemable paper," having led to all kinds of monetary troubles and speculations, should be retired as rapidly as possible. Later, he stated that he was " raised in the Democratic party on the pot-metal basis, not on the greenback, lampblack, rag paper currency basis. . . ." [48]

On June 7, 1870, while he was demanding in Congress a return to gold, two members from Pennsylvania came over to where he was speaking and presented him with two twenty-dollar gold pieces. These he clinked together in his hands, declaring that it recalled " a better day of the Republic when people knew what they had to deal with." He proposed a gradual retirement of greenbacks and national bank notes with the eventual establishment of a gold and silver basis. Although unable to get any official statement of intended resumption, he helped defeat a bill to increase by $45,000,000 the amount of greenbacks outstanding.[49] Here the vote cut across party lines, Eastern Democrats voting with Eastern Republicans to defeat the additional greenback issue.

One evil growing out of a double currency of metal and inconvertible paper had been realized the preceding September with the Jay Gould-Jim Fisk corner on the gold supply and the resultant " Black Friday " disaster. The Banking and Currency Committee conducted an investigation into this episode, holding hearings in New York during Christmas week of 1869. As a committee member, Cox presented the minority report in opposition to Chairman James A. Garfield's majority report. Both reports agreed substantially that the cause of the gold panic was a conspiracy to create a " wholly artificial and unnatural shortage " of gold. The majority held that the national Administration had no responsibility for the affair and that the remedy lay in a tax on New York Gold Exchange transactions. Cox, however, who had tried in vain to compel the President to testify, contended that much of the blame rested on the shoulders of A. R. Corbin, Grant's brother-in-law, and that " unconsciously or consciously, the President in his letters to Mr. Boutwell [Secretary of the Treasury] worked in unison with the conspirators." He recommended resumption of specie payments to place paper on a par with gold and thereby to eliminate the differential in values which bred speculation.[50] His conclusion regarding the President tortured the facts for purposes of political propaganda but in a private letter he remarked that the evidence " compels me . . . to believe that some of them [the Grant family] were in . . . on the New York Gold Corner." [51]

Regarding the even more serious problem of Southern reconstruction, Cox was anxious to readmit those Southern states still outside the Union and to remove political disabilities imposed upon ex-Confederates by the Fourteenth Amendment. By December 1869, Virginia, Mississippi, and Texas, having met the requirements of the Reconstruction Acts, applied for recognition as states within the Union. A new bill proposed more conditions for Virginia to meet. In January Cox bitterly denounced this bill and urged immediate, unqualified admission of Virginia. In support of his position, he quoted President Grant's December message to Congress. Asserting that Virginia should come in " unshackled, like an upright man " rather than " handcuffed, like a criminal," he called upon Congress to exercise " something of that divine grace of forgiveness." The restrictive bill passed, however. Virginia came in at the end of January, after having accepted the new conditions.[52] Similar disputes arose over the admission of Mississippi and Texas, with Cox fighting in vain against restrictions proposed by the Radicals.[53] The bases of his opposition were three: 1) as a matter of Democratic political strategy, speedy readmission of Southern states would give Democrats a fighting chance to recover control in Washington; 2) a state's internal affairs should be determined by the state itself under the federal constitutional system; 3) the South through war and destruction had already suffered punishment enough.

These views were most clearly expressed in the case of Georgia. That state had been " reconstructed " earlier, after which the legislature had expelled its Negro members. As punishment for this action, the Radicals in Congress proposed to re-establish martial law in Georgia, reform the legislature under Radical control, and eliminate native white influence. A bill to this effect in Congress was characterized by Cox as one " without parallel or precedent." " If Georgia is a State," he said, " the bill is a usurpation; if Georgia is not a State, the bill should be an enabling act for her admission." Citing the Supreme Court's view in *Texas v. White*, he maintained that Georgia did not lose statehood by supposed secession, since secession was illegal. If he were a Georgian, Cox declared, echoing Tom Corwin's Mexican War speech, " I would welcome with open hands to hospitable homes the whole military satrapy of the Federal Union to my State rather than be made the unwilling instrument of this Congress to destroy my State . . . and crawl beneath the yoke of abject submission." Once more Cox was beaten by congressional vote, and Georgia had to accept military rule and the Fifteenth Amendment. This action made Cox feel that " it is almost an insult . . . to ask a man if he is a member of Congress " when " Congress is a despotic majority " and " the Constitution as a federate bond is almost obsolete." [54]

Against the political disabilities imposed upon ex-Confederates, Cox began in December 1869 a long fight, which he continued for the next fifteen years. An act of Congress of July 2, 1862 had established the " ironclad oath," making it impossible for anyone who had held office in state or federal government in 1861 and who had aided the Confederacy to hold a position in government thereafter. This had been strengthened by the third section of the Fourteenth Amendment, which restated this political disability and authorized its removal by a two-thirds vote of both houses of Congress. The Republican Congress found this a convenient instrument to bar ex-Confederate Democrats from politics and to admit those ex-Confederates who had become converted to the Republican party. As early as the spring of 1868, Congress had passed special amnesty bills for several hundred individuals.[55]

Cox condemned this " peddling out of the amnesty of the Government." Instead of special bills which served as " premiums given to certain parties for their profligacy," he " would give amnesty to all." Strengthened by demands for general amnesty in both party platforms of 1868 and in New York papers, such as the *Tribune*, the *Times*, and the *World*, he began a frontal assault. He secured passage of a resolution instructing the Reconstruction Committee to report out a bill " to remove all political and legal disabilities." When this resolution passed by more than a two-thirds vote, a direct resolution of general amnesty was tried and came within two votes of the required two thirds.[56]

Had Cox been able to secure adoption of the measure by both houses of Congress at this time, Southern leaders would have been spared many years of political exile and the country would have been spared the hot words that reopened old wounds and revived bitter feelings during the next decade.

Under the newly-adopted Fifteenth Amendment, the first Enforcement bill was submitted to Congress in May 1870. It was intended to protect the vote of the Negro by giving United States marshals and courts the authority to intercede in elections when necessary to prevent intimidation, bribery, and fraud at the polls. Cox objected on several grounds. The bill violated the constitutional provision that left elections in the hands of the states. This " large . . . and sudden grasp of power " by Congress " would institute a federal police, spy and informer system, so as to control by force state elections." The bill was also directed at elections in New York City, but, he asserted, there was no necessity for federal supervision of New York elections. He hoped that in defiance, New Yorkers would " break the yokes now forging for them in this federal capital." Once again, in spite of his opposition, Congress passed the bill, the first in a series of three.[57]

Meanwhile, he continued his work as a member of the Foreign Affairs Committee. Of concern to his constituents, a large portion of whom were Irish immigrants, was the British government's imprisonment of Irish Fenian revolutionists who were trying to overthrow British rule in Ireland. Some of these were naturalized American citizens who had returned to their native land. Many had relatives living in America. When Cox's resolution condemning British action bogged down in committee, he declared that he was willing to risk war with England and he again waved the flag of " manifest destiny," holding that Canada would sooner or later become American by " inevitable gravitation of interest." In Latin American affairs he tried without success to get House approval of a demand on the President to submit documents regarding claims of American citizens against Venezuela under the convention of 1866.[58] He also inquired personally into the status of American claims against Colombia.[59]

Speaking for such New York commercial promoters as George Earl Church, Samuel L. M. Barlow, and Jerome E. Chaffee, he secured House passage of a bill to incorporate the National Bolivian Navigation Company, which proposed to develop commerce from Bolivia via the Madeira-Mamore-Amazon route. But for domestic railroads seeking special favors from the government, he had nothing but opposition. He had voted against the original Pacific railroad bill; now he fought further grants to railroads under the subsidy system, which he branded " a great running sore upon the body politic." [60]

When a suggestion was made to cut out the *Congressional Globe* because it was getting too bulky, Cox observed that it would not be so large were it not for " a new order of politics " under which the " Federal Government . . . has absorbed the business of the country." One means of improving government procedure, he suggested, would be to cut time-consuming roll calls. Also, he felt the federal government could well set an example for other employers. To illustrate this, he proposed a bill declaring an eight-hour day for " all laborers, workmen and mechanics in the employ of the Government of the United States," but the bill never got out of committee. He thought that postal workers, especially, were not receiving fair treatment. At some length, he described the letter carriers, who " trudge their weary rounds through the winter's snow and under the summer's sun " twelve to fourteen hours a day for a paltry $800-$1,000 a year. His efforts for a 20 per cent raise were lost in this session but marked the beginning of his long fight to improve the position of the letter carriers, who ultimately erected his statue in Astor Place, New York.[61]

RE-ELECTION AND OPPOSITION TO GRANTISM, 1870-1872

Before Congress adjourned, Cox sounded the keynote for his campaign for re-election. The Grant Administration, he announced, was " an utter and conspicuous failure . . . run by land jobbers, foreign jobbers, by traffic jobbers, by railroad jobbers." [62] His campaign was based not only on the Administration's corruption but also on its centralizing tendencies and indifference to the interests of commerce and agriculture. Thus, in a speech to his old constituents in Columbus, he called for Ohio and New York, for " agriculture and commerce," to stand together. He also lambasted the Republicans for their failure to reform the tariff system of " indirect and insidious bounties." [63]

In a Fourth of July speech at Tammany Hall, he once again protested federal intervention in state affairs, which, New Yorkers feared, might influence their elections.[64] The New York *World* backed the protest against the use of federal troops on election day.

Accepting the Democratic nomination in the Sixth District, Cox stated: " I have endeavored to reflect the best sentiment of this constituency." He reviewed his record: he had opposed the high tariff, greenbacks, railroad land grants; he had fought for general amnesty, resumption, and " the commercial independence and integrity of this great city."

As the campaign moved on and the Republicans nominated protectionist Horace Greeley, editor of the powerful *Tribune*, as their candidate for Congress to oppose Cox, the *World* was uncertain about Cox's chances. However, the free-trading New York *Evening Post* declared for Cox, and he received the united support of the Democratic factions—the Mozart Hall Democrats and the Young Men's Democratic Association—as well as that of Tammany. When he appeared at a giant rally on October 27 at Bryant's Opera House, he expressed surprise that the Republicans in nominating " no less a man than Horace Greeley . . . should bring in a farmer—an alien from Westchester," referring to Greeley's country residence. The issue was clearly " free trade against protection." Greeley, obviously, stood for a high tariff " in direct antagonism to the interests of this city." The final campaign rally was held on Fifth Avenue, just around the corner from Cox's Twelfth Street home. A big brass band played " Hail to the Chief " for Cox and the Avenue was " all ablaze with calcium lights, Bengal rockets, Greek fire, and bombs, while a huge bonfire of tar barrels in the middle of the street lit up the neighborhood." Here, from a platform shared by Mayor A. Oakey Hall, Cox denounced the " Goliath of protection " and a tariff that " does not so much rob Peter to pay Paul as it robs both of them to pay Judas Iscariot."

Greeley, who was in poor health, did little speechmaking. But the Republican press centered its ire on Tammany, which was supporting Cox. The press charged that Tammany agents were distributing " bogus naturalization papers." The election results were close, 9,228 votes for Cox to 8,203 for Greeley, the *Tribune* attributing Greeley's defeat to feuds among the Republicans. " Sunset " Cox had defeated New York's best known Republican.[65]

Even with this vote of confidence behind him, Cox returned to Washington in one of his periodic moods of discouragement. He thought the political outlook dark. Too much " jobbery " in the government had driven many capable men of pre-war days out of politics, leaving the field to newer, less able men. He suggested to Manton Marble that the *World* might use his services " as a foreign correspondent." The only thing that kept him interested in politics was " the Big Issue "—the tariff.[66]

In Congress Cox hammered away at the tariff issue. In 1872 a Republican-sponsored bill asked for a 10 per cent across-the-board reduction of duties. Cox responded that the proposed bill did not go far enough and that a 10 per cent horizontal reduction could be too easily restored. He offered amendments reducing the pig iron duty to $5 a ton and placing salt, coal, lumber, and cotton goods on the free list. The tariff, he estimated, transferred $500,000,000 annually from the consumers to the " protected classes." " This great tribute " had affected most Americans adversely, and, even for manufacturers, it was a short-sighted policy, considering that the export of American manufactured goods had declined 62½ per cent between 1860 and 1870 even though total American exports had increased 12½ per cent.

The factors that had degraded people in Europe were now beginning to affect the United States. A costly army and navy, a large national debt, and an " infamous tariff system . . . will produce the same poverty and degradation of the working man here." It was sheer delusion, Cox said, to view the new tariff bill as a reform; rather it was a form of stealing. " Michigan steals on copper; Maine on cotton goods; Connecticut on hair pins; New Jersey on spool thread; Louisiana on sugar." Then, describing a breakfast at which the guests walk off with the salt, plates, bread, potatoes, mutton, table, stove, and coal, he imagined the guests as saying: " We have done all this to increase the general

comfort and to make free with the breakfast table. . . . Is
there not left coffee unground and unburned, tea undistilled,
sweetened by the memories of sugar upon an absent cloth,
and covering an invisible table! " Summing up his views he
said: " I believe that free trade, free labor, and the right
of the interchange by trade of the products of free labor, is
just as much a right, under God, as the right . . . of personal
freedom, guaranteed now to all . . . by the Constitution."
The 10 per cent reduction passed, nonetheless, and with it,
the GOP made a slight nod in the direction of reform with
which to face the Liberal Republican revolt in the campaign
of 1872.[67]

Cox was again aroused against various proposals for more
land grants to railroads like the Central Pacific. These " conspiracies against the people," he protested, " seize lands . . .
make towns . . . get the bulk of the public lands and obtain
an amount of power greater than that of the Government
itself." These " corporate leeches " had already acquired
" nearly all the arable land in this country," which should
instead have been granted directly to settlers.[68]

Only on the question of amnesty for Southerners was he
more vehement. For several years circumstances had been
working in favor of general amnesty. Many Republicans,
among them Horace Greeley and Carl Schurz, felt that their
party should deal justly with the South. Southern states were
sending representatives to Congress who were unable to take
the required oath. In December 1870 Schurz in the Senate
introduced a liberal general amnesty bill, similar to the one
Cox had offered a year before, removing all political disabilities. In the House Ben Butler offered a general amnesty
bill containing so many exceptions and qualifications that
few ex-Confederates could benefit by it. After examining the
Butler bill, Cox concluded that its " tautological, complex,

multifarious " provisions were hardly amnesty at all. " It was grace which was grudged . . . punitory pardon." The *Nation* remarked that " as a means of soothing the South, the measure is worth little or nothing." Referring to it as " Butler's Damnesty bill," Cox observed that Republicans would do well to follow General Grant's report of 1865, favoring immediate forgiveness for the South. Cox urged full, general amnesty: " Let it be done without discrimination and spite. . . . Let us overcome evil with good. Revenge only harms him who cherishes it. . . . In this spirit of Christian grace I would . . . erase all the reservations out of this bill. . . ." The Butler bill was postponed, and the Congress came to an end before any action was taken.[69]

Closely associated with amnesty was the question of required oaths. The " ironclad " oath, established in 1862, required all federal officials to swear that they had never taken part in nor given aid to rebellion against the United States. An 1868 modification provided that those whose political disabilities had been removed by two-thirds vote of Congress under the terms of the Fourteenth Amendment need not take the " iron-clad " oath but only a simple oath of allegiance to the Constitution. In 1871 a bill was drawn providing that those who had held no office before the war (and therefore were not barred by the Fourteenth Amendment) but who had taken part in rebellion would be excused from the " iron-clad " oath by simply taking the 1868 oath. Although favoring the bill's objectives, Cox delivered a long denunciation of the whole system of oath-taking as inconsistent, encouraging to liars, and paradoxically requiring " those who were innocent of rebellion " to take the " iron-clad " oath. Congress, however, passed this bill on February 1, 1871, and it became law without the President's signature.[70]

The amnesty question was revived with broader support

in December 1871, when President Grant recommended passage of a general amnesty bill.[71] A new Butler-sponsored measure for general amnesty with fewer exceptions was adopted by two-thirds vote of Congress the following May. Cox, disappointed that exceptions were still made, noted that the bill passed only after the Liberal Republican faction forced the step upon the regular Republicans, who were trying to steal the glory from the Democrats who had fought for amnesty for seven years. He foresaw that in the coming election of 1872 the Republicans would pose as the one " who gave you grace and amnesty." But, he philosophized, " anything that is in accordance with a spirit of Christian grace I am happy about." By the end of May 1872 every seat in the House was filled for the first time since 1860, with ex-Confederates being seated.[72]

In another area, Cox also worked to end the repressions laid upon the South. He had opposed the first Enforcement Act of May 31, 1870, which sought to guarantee Negro suffrage, and the second Enforcement Act, passed in February 1871, which added more stringent penalties and gave greater powers to federal officers during elections. Although the Ku Klux Klan had officially disbanded in 1868, violence and intimidation continued in some parts of the South. Radical Republicans, noting the rapid revival of Democratic strength in the South, determined to put reports of violence to good political advantage. Again Ben Butler led the congressional forces in pushing through the third Enforcement Act on April 20, 1871, which authorized the President to declare martial law and suspend *habeas corpus* in those areas where the Ku Klux Klan was found operating. Cox condemned this bill as " a coercive act backed by the unrestrained violence of any army commander, whose will is to be the only law! " He pleaded with Republican leaders: " Gentlemen, I pray you to pause . . . to stay your invasion of the Constitution." Congress might better leave the South alone and attend to more pressing problems like the tariff, shipping, and currency.[73] It was while listening to this speech that Bourke Cockran, later prominent as a politician but in 1871 a recent immigrant from Ireland, sat spell-bound in the House gallery admiring Cox's eloquence.[74]

On the same day that the "Ku Klux law" passed, Congress established a joint committee to investigate conditions in the South. Cox was a member of this committee. Its chairman was Luke P. Poland of Vermont. The committee heard many Southerners in Washington and in some parts of the South intermittently from May 1871, until February 1872. Cox attended the Washington meetings in May, September, and December 1871 and again in February 1872. Very little reliable testimony was secured, although it filled thirteen printed volumes. The final report, which was made to Congress in late February 1872, included majority and minority sections. The majority urged the necessity of continuing vigorous federal protective measures in the South. The minority, including Cox, disagreed, holding that violence in the South occurred only in isolated areas and was caused by repressive federal measures, which aimed at punishing the South for failing to elect to Congress men "who would blindly obey the orders of" Radical Republican leaders. The last part of the minority report arraigned the President for allowing himself to be used for "the dictates of party vengeance, . . . rather than to do equal and exact justice to all classes of citizens."[75]

As a member of the Foreign Affairs Committee, Cox opposed Grant's effort to annex Santo Domingo. Annexation was spurred by American promoters who hoped to profit from speculations there. A treaty of annexation failed in

1869-1870 when Senator Charles Sumner blocked ratification, and when a new effort was launched in December 1870, a caucus of House Democrats declared they wanted no part of the Santo Domingo " fraud." [76] Cox labelled it " an unnatural, corrupt and noisome scheme " to revive the " sinking party " in power. " You are not content with our buying icebergs, seals, Indians, and misery at one end of the world, but you are dickering for earthquakes, hurricanes, negroes, and bananas at the other." Later he denounced the original treaty with its attached list which showed the grants of land, mines, franchises, and concessions already made to American speculators. He still believed in expansion, but he thought Americans should be " more heedful of the modes and motives for the enlargement of our domain." [77]

In regard to Cuba, however, he was less than " heedful." He thought that Cuban belligerency, in the insurrection against Spain, should be recognized. President Grant had at first leaned toward such a policy but, acceding to Secretary of State Hamilton Fish's views, he reversed himself. This shift caused the defeat in June 1870 of Nathaniel P. Banks's House resolution favoring recognition. Nevertheless, Cox introduced a similar resolution in January 1872 and spoke in favor of it several times, referring to Spanish cruelty and arguing that " American citizens engaged in legitimate commerce " should be protected.[78]

In the interests of other special groups, Cox continued to be active during these years. For the letter carriers in large cities he urged that the annual pay be raised from $1,000 to a maximum of $1200.[79] It was in 1871 that he became the champion of a new group and an advocate of a new government service. Since 1848 Congress had made small appropriations for maintaining boathouses and life boats along a section of the New Jersey sea coast, the boats being manned by volunteers when ships were wrecked. In 1870 it was proposed to eliminate even this small amount from the appropriations bill. Cox, who himself had narrowly escaped shipwreck off the Scilly Islands on his trip abroad, had been much impressed by the good work of the British coast guard, and he spoke in favor of restoring the amount of the proposed cut. He made his case so effective that Congress voted not only the boat house appropriation but an additional sum " for pay of six experienced surfmen to man the boats at alternate lifesaving stations upon the New Jersey coast." In the following session Cox continued the fight and, in April 1871, secured a more substantial appropriation ($200,000 in contrast to the usual $10,000) and an authorization for the Secretary of the Treasury " to employ crews of experienced surfmen at such stations and for such periods as he might deem necessary." The result was the establishment of the United States Life-Saving Service under Sumner I. Kimball, chief of the Revenue-Marine Division of the Treasury Department. Here was a cause to which Cox could bring his boundless energy. His inexhaustible devotion to it won for him the title of " Father of the Life Saving Service." [80] This service in the twentieth century has been amalgamated into the United States Coast Guard.

Such work gave Cox high rank in congressional circles. Leading Democrats at the opening of the Forty-second Congress talked of giving him their complimentary nomination for speaker. When Morrison R. Waite passed through Washington on his way to Geneva in 1871, Cox introduced him to President Grant, little realizing that he was preparing the way for a future chief justice of the Supreme Court.[81] During these years (1870-1874) he found time also to serve as national president and as one of the board of governors of his social fraternity, Delta Phi.[82]

Cox's theme for the operation of the government was always economy and simplicity. The Grant Administration, which was anything but economical and simple, came in for a major share of his invective. He criticized the President for running around the country and " making a public exhibition of himself " at " all the horse races . . . to the neglect of the public business." Washington lobbyists " swarm all around us like the frogs and lice of Egypt." Cox felt that great forces were pushing the country and the government into a new and different mold: " Our government is undergoing just now a great many transitions. We are changing our characteristics." The new " characteristics " did not look attractive. " This session . . . has been pernicious, pestiferous, in almost every conceivable way." But Cox approved his fellows' " Address of the Democrats in Congress to the People " of April 20, 1871 which arraigned the Administration for its use of " despotic powers," " pernicious patronage," " widespread corruption." [83]

Meanwhile, the Democrats of New York might well have looked to keeping their own house in order. The corrupt Tammany Ring under the notorious Tweed was stealing millions yearly from the city's treasury. By September 1871 the situation had grown so obnoxious that a " Committee of Seventy " prominent citizens under the leadership of Samuel J. Tilden declared war on the Ring. The Ring leaders were convicted and the Tweed machine was swept from power. With this coup Tilden made a reputation that carried him to the door of the White House.[84] Cox did not take an active part in the war on Tweed. When charges were later made of his failure in this connection, his only explanation was that he had been in California at the time of the exposures (which was true) and that he " did not speak for Mr. Tweed at any time." [85] A new list of Tammany

Sachems in 1872 carried the respectable names of August Schell, Charles O'Conor, Horatio Seymour, Samuel J. Tilden, Abram S. Hewitt, and August Belmont.

DEFEAT ON A LARGER STAGE, 1872

In 1872 the signs of the times pointed toward Democratic victory. The country was growing restless under Grantism with its corruption, nepotism, military rule of the South, fantastic foreign schemes like Santo Domingo, special favors to railroads, and protection for manufacturers. The margin between Grant and Seymour in 1868 had been slim. And now the Republican party was splitting. The Liberal Republican movement, starting with Carl Schurz and B. Gratz Brown in Missouri, was attracting many idealistic Republicans, especially the founding fathers of the party, who wished to end the misrule of Grant and his crowd. Democrats looked to the enthusiastic Liberal Republican convention at Cincinnati for a nominee whom they, too, could support. They were astounded when that gathering named Horace Greeley of New York, a life-long enemy of the Democratic party, whose attitude had been expressed in the words: " I do not say that all Democrats are rascals but it is undeniably true that all rascals are Democrats." When the platform failed to include any mention of tariff reform (out of deference to Greeley's strong protectionist views), it was almost too much for some Democrats to swallow. Manton Marble of the *World* urged his party to choose a different candidate.[86]

The Democratic convention met in Baltimore in July. Here the Democrats were forced to the bitter conclusion that the one chance to defeat Grant lay in selecting the Liberal Republican candidate. The New York delegation included Cox, James Brooks, " Honest John " Kelly (embryo boss of Tammany), and August Belmont, who was serving the last of his twelve years as national Democratic chairman. After adopting the Liberal Republican platform intact, the convention, by an overwhelming vote, named Greeley to oppose Grant.[87]

In New York state, Democrats and Liberal Republicans combined to nominate a joint slate: Francis Kernan for governor, Chauncey Depew for lieutenant governor, and Samuel Cox for congressman-at-large. This last office was the result of a legislative gerrymander of the state following the 1870 census, which, by reducing the number of New York City districts, placed Congressmen Cox and Brooks in the same district, thereby attempting to remove one of them from office. The Democratic response was to nominate Cox at-large. He accepted in a speech calling for repudiation of Grant and reconciliation toward the South. Cox's new-won prominence in his adopted state was recognized early in 1872 by editor George W. Curtis's usually unfriendly *Harper's Weekly*, which devoted an article to his career. Calling him " a successful author and a popular lecturer " and praising " his consistent and persistent efforts against the tariff," it noted: " Few men in the House, ' hold the House ' better than Mr. Cox . . . a ready, graceful, self-possessed, vigorous debater, so mingling argument with wit, and sarcasm with good humor, as always to command attention and respect . . . a high personal favorite with members, irrespective of parties . . . ever on the alert to serve his constituents, regardless of politics." [88] Cox's campaign opponent was an upstate Republican, Lyman Tremaine.[89]

The subsequent campaign was perhaps the most peculiar in the annals of American politics. The Democrats were forced to eat " boiled crow," as editor Edwin L. Godkin put it, by accepting Horace Greeley who held the paradoxical

position of advocating protection while being supported by
the low-tariff party that he had repeatedly denounced. The
Democrats campaigned, as usual, for reform and conciliation
The Republicans made much the same argument, " pointing
with pride " to their " tariff reform " act and general amnesty
act of the previous May. The situation was neatly described
by General William T. Sherman who said that the Democrats
with Greeley had nominated a man " who never was a
Democrat " while the Republicans with Grant had chosen
a man " who never was a Republican." Greeley, with his
odd appearance and personal eccentricities, became the butt
of so many of Thomas Nast's cartoons and of so much
ridicule that he declared he was not sure " whether he was
running for the Presidency or the Penitentiary." [90]

Cox's campaign opened on August 30 in New York City
with a speech urging the nation to return from the present
evil days to the " old simplicity and purity and frugality."
He characterized the " Gilded Age " as an outgrowth of the
war, which brought on " an insane greed for wealth, the
enormous growth of capital, shoddy display and superficial
fashion, monopolizing corporations and family greed—the
desire to shine in the calcium glare of the present feverish
round of social and political junketing." This new Liberal
Republican-Democratic alliance arose from the necessity
to protect the government from the current despotism, mer-
cenary politics, and repression. The policy that was advocated by the alliance was the one laid down by Jesus many
centuries ago in the Sermon on the Mount—" ' Love your
enemies, bless them that curse you, do good to them that
hate you '. . . . God and time will help us carry it into our
political ethics." [91]

In mid-September Cox complained to Parke Godwin that
the New York *Evening Post* did not stand by him although

he had consistently championed the cause of free trade—
" I converted Wells and others to our favorite doctrines. . . .
I am a defiant antagonist of monopolies." To the charge
that in the war on the Tweed Ring he had been on Tweed's
side, Cox replied that this was false, that he had actually
" tried to reform the Ring." [92] On September 21, 1872,
Harper's Weekly branded Cox " amiable and generous "
but " an unswerving party man." Despite his critics, Cox
was optimistic during an upstate tour in October. " The
cream of these dairy counties is for H. G.," he wrote from
upstate New York. His schedule was strenuous: on October
22 in Auburn, he paid tribute to his friend Seward who had
just died; on October 23 in Elmira he denounced Grant's
repression of Southern rights; on October 24 in Buffalo he
condemned the Grant frauds and urged reconciliation with
the South; on October 27 in Albany, " amid wildest enthusiasm," he spoke again; on October 28 in Troy he " added
fresh laurels to his already wide-spread reputation as an
orator " in describing the " utter demoralization of the public
service "; on October 29 in Brooklyn, in reply to the charge
of Greeley's shift of party, he pointed to party shifts by
Grant, Tremaine, and John A. Dix, Republican gubernatorial
candidate. On election day the New York *World* urged its
readers to vote for Cox as the champion of ships, coal,
dresses, and blankets free of tariffs, the foe of high taxes,
the friend of the working man, and a representative of " 15
years experience in Congress." [93]

The election results were a heavy blow to the Democrats.
In the country at large, Greeley was snowed under by a
majority of more than 700,000 for Grant. He even lost his
home state by 43,000 votes. Cox ran somewhat better,
Tremaine's statewide majority being only 37,000. The *World*
suggested that the defeat was caused by the taint left over

from the Tweed Ring and that the result might have been different had not Greeley been the candidate. Cox thought the defeat due mainly to the Republican " waving of the bloody shirt." [94] When he sent his congratulations to his successful opponent, Tremaine replied that he felt honored to have won over a " gentleman so universally esteemed for his genial qualities." [95] With the election over, Cox, believing his political career at an end, began to look seriously toward writing. [96]

On the opening day of what he believed to be his last Congress, he delivered a eulogy on Horace Greeley who had died a few weeks after the election. In the speech he praised Greeley's " independence and courage " and " large-minded amnesty toward all people." On the theme of amnesty, he pushed a bill to remove all civil disabilities under the Fourteenth Amendment, but, lacking a two-thirds vote, the bill failed. [97]

During the 1872 campaign the full extent of the graft and corruption of the Grant regime had been only conjectured. Not yet clearly seen were the outright sale of offices in the War Department, the high-jacking of almost a half million dollars by Treasury tax gatherers, the loss of millions of dollars of revenue through government collusion with St. Louis whiskey distillers, and the wholesale corruption in the customs houses. Even Congress had become directly involved. The fraudulent Crédit Mobilier, to cover its bilking the Pacific railroad of construction funds, had shrewdly distributed stock to key members of Congress. In the House, Speaker Blaine, one of those accused of receiving Crédit Mobilier stock, called Cox to the chair, and Cox appointed an impartial committee under Luke Poland, capable chairman of the earlier " Ku Klux " committee. [98] Testimony taken by the committee clearly implicated Republican Oakes

Ames and Democrat James Brooks, while throwing an unsavory cloud over James A. Garfield and Vice-President
Schuyler Colfax. The House dodged the taking of any clearcut action by voting not to expel but to " absolutely condemn " the conduct of Ames and Brooks.⁹⁹ These men had
been made the scapegoats of a giant swindle. The Crédit
Mobilier incident involved many leaders of both parties, but
Cox, who had had no connection with the stock distribution,
emerged as a leader in the movement to uncover the fraud.

While still congressman, Cox introduced a resolution,
written by Parke Godwin of the New York *Evening Post*,
declaring the United States government to be " not a supreme, unlimited, imperial Government," but " a Government of limited powers " under which " the separate spheres
of action " of the states and nation " should be kept forever
distinct and inviolable." Following a brief debate, the House
dropped the question. Continuing along the same line of
thought, Cox opposed establishing a federal bureau of education and objected to continued aid for agricultural colleges.
These operations, he said, were outside the true sphere of
federal activity. Nor, in the matter of reviving American
shipping, should the federal government grant subsidies.
Rather, the best way to revive American commerce was to
eliminate duties on materials used in shipbuilding and to
allow shippers to purchase ships anywhere in the world. As
for the American navy, the government, instead of continuing
to build wooden vessels only, should develop a systematic
plan including steel ships, some to be built in private ship-
yards as well as in regular navy-yards.¹⁰⁰

Toward the end of the session a bill providing for a 50
per cent increase in future and retroactive salaries for members of Congress was introduced by Ben Butler. Cox entered
a strong protest " against increasing my own salary by my

own vote," and voted in the negative. When the Treasury sent him his pay under the " Grab Act," he returned it promptly with the explanation: " I didn't expect it when I served; I did not contract for it; I am happy in being rid of it." With the adjournment of this Congress in early March, the New York *Tribune* judged that it went " into history . . . with . . . a reputation for fair intentions but great feebleness " in execution.[101]

6

DEMOCRATIC REVIVAL,
1873–1877

Early in 1873 with his political career seemingly ended, Cox determined on another trip abroad. He abandoned the plan in May, however, when his father died and he was called to the family home in Zanesville. At the same time, the death of New York Congressman James Brooks moved Cox to seek election to Congress in Brooks's place in the Sixth District. This was not the same Sixth District that Cox had previously represented, but a new one carved out on the lower East Side of Manhattan between the East River and Avenue D and Division Street, with 14th Street on the north and Catherine Street on the south.[1]

Of the 140,000 inhabitants in the district, 65,000 were foreign-born, mainly Irish, German, and Jewish, while many others were first-generation Americans. Most were tenement-dwellers, and the illiteracy rate was high. There were unskilled laborers in the ship-yards, docks, warehouses, stores, small workshops, and offices of the area, including truckers, draymen, clerks, porters, mechanics, and stevedores.[2] Tenements were crowding out the old Knickerbocker element, although a few of the latter still hung on. The Astors still owned properties along Avenue A; Secretary of State Hamilton Fish maintained his home on Second Avenue at 17th Street; and William M. Evarts lived nearby. On the east side of Avenue A between 7th and 10th streets spread the park, known as Tompkins Square, where Germans gathered for singing and band concerts, where the militia drilled, and where gangs of boys engaged in extended fights. The Green horse-car line zig-zagged through the district to Union Square within two blocks of Cox's house on 12th Street. Traffic regulations on the streets were non-existent, but policemen were posted at the busier intersections. They wore plain visorless caps, which were soon to be replaced by high blue derbies.[3]

Although political methods had remained about the same, a change had come over New York politics since Cox's first appearance in the metropolis in 1865. The break-up of the Tweed Ring resulted in a realignment of forces in both city and state. The Republicans took control of the state when John A. Dix became governor in 1872. Tammany Hall, out of power, was rebuilding its muscle under the leadership of " Honest John " Kelly, who had gained a reputation along with Tilden in the prosecution of the Tweed Ring. Some dissident Democrats formed the separate Apollo Hall organization, while the ex-pugilist, John Morrissey, made preparations to break with Kelly and to set up the Irving Hall Democracy. Among these factions, Cox found it necessary to tread warily, although he often remained close to the Tammany organization.[4]

While political factions struggled for power, the nation's

economy reeled under a rude shock in September 1873. Since the end of the Civil War, the country had seen economic expansion, large-scale business consolidations, and rising monopolies. In steel and oil, the big-business trend was most spectacular. Railroad construction and development, plus railroad stock-watering and manipulating, became almost a mania with many Americans during these years. The post-war boom of business had spiraled dizzily upward until the sudden financial collapse of the Jay Cooke banking firm in September 1873 pulled down other businesses. Then the country's economic wheels ground to a halt. The business cycle, having passed through its phase of wartime and post-war prosperity, plunged into a depression that would last until 1878. Even before the actual panic, agrarian discontent in the Midwest had fostered the rise of the Grangers who sought at first to reduce exorbitant railroad rates, and then turned to anti-monopoly agitation and demands for inflation through increased issues of greenbacks. All of these factors had a depressing effect in New York, where business activity slackened and thousands were added to the normally large ranks of the unemployed.[5]

Against this economic setting Cox returned to the political wars after his defeat of the year before. Over 400,000 people had voted for him in 1872, and his name was well known throughout the state. Recognition of his work for tariff reduction came early in the year when he was chosen an honorary member of the Cobden Club of England, along with Henry Adams, William G. Sumner, and Henry Watterson.[6]

In August 1873 a group of independent German Democrats of the new Sixth District nominated Cox to fill Brooks's place in Congress. The New York *World* pointed out that Cox had run considerably ahead of the Greeley-Kernan state ticket in 1872: " Mr. Cox's personal popularity is indisputable." By mid-October Cox received official Tammany endorsement and denounced the frauds and extravagances of the Grant regime. In his final canvassing appearance he shared the platform at Tammany Hall with Samuel Tilden. The September panic, Cox said, was due to " administration mismanagement."

The Republicans, who controlled the Customs House patronage and were in league with the Apollo Hall Democrats, expected to beat Cox with Lucius Wadsworth, former president of the Second Avenue street railway.[7] But the Republican effort failed. Election night found Cox with a strong 7,000-vote majority over his opponent. The delighted *World* told its readers that " a great commercial city . . . should be represented by men who really . . . understand its permanent interests. Mr. Cox has proved himself . . . to be such a representative." He " is second to no one in his practiced familiarity with the principles . . . of public legislation." He would oppose all " insane financial schemes and idiotic fiscal experiments." His election was " a practical contribution to a genuine civil service reform." [8]

When Congress convened on December 1, 1873, William S. Holman, an old Hoosier friend, placed Cox's name in nomination for Speaker. Cox arose, stated that he was not a candidate, and deferred to Fernando Wood. It made little difference whom the Democrats named anyway, since the Republicans controlled the House by 195 to 92. Blaine was re-elected Speaker, Cox received two votes in spite of having declined. Committee assignments placed Cox again on the Rules and the Foreign Affairs Committees.[9]

Although he did not serve on the Banking and Currency Committee in this session, his interest in financial matters led him to propose that revenues, lower as a result of the panic, be increased by reducing tariff duties. Congress, however, failed to take any action other than to enact, as part of the revised statutes, those tariff changes made by earlier laws and by the Secretary of the Treasury under his discretionary power. In mid-1874 importers found to their dismay that some tariff rates in the revised statutes appeared at a higher level than in the tariff act of 1872. Cox was thoroughly discouraged on the tariff issue, especially when some Democrats under Samuel J. Randall of Pennsylvania supported the Republican position. But he planned to win the rising Grangers to the cause of tariff reform. Consequently, he wrote Marble: " Hammer away at free trade, as you are [doing], in the *World*, and fill the Grangers full of it; so that when they discard men of both parties, they will be sure to get a free trader." [10]

The panic had brought renewed demands for more greenbacks to bolster falling prices. Before Congress gathered, Secretary of the Treasury George S. Boutwell had issued some $26,000,000 in greenbacks from the so-called " reserve " greenback fund. Earlier Secretary McCulloch had retired $44,000,000 of greenbacks from circulation in the late 1860's, reducing the total amount of paper notes from $400,000,000 to $356,000,000. A bill to approve Boutwell's $26,000,000 issue and authorize a return to the $400,000,000 level touched off a vigorous debate in Congress that put Western Republicans side by side with Southern Democrats in support of inflationary measures.

Cox lined up the Eastern opponents of inflation and delivered several attacks on the bill. At one point he branded the scheme " the fraud of the land—the swindle of the ages." Greenbacks, Cox maintained, were a cause of the " Black Friday " swindle and of the panic of 1873. A further greenback issue would simply aggravate the already serious depression. "An unequal tax upon the working classes," they showed that since 1868 Congress "has legislated for the benefit of the rich." He urged, instead, a gradual resumption of specie payments. Nevertheless, a bill to authorize greenback issues up to a total of $400,000,000 passed Congress, only to meet a presidential veto. By the end of the session a compromise had been effected, authorizing the already-issued amount of $382,000,000 but forbidding further issues.[11]

In the field of foreign relations, Cox, like most of his countrymen, was deeply aroused over the *Virginius* affair. This vessel, flying an American flag and carrying men and supplies to Cuban insurrectionists, was captured on October 31, 1873, by Spanish authorities in Cuba, who executed fifty-three crew members and passengers, including eight American citizens.

The outcry in the American press was vehement. The State Department immediately lodged a protest with Spain and called for an official apology. Mass meetings were held in New York. On November 17 an overflow crowd in Steinway Hall heard Cox join Nathaniel P. Banks in a call for vigorous action, "like ginger hot in the mouth." Early in December Cox again offered a resolution in the House to recognize the legal status of belligerents for the Cuban insurrectionists, only to have it turned down. By the end of the year, when it was discovered that the *Virginius* had illegally flown the American flag, the affair was settled peacefully. Cox, nevertheless, felt that the United States had not taken a strong enough stand. "There is not enough fight in this House to kill a mouse," he said. The navy ought to be made "stronger and better than it is." Ridiculing the Administration for sending Colonel A. B. Steinberger to the Samoan Islands, he asked why the Administration did not take more interest in Cuba, which was nearer home and more important.

In this session Cox began the long Democratic fight, based on grounds of economy, against the military reconstruction measures in the South. On the army appropriations bill, which was to become a favorite Democratic target, Cox argued that army expenses were far too high. A large army was unnecessary. Its only purpose was to keep the South within the Republican party fold. Likening the army in Louisiana and the Republican party to Siamese twins, he jeered: " When the one died, the other died shortly thereafter. . . . Louisiana is your corpse; it is tied by a ligature to your party." The continued use of the military in Southern civil affairs was a " godless tyranny and detestable usurpation " and a " blazing outrage." In other matters of economy, he called for lowering government expenditures, reducing appropriations for the executive mansion, and ending the franking privilege for congressmen. Facing an overwhelming Republican majority, he could scarcely hope for adoption of these proposals, but they provided material for future political campaigns.

About his own party, Cox asserted that Tweed's influence was " now as extinct as the dodo. . . . Our party in New York City . . . has been entirely reformed and reinvigorated," and he wished that the Republican party " would take the same pains to reform itself." [12] Meanwhile, he wrote a number of individual Republicans like Banks, and tried to convert them to the Democratic party.[13]

DEMOCRATIC TIDAL WAVE OF 1874 AND LAME DUCK REPUBLICANS

With their perennial optimism Democratic leaders looked

forward to the 1874 campaign. In the spring the Manhattan Club, of which Cox was a member, issued a statement of its "political doctrine," emphasizing particularly free trade, hard money, free ships. Important as these may have been as issues, the depression and the corruption in government provided the raw materials of discontent from which the "outs" hoped to fashion political victory. "Reform" became the keynote of the year. The Grant Administration and the "canal ring" in Albany became the principal targets. Breathing the spirit of the times, the Democrats named Samuel J. Tilden for governor on a platform demanding local self-government and denouncing Republican corruption. Tammany Hall endorsed Tilden as a man of "integrity, decorum, administrative ability, and shrewd political management." Having cleaned house since the days of Tweed, the reorganized and reformed Tammany sported a new front in the person of "Honest John" Kelly, who, in contrast to Tweed, was a deferential, retiring, sensitive man whose private life was above reproach. Within a few years Kelly was to emerge as the autocratic boss of a highly disciplined machine. In 1874 the Democrats claimed simply to be the "only reform party in existence here today." [14]

For Congress, the old reliables, Cox, Abram Hewitt and Fernando Wood, were nominated. Accepting his tenth nomination, Cox reviewed his record in opposing "bad tariffs," "the scandalous farming out of the revenues," and "the spoliation of your domain by the railroads." "The little band" of Democrats, "which is now growing," he said, must take over the House from the Republicans, the "party of centralization, usurpation, protection, and spoils." He appeared on the platform with Seymour, Montgomery Blair, and Francis Kernan at the grand Tammany rally at the end of October. The audience waited from 7:30 until after 10:30 for Cox to speak and then " heard him with a laugh at every other line and a cheer in between." Cox expressed his thanks " that I am permitted to run for a once reputable office without the reproach of either party." He then scored the Grant Administration for military tyranny in the South and for general corruption.[15]

Political fortune was with the Democrats that year. Tilden romped into office with a solid 50,000-vote majority. Cox trounced Republican J. H. Campbell with more than 10,000 votes to spare. He exclaimed at the Tammany victory rally, " There is music in the air. The days of radicalism are numbered. . . . I worked like you until sunset. If I didn't work for ' Sunset,' it was because ' Sunset ' didn't require work to be done." Throughout the country, too, there was " music in the air " for the Democrats who captured 168 seats in the lower house of Congress compared to 114 for the Repubicans—a clear Democratic majority for the first time in twenty years.[16] Little wonder that on December 12, 1874, Cox wrote the successful Tilden: " The Repub'ns here are stunned by the blow of Nov'r. They have begun again to flounder." A " tidal wave " had truly engulfed the Republicans, and on its crest the Democrats rode hopefully toward 1876 and the White House.

In the lame-duck session from December 1874 to March 1875, the Republicans sought to consolidate their political position before the Democrats took over the House in the next session. A bill was brought in to restore the 10 per cent tariff cut of 1872. Cox led the opposition to " this miserable little bill." Repeating his usual arguments, he added some new notes. " The true principle of taxation . . . should reach property not labor," he maintained. A higher tariff would simply place an additional burden on labor when workingmen were unable to afford it. Protection was uncon-

stitutional since it obviously favored one class of people at
the expense of another. Furthermore, duties on eight items
had brought only $41,000,000 into the Treasury since 1870,
yet they had transferred $852,000,000 from " working class
consumers " to wealthy manufacturers. Instead of raising the
tariff, Cox proposed to reduce government expenditures by
cutting the President's salary, eliminating unimportant con-
sulates, and lowering salaries of small town postmasters. His
efforts, however, failed, and the 10 per cent tariff increase
was adopted. He was especially disgusted with such Democratic protectionists as Randall, who " actually bargained on
the floor to help the bill through, in a hurry." [17]

However, Cox gave support to the Republican-sponsored
measure for resumption of specie payments. Acting upon
a proposal in Grant's session-opening message, the Republican leaders had rushed a resumption bill through the Senate
by the end of December. The House gave approval early in
January. The bill provided gradual retirement of greenbacks,
to be redeemed at par in gold, beginning on January 1, 1879.[18]

To bolster their gradually deteriorating position in the
South, Republicans now pushed an additional force bill,
against which Cox and his Democratic cohorts used all the
delaying tactics they could muster—amendments, roll calls,
and motions to adjourn. When the Republican-dominated
Rules Committee brought in a new rule forbidding more than
one motion to adjourn, Cox and Randall resigned from the
committee in protest. In this fight, " Cox was truly our
Parnell," Congressman Richard P. Bland declared later.

As this session came to a close, it was evident that the
era of radical Republican dominance was ending and that
the Democratic party had not been destroyed by the war
and reconstruction. Symbolic of the change was Blaine's
valedictory as Speaker, delivered on the closing day of the

session. Listening, Cox realized that the long, dark years of
" hate and persecution " were over. To an observer in the
gallery, it seemed " as if nothing short of a somersault would
adequately express . . . [Cox's] feelings." [19]

A DEMOCRATIC HOUSE, 1875-1876

At the end of the session, Cox prepared for a lecture tour
through New England, hoping to sandwich in a few hours
of work on the book he was currently writing and to visit
his friend, Mark Twain, in Hartford.[20] Before his departure,
he canvassed his chances for Speaker in the next House and
found them good. In a long letter to James M. Comly,
editor of the *Ohio State Journal,* he was optimistic: " Most
of the Northern or Eastern men are for me. . . . I have active
friends South and West." About his rivals, Cox felt that
Wood would " retire from the ring "; Randall would be out
because of his stand on " back pay and protection "; but
Michael C. Kerr of Indiana " will prove more formidable."
The whole political future looked bright, for the Democrats
" will make '76 lively, and the centennial gloriously belligerent." [21] By October Cox's tone had changed somewhat.
Hearing of the election of Rutherford B. Hayes to the
governorship of Ohio, he remarked: " Ohio is gone! It
makes me blue—for it makes twenty years work and waiting
a doubt; 1876 is in peril." [22]

As December 1875 approached, the fight for the speakership became " an unseemly scramble." The aspirants reached
Washington several weeks early to line up support. Randall's
chances improved at the end of November. Wood withdrew
from the race but gave Cox little aid. When Kerr was
finally chosen, the New York *Tribune* remarked that Randall
and Cox could " both be quite useful on the floor or in the

committee room." As for affecting the presidency, Kerr's choice " is the success of the friends of Mr. Tilden, aided by Mr. Cox." [23]

Cox was keenly disappointed over his defeat. The speaker-ship seemed at the moment the one attainable, worthwhile goal of his career. The records, however, reveal no bitter-ness on his part toward Kerr. In fact, the two men remained extremely close friends. Cox received some consolation in being appointed (along with Kerr, Randall, Blaine, and Banks) to the powerful Rules Committee and in being made chairman of the Banking and Currency Committee. As usual, he was optimistic about the future. When Kerr became ill in mid-February, he was chosen Speaker *pro-tempore.* Since Kerr's was a recurrent illness, Cox was in the chair regularly from February to June. As presiding officer he shed his customary jocularity and ruled over the House in a dignified, impartial manner. When his secretary remarked that it seemed curious for a man who loved fun so much to be so stern, he replied, " I know it, and if I don't get down on the floor pretty soon and let off some steam, I'll explode." When not in the chair during this session, Cox acted as majority floor leader.[24]

Other Democratic leaders in this session were Randall, Kerr, Hewitt, Alexander H. Stephens, Lucius Q. C. Lamar, J. Proctor Knott, and William R. Morrison. The presence of Stephens and Lamar, both former high Confederate officials, spotlighted the return of Southern Democrats to positions of influence in Washington. Republicans Blaine, Garfield, Kelley, and George F. Hoar led the opposition. The Democrats, who had developed great skill in criticism and opposition, now found that " they had not yet learned how to frame and carry constructive legislation." [25]

The problem of restoring the South and Southerners to

full political status received early attention in the House.
A general amnesty bill making no exceptions was quickly introduced and moved along rapidly until early in January when
Blaine moved to amend the bill, excepting Jefferson Davis
from its provisions. He delivered a powerful phillipic against
" the man who organized . . . the hideous crime of Andersonville." This was a shrewd political maneuver. It could
easily persuade many Northeners to oppose amnesty, since
Jeff Davis personified to the North all the things it hated in
the South. Blaine, with his eye on the Republican presidential nomination, expected this move to keep the political
spotlight centered upon him.

The Democrats were thrown into confusion by the unexpected ruse. Cox, who had no prepared speech, determined
to show up Blaine's artifice in using the " bloody shirt " to
gain political favor. The New York *World*'s Washington
correspondent was not at first impressed when Cox arose to
reply to Blaine. " I had heard the gentleman make campaign
speeches," he wrote, " and did not consider him equal to the
situation. In person he seemed insignificant " compared with
Blaine's " fine stalwart figure." " But before long it was
clear that he was master of the situation. . . . His speech
varied from lofty declamations to irony, invective, wit, and
even burlesque." As he continued speaking,

> Blaine, himself . . . began to wince as blow after blow fell.
> . . . He rose over and over again to retrieve himself, and at
> every interruption was knocked savagely back. . . . [Cox] re-
> marked with grim humor . . . " You are like the boy in Memphis
> who undertook to twist the mule's tail; you will never again
> be near so handsome as you were; but you will know a great
> deal more than you did."

To the *World* reporter, Cox was " a David " engaged in

" the slaughter of the political Goliath of the Republicans."
Cox attacked " the malice, dishonesty, and hypocrisy of Mr.
Blaine and his party in dealing with the amnesty question."
He showed that the man responsible for the Andersonville
prison atrocities had long since been hung. Blaine himself,
Cox stated, as a member of the Rules Committee in 1873
had approved just such a bill as the present one for general
amnesty (including amnesty for Jefferson Davis), which the
House had passed by an overwhelming 141-29 vote. Now,
said Cox, Blaine had shifted positions " and was raking up
all the embers of dead hate " because he was led " like
Macbeth by the dangerous vision of a crown " in the form
of the Republican nomination. But " the apocalyptic angel "
from Maine " would never be elected to the presidency if
he lived a thousand years." The amnesty bill missed the
needed two-thirds majority by a vote of 184 to 97. Undoubtedly, Blaine had influenced more than the four votes
that made the margin of difference. But Cox's speech, in
dramatizing Blaine's hypocrisy, did much to puncture " the
plumed knight's " presidential balloon.[26]

Even though full amnesty failed, Cox worked in other ways
to help relieve the South. His bill to remove the political disabilities of his pre-war congressional friend, George Hawkins
of Florida, secured the required two-thirds vote. He won
House approval for his resolution that the " Government of
the United States is a Federal Union " in which " the rights
of the States have the same sanction and security in the Constitution as those of the Federal Government " and in which
" the doctrine that a state has the right to secede " is " forever extinguished." The Negro question Cox considered
settled by the war amendments. " I do not see why we
should be all the time keeping up this race contest," he
complained. A man patronizing a butcher shop asks, " Is it

good mutton," not whether it came from a white or black sheep. " And so the good Lord on Judgment Day will not ask whether we are white sheep or black sheep but whether we are good mutton. . . ." Finally in late July with the presidential campaign already under way, Cox decried the misrule and robbery of " Republican adventurers " in South Carolina, quoting James Pike's *A Prostrate State* to illustrate his points.[27]

As chairman of the Banking and Currency Committee, he argued for a sound currency, which to him meant gold and silver money, and he secured congressional approval of his bill to establish a commission to study the monetary system and to make recommendations. With silver agitation mounting in the Western states, a bill for the issuance of $10,000,000 of silver coins to replace a like amount of retired greenbacks received Cox's and the House's approval but failed in the Senate. Referring to the " Crime of '73," Cox argued that " silver should not be demonetized . . . [for it is] legally [and] . . . morally . . . a part of the coin of this realm." He thought that the act of 1875 fixing January 1, 1879 as the date for specie resumption was " hopeless of execution." Thereafter, he proposed a bill repealing that act, which the House passed, but at the same time he declared that " resumption is the great desideratum." This obvious political straddle fitted Democratic strategy in the 1876 presidential campaign.[28]

Although Cox often looked abroad in the field of foreign relations, he kept in touch with reactions from his constituents at home. Remembering the heavy concentration of Irish and German immigrants in his district, he offered a resolution inquiring into the fate of one Edward Condon, an Irish-American citizen, who had served four years in the Union army and who, when last heard of, had been imprisoned by

British officials. Condon was under life sentence for murdering a constable during a Fenian disturbance in Ireland in 1868. Cox sent to the State Department resolutions of a New York mass meeting which called for efforts to secure Condon's release.[29]

To aid German-Americans, he denounced Minister George Bancroft's treaty of 1868 which permitted the German government to claim military service of naturalized American citizens who returned to the fatherland for visits of longer than two years. Cox was happy that this treaty would expire in 1878. His denunciation implied that Republicans were "tinged with Know-Nothingism" and would not protect naturalized Americans.

A more pressing problem concerning immigrants he presented in the form of a memorial signed by the New York State Commissioners of Emigration, the mayor of New York, and the representatives of German and Irish-American societies. The memorial asked Congress to take immediate steps for the care of immigrants arriving at New York. Such care had previously been provided by state commissioners but a recent Supreme Court decision had held that a state had no power in this field. The result was that thousands of immigrants arriving in New York were uncared for. Of the 5,500,000 immigrants who had entered at New York since 1847, over 1,717,000 had received aid from the state. The job would now have to be handled by the federal government. Despite Cox's urging, no action was taken at this session.

In regard to Latin America, Cox presented two petitions. One called for printing three hundred copies of Lt. Frederick Collins' report of his recent survey of the Panama Isthmus for an interoceanic canal. The other proposed that Americans would be justified in pursuing across the border Mexican bandits who had caused $2,000,000 damage on the American side.

Regarding technical government operations, Cox fought the proposed transfer of the Bureau of Indian Affairs from the Interior Department to the War Department. It was absurd, he said, to place the Indians under the care of the War Department which believed, with General Philip H. Sheridan, in a policy of extermination. Not that Indian affairs were skillfully handled in the Interior Department— far from it. But " if the present system is hell, and the Indian himself is in hell and the lowest deep is the Interior Department, where is the lower deep, lower even than the lowest, threatening to devour him, unless it be found in the War Department? " The best Indian policy, he said, was one of friendship, as practiced by William Penn and the Quakers, and more recently by Canada. In other technical matters, he introduced a bill to reform the civil service and proposed a postal savings bill—this some twenty-five years before a postal savings scheme was finally adopted.[30]

In his attacks on the Administration and in his efforts to expose Republican scandals Cox appeared at his best. He used all kinds of devices to embarrass Republicans and the Grant Administration, usually with consummate skill and good humor. Early in the session the House instructed the appropriate committees to investigate administrative agencies dealing with Indians, the army, navy, post office, public lands, and foreign affairs. The Democrats, of course, hoped to uncover evidence of scandal for use in the presidential campaign. Arguing that such investigations were necessary in view of the Crédit Mobilier scandal and the whiskey frauds, Cox was interrupted by hefty Representative Joseph G. Cannon, who shook his finger at the diminutive New Yorker. Cox retorted: " Don't shake your finger at me that way. . . .

I will get scared if you do. . . ." Then Cox consented to Cannon's having the floor " if the gentleman will keep his hands in his pockets." Cannon agreed and began to talk. Immediately Cox broke in: " The gentleman has his hand out of his pocket and is shaking his finger at me again. . . ." Cox then resumed his scathing denunciation of the Grant Administration, especially of Orville E. Babcock, Grant's private secretary, and of Secretary of War William W. Belknap. Democratic revelation of executive scandals had forced resignations until only Hamilton Fish was left of the original department heads. Cox denounced opponents like Blaine and Roswell Horr, who would not push impeachment of Belknap after the latter's resignation: " This mode of defense does not look like the high moral tone of the party which claimed to be based on moral ideas. . . ." Recalling the " Black Friday " investigation, Cox pointed out that the Republicans had " slammed the door in our face " by closing off testimony from the White House; they were trying to do the same thing now. *Harper's Weekly* caricatured Cox with a full-page cartoon on the front cover of its June 3 issue, showing him at the Speaker's desk swamped under piles of impeachment articles that bore Grant's name.

The net result of Democratic charges and investigations was to reveal an Administration honey-combed with graft, nepotism, and corruption. By this means, effective campaign tinder was provided for the Democrats who sniffed a White House victory bonfire in the offing.[31]

CENTENNIAL-YEAR ELECTION AND DISPUTE, 1876-1877

Before it actually began, and for many months after it was over, the campaign of 1876 cast its shadow across the proceedings of Congress. Frequently speeches were slanted toward influencing the November voting. As early as February, looking toward the election, Cox wrote Manton Marble that Democrats should stress " retrenchment " to make the strongest appeal to voters in this year of depression. He estimated that to win the presidency, Democrats would have to carry New York, New Jersey, and Connecticut, as well as the South. Western Democrats might cause trouble, since they were becoming " very cross and arrogant toward those of us who are trying to hold the [money] question in hand until we can secure some harmony." Meanwhile, Cox carried on as Speaker *pro tem* of the House and felt that " everyone here (Dems. and Repubs.) are satisfied with my running the Chair and doing it easily." [32]

In June, while still Speaker, Cox was chosen as delegate from New York to the Democratic National Convention in St. Louis. He went to St. Louis, with the understanding that on his return his substitute would relinquish the chair to him. Why this arrangement did not work out on Cox's return is not at all clear. It is curious that Cox was willing to abandon, even temporarily, the important position of Speaker *pro tem.* His opponents later charged that he was ordered to St. Louis by Tammany boss Kelly. His explanation, which seems too simple, was that he had been elected by his home district and had to go. He vehemently denied the suggestion that he " left the chair at the beck of any man." It seems a fair inference that he went to St. Louis because he wanted to have a hand in naming the man who appeared certain to be the next President. The result was that he lost the speakership, which, on Kerr's death in August, might have been his for as long as the Democrats controlled the House. [33]

To choose a presidential candidate that would satisfy the various factions of the Democratic party in 1876 was no simple task. Northern merchants, shippers, poor laborers and immigrants of the cities, old-fashioned Jacksonians in the West, Southern farmers, and small-town folk had little in common. Certainly, Southern and Western Democrats lost little love on their hard-money Eastern brethren. Even in New York itself the choice of a favorite son caused a battle between Tilden-led reformers and the Tammany men. New York's delegation to St. Louis, headed by the eminent Francis Kernan, lined up mainly behind Governor Tilden, but Tilden's manager, Abram Hewitt, found difficulty in dealing with boss John Kelly, who opposed Tilden in the hope of nominating the more manageable Winfield Scott Hancock. Cox joined the New York delegation in St. Louis on June 27. The New York *World* reported that he was preparing to make a speech opposing Tilden.[34]

Cox did make a speech on this first day of the convention but not in opposition to Tilden. He declared that " ' he who hath a pure heart and clean hands ' . . . is my man for President." Praising the Democratic House for its fight against " profligacy, robbery, ringdom, and all that rake-helly brood of ragged rascaldom that has been let loose on the country since the war," he urged an end " of the everlasting malfeasance in office . . . [of] Grantism and Babcockism and Belknapism . . . and every other ringism." Let Democrats unite to defeat Hayes and Wheeler. Let there be " none of your sectional hates and asperities; no party cries, no sectional shibboleths. Stand by the whole country . . . and good old Democratic Government. . . ."

Tilden, the strongest candidate the Democrats could offer, was nominated. Hunger for federal offices melted the opposition, and even boss Kelly came out for Tilden at the close of the convention. The platform, drafted mainly by Manton Marble, rang the keynote of reform, denouncing Republican corruption, calling for reform of taxes, tariff, and civil service, and for repeal of the 1875 Resumption Act which was a hindrance to the speedy return of specie payments. The paragraph dealing with economy and retrenchment was inserted largely at Cox's insistence.[35]

The Republicans, who had nominated Rutherford B. Hayes of Ohio, also talked of reform, but some Republicans, Charles Francis Adams among them, feared " stalwart " influence over Hayes, and refused to go along. The underlying campaign issues were the depression and the money question. The cautious Republican orators stayed away from " hard times, which is our deadliest foe "; instead they waved " the bloody shirt " from every stump, painting the horrors of the return to control in Washington of the Confederate brigadiers with their threat of repudiating the national debt and undoing of the war amendments.

Democratic arguments stressed the economic depression, disgust with Grantism, and the desire of rational men to forget war and its aftermath. It was " the ragged shirt versus the bloody shirt " with " a mass of desperate unemployed, desperate [Southerners] . . . groaning under black rule, desperate battlers against national corruption " contesting with " men fearful of the South, of low tariffs, of cheap money." In many ways it was the most exciting campaign since 1860.[36] The Democrats under National Chairman Hewitt's astute guidance rushed spell-binding orators to key states. When Congress adjourned in August, Cox made a brief visit to the death-bed of Speaker Kerr at Alum Springs, West Virginia. From there he proceeded westward to join Senators Thomas F. Bayard and Allen G. Thurman, Congressmen Samuel Randall, Henry Watterson, and Daniel Voorhees, who were stumping in Ohio and Indiana, where the campaign was hottest. After two months of speaking, Cox returned to campaign in New York, repeating the rigorous upstate tour he had taken in 1872. In the October voting, Democrats carried West Virginia and Indiana, but Republicans salvaged Ohio.[37]

Confident of his popularity, Cox paid little heed to his home district until the last few weeks before election day. An " S. S. Cox Campaign Club No. 1," formed by Irish voters in his district, and German groups endorsed him. Appearing at many rallies and frequently visiting Everett House, the Democratic national headquarters in New York City, he not only spoke for Tilden but also gave advice on running the campaign. The *World* reported him as one of the prominent guests at the Manhattan Club's reception for Tilden on October 30.[38]

On election day, November 7, the New York polls " opened at the early hour of 6 " and " the first votes were cast by gaslight." After a day of balloting, Democratic bigwigs, including Hewitt, Edward Cooper, Cox, and McClellan, gathered at Everett House to watch the returns come in. New York state results were encouraging—so much so that Tammany held a big rally in its hall. Cox dropped in on the rally during the evening to offer " commendation for your united show. There never was an organization more harmonious, so perfect, so democratic as that organized by Mr. Kelly." He added, " We have won, and there is nothing to do but enjoy ourselves." By midnight it was clear that Tilden had carried New York, Indiana, and New Jersey. Shortly after midnight at his Ohio home Rutherford Hayes went to bed all but certain of defeat. The following morning, newspapers proclaimed Tilden's victory. The Democratic *World* carried the headline: " Tilden Triumphant, Great Democratic Victories." Even the Republican *Tribune* conceded: " Tilden Elected; His Electoral Majority Small." But the New York *Times* refused to acknowledge defeat. At the urging of one of its editors, Republican Campaign Chairman Zachariah Chandler telegraphed party leaders in Louisiana, South Carolina, and Florida to " hold your State." Later in the day Republican headquarters announced: " Hayes . . . is elected." Despite this announcement, many Republicans, including Senator Roscoe Conkling of New York and the editors of the New York *Evening Post* and the Springfield *Republican* conceded a Tilden triumph.[39]

Cox wrote to one correspondent: " I spent yesterday with our Elect Pres't. He is sure he will go in. I fear the counts. The *mist* may obscure and trouble our dawning day. God help us to see the *mist* roll away, and that without further suspense and violence." [40]

Attention focused on Louisiana, Florida, and South Carolina, upon which the election now hinged. Both parties dispatched unofficial observers to those states. The Republicans had control of the state canvassing boards which would check the returns from local voting districts. On the grounds that Democrats had allegedly used intimidation, " bulldozing," and violence at the polls, the boards threw out many Democratic returns. In Louisiana a Tilden majority of 8,000 was converted into a Hayes majority of 4,000. In Florida and South Carolina the count gave the Hayes electors an average majority of 815 and 924 respectively. Democratic observers protested but without success against what they labeled " fraudulent proceedings." [41]

Back in New York, Tilden, who had received hundreds of congratulatory telegrams, saw victory slipping from his grasp. National Chairman Hewitt raised the question of Oregon's electoral vote. He charged that one Republican elector was also a postmaster and hence not qualified for the electoral college under the Constitution. Cox, who was staying at the Manhattan Club, advised Tilden to wire

Oregon and " have the telegraph repeated back: not merely answered . . . have James Beard (a special friend and confidential one, too, of ex-Senator Eugene Casserly) go " to Oregon. Raising the Oregon question was no mere political trick, but rather a means of deciding whether the federal government could go behind a state's returns. If it could not do so in the Southern states, as Republican leaders contended, then it could not do so in Oregon, where the Democratic governor was ready to certify a Democratic elector in place of the challenged Republican elector.[42]

Meanwhile, Cox had his most impressive success in the New York local election. He piled up 17,098 votes to 41 for his rival, A. J. H. Duganne. Cox gloated: " The 17,000 majority, by which a grateful constituency signalized my return " made the race seem more " theatrical than political." [43] With this overwhelming triumph, he became hopeful of regaining the speakership that he had lost the previous summer. " I have quite a reasonable assurance from a majority of our folks," he informed a Southern representative, " for my elevation to the Speakership." The New York *World* observed that Cox's chances were fair in a four-cornered contest for Speaker against Samuel Randall, Milton Sayler of Ohio, and William R. Morrison of Illinois. But Cox's hopes faded as the Democratic House caucus decided on Randall, who was duly elected over James A. Garfield. This choice must have hurt Cox the more, since Randall was one of the few protectionists among the Democrats, who generally favored a low tariff. Also, the new Speaker would be an important figure during the next three months while House members would be disagreeing over the decision in the presidential contest.[44]

" Clouds thick and threatening were obscuring the horizon," Cox recalled later when " Congress met . . . in December, 1876. Who was to be the next President? " The national chairman of each party issued a statement claiming victory for his own man. Several sets of returns reached Congress from Louisiana, Florida, and South Carolina. In the dispute over who was to open the returns, some Republicans interpreted the constitutional provision to mean that the president of the Senate, a Republican at the moment, had discretionary power in counting the returns, an interpretation that the Democrats naturally rejected. Further complications arose because the Republicans controlled the Senate, the Democrats the House. Democrats argued that the former joint rule of Congress providing that no returns should be counted unless agreed to by both houses was still in force. This would have permitted the Democratic House to block acceptance of the disputed Republican returns. " Peace," Cox wrote, " unless one party surrendered its claim of victory, seemed out of the question. No middle ground appeared possible. The horrors of civil war loomed up." [45] The " situation is indeed perilous," exclaimed Hewitt, whose hopes for revival of the joint rule had just been blasted by the Senate.[46] By Christmas, however, Congress proposed an Electoral Commission composed of five senators, five representatives, and five Supreme Court justices. Each party also appointed an advisory committee to work on this plan and to select Commission members. The Democratic committee met in Cox's Bank and Currency Committee room, with Cox providing the services of his own secretary, Milton H. Northrup.[47]

While these negotiations were proceeding, Cox, early in December, denounced the " frauds " of the Louisiana returning board. He contended that Congress should go behind the returns and " get at the truth." A House committee went to each of the doubtful Southern states to try to discover

" the truth." " On it," he observed, " hangs all our business, now suspended and paralyzed. . . . On it hang, I was about to say, peace and war." He demanded that the President report on the use of troops in the South during the election.[48] Convinced that the election rightfully belonged to Tilden, Cox was unhappy over the Electoral Commission arrangement but voted for it in the belief that it would insure the official choice of Tilden. Like most Democrats, he was sure that David Davis, the fifth Supreme Court member of the Commission, would sustain the Tilden returns. On the same day that the bill passed Congress, however, the Illinois legislature chose Davis as senator from Illinois, and he resigned forthwith from the Court. This was a blow to Democratic hopes.[49]

Counting of the returns began on February 1, when the senators filed in and took their places with the representatives in the House. Cox wrote:

> The galleries are packed. . . . Public expectation stands upon the tiptoe of trepidation. The certificates containing electoral votes are opened by President [of the Senate] Ferry. . . . The votes of state after state, in alphabetical order, are duly recorded. . . . All goes serenely for a time; when lo! a wild excitement and a hush of expectation! . . . The Chair announces that from Florida there are two sets of returns. . . . These two sets, he declares, must go before the Electoral Commission to which Congress had so improvidently delegated its duties.[50]

After hearing arguments by the learned counsel, Charles O'Conor, Lyman Trumbull, William C. Whitney, William M. Evarts, and Samuel Shellabarger, the Commission ruled that it could not go behind the returns and on February 5, by a vote of eight to seven, it accepted the Hayes returns for Florida. When the report reached Congress, the Senate voted to accept, the House to reject. When Louisiana was reached in the counting, the same process was repeated. It was when the House considered the Commission's report on Louisiana that two Republicans refused to go along with the decision and voted against it. Cox, too, was incensed and delivered a powerful speech, agreeing with Massachusetts Republican Julius Seelye that

> No facts were ever proved more conclusively than the fraud and corruption charged on the one side and the intimidation and cruelty charged on the other. Which of two sides went farther, did the worst, in this wrong-doing, would be very hard to say. . . . I find it quite impossible to say which set of returns . . . voices the true will of the people of Louisiana . . . and [it is] therefore equally beyond my power to assent to the propriety of accepting either.[51]

Cox was appalled that "the verdict of the American people . . . should prove a fruitless verdict." The judgment on the case being a foregone conclusion, he made this speech for history:

> Peril gives the lessons of years in a day. . . . The people of the United States, desiring peace and unity . . . spoke . . . in favor of a party whose tradition, principles, and history have rendered it deathless. . . . It was unmistakably called to the high places of the land. . . . [The Electoral Bill] is the law. . . . We knew and felt that some virtue had gone out of this House when we passed it. . . . It was voted for in a spirit of confidence and in a moment of peril. . . . We are bound by its decisions but not by its reasons. The faith of those who voted for it was strong in the integrity and purity of their case; and next in the fidelity and independence of the tribunal. We placed our faith in the ermine. But one strange thing about the bill is this: while we are permitted to vote in this House, yet after all it is a sort of post mortem vote. . . . [It is] the old rule of hanging a man and trying him afterward. And what is it we try? Why, sir, everything as to testimony and facts and forgery and perjury and force is *aliunde*—outside—not to be considered.

The House is *aliunde*. All its acts and the acts of its committees and their reports, all the facts gathered in these Southern States —*aliunde*! Nothing to be considered but the bare naked fact of a certificate based upon what? On forgery and chicanery. On a returning board, which returned the fact that 10,400 Democratic votes were not counted. . . . Truth and justice and morality and fair dealing—*aliunde*. . . . Earth is sick and heaven is weary of the hollow words which the statesmen and the judges use when they talk of right and justice, when such things can be accomplished. . . . Ah! they called in the ermine to help them. The ermine is a little animal. It is an emblem of purity; it would rather be caught than be bedraggled in the mire. . . . But where is the ermine now? Ah! the fox has become the ermine. But no cunning, no craft, no human law, no divine law can ever condone fraud. All codes and the histories of all nations cry out against it. . . . Ask the people of this country. Fraud is to them an endless offense. . . . With the permission of this House, I will read from the Psalms, xciv, 20: " Shall the throne of iniquity have fellowship with thee, which frameth mischief by a law? "

Mr. Kelley objected. But Cox continued: " The Bible is *aliunde* with these gentlemen." [52] This was Cox's final shot against the electoral proceedings, and it was followed by great laughter.

Although some Democrats attempted filibustering to block a settlement before March 4, the proceedings continued. On February 27 a number of practical men arranged the Wormley's Hotel deal whereby Democrats were promised control of Southern state governments in return for accepting Hayes as President. Meanwhile, economic pressures were forcing acceptance of the compromise. The House made its final, futile gesture of protest with a resolution asserting Tilden to be the rightful President. House Democrats, Cox among them, proclaimed that the presidency had been stolen from the Democracy and handed to " Rutherfraud " B. Hayes.[53]

At various times in this session, Cox filled in for Randall as Speaker. He also delivered an impressive eulogy of deceased Speaker Michael Kerr. Alexander Stephens, who lay ill at the National Hotel, sent for Cox, and when Cox reached Stephens' bedside, the latter said, " I have read your eulogy . . . and have sent for you to make a request. . . . Will you promise to deliver my eulogy when I am gone? " Cox shrugged and replied, " I would like you to make my eulogy. You will be the survivor."

His greatest efforts during this session were made in behalf of the letter carriers. These men, he insisted, who performed " an immense labor . . . from before daylight till late at night," were " now very inadequately paid." He fought a proposal to cut appropriations for their salaries and got the amount of the proposed cut restored. To do this, he had to stave off the attacks of economizers like Charles Foster of Ohio. When the latter accused Cox of angling for the letter carriers' vote, Cox replied that he didn't have to, since in the last election only forty-one votes were cast against him and therefore he was in an independent position to " speak for justice for these men," especially those carriers who received less than $1200 a year. The proposed salary cut was defeated.[54]

At the session's close Cox stayed on in Washington long enough to attend the inauguration. Hayes recorded in his diary his meeting at this time with Cox and other congressmen just before the ceremony.[55] After the inauguration Cox and his wife proceeded on a lecture tour through the Carolinas, Georgia, Tennessee, and Kentucky. Delighted with the South, he wrote: " We have had since we left Columbia a floral procession, and such times! If you had come along you would recognize that I never understood, the ' Sunny South ' in its kindest sense." The trip proved profitable as well. " I have lectured at Rome, Atlanta, Macon . . . to big crowds; and really am making money. Think of that! The noble pursuit of avarice! " [56] While on this trip he was entertained by various pre-war congressional colleagues, such as William N. H. Smith in Fayetteville, North Carolina, and William T. Avery in Memphis.[57] Noting the political climate, he sent to President Hayes from South Carolina " some observations " on " the prostrate state," offered as " my best judgment as to the policy which ought to be pursued." He followed this with a ten-page letter describing his talks with " men of both parties " which had convinced him that " the federal troops can be removed with safety and peace and unity restored. I believe that ready acquiescence will follow." By the time he reached Cincinnati, he felt almost overwhelmed by " two months oration ovation. . . . Such a generous people I did not dream of." [58]

Looking back over the eight years since his election to Congress from New York, Cox felt that his efforts had not been completely in vain. His party, in 1869 " a helpless, demoralized, suspected " minority, had by 1877 reached the very threshold of the White House. The seventy-three Democrats in the Forty-first Congress had grown to one hundred and eighty-three in the Forty-fourth Congress. With them as colleagues, Cox had fought against the ruthless reconstruction policy of the Radicals. His efforts were also directed against the protective tariff, which he considered an unfair tax on the farmer and on the laboring man for the benefit of the manufacturer. If he had not secured its repeal or modification, he had a least focused some public attention on the problem. He had opposed granting subsidies in land, money, and bonds to railroads or other corporations. These practices had at least been halted and the groundwork laid for future regulation in the public interest. He had sought to eliminate the inflationary greenbacks. Practically alone, he had effected the retention and extension of the United States Life-Saving Service. He had protected the mail-carriers from slashes in salaries which were already too meager. Although the rewards had not matched the labors, his satisfaction in a fight well fought was basic to his optimism about the future.

four

SUNSET:
YEARS OF HOPE AND
TRIUMPH, 1877–1889

7

CONGRESSIONAL UPS AND DOWNS,
1877–1883

TARIFF, CURRENCY, FOREIGN AFFAIRS, AND
LABOR, 1877–1878

During the years between Hayes's inauguration and that of Grover Cleveland, Cox remained an active, prominent leader of the House. His party controlled the House, except from 1881 to 1883, and even held a majority in the Senate in 1879-1881. Cox had two-year stints as chairman of the committees on Foreign Affairs, Census, and Naval Affairs. His interest in the tariff, shipping, currency, full amnesty, foreign affairs, the Life-Saving Service, and the letter carriers remained as keen as ever. To these were added new interests in the census, civil service, and railroads. Literary activity occupied some of his time, for he published three books during this period and carried on a full correspondence with such writers as James Russell Lowell, Oliver Wendell Holmes, Bret Harte, George William Curtis, Joaquin Miller, and John G. Saxe.[1]

Congress in these years came in for criticism from all

quarters. It became the fashion to belittle congressmen as nothing but petty place-seekers and appropriation-hunters. But the House in the 1870's and 1880's boasted a far higher level of ability than those who sneered at it supposed. Such an eminent observer as James Bryce, who came expecting the worst, was surprised to find " so much of character, shrewd-ness and keen though limited intelligence among the repre-sentatives." He felt that its capacity compared favorably with that of the British House of Commons. " Congress-men," he commented, " have almost certainly made their way by energy and smartness, picking up a knowledge of men and things all the time." With this judgment Cox agreed, but added that " something more is needed than mere current knowledge. . . . A member should know something about everything . . . science . . . history . . . physics, metaphysics . . . philosophy. . . ." Bryce was astonished at the short tenure of the average congressman and remarked that " the chances are about even that he will lose his seat at the next election." Cox, whose frequent successes at the polls quali-fied him to speak on this point, explained: " The mere businessmen in Congress are not the most successful legis-lators. They seldom " engage " in general thought. . . . It is the full-rounded development of all the faculties, including that of humor, which is the secret spring to political success and the test of our greatest men." [2]

Congress' chief difficulty stemmed from its unwieldy, awkward machinery that encouraged delay and blocked action, with one House often canceling out the other. In the House of Representatives, " a huge chamber . . . [with] desk-lids clapping, pens scratching, pages scampering about, groups talking and laughing, galleries humming," time wasted in roll calls and motions to adjourn, it was surprising that any business was transacted at all. These factors " were most noticeable during the late seventies and early eighties when the House and the Senate were of opposite political complexion. The result was that issues were simply evaded and constructive action failed to materialize." [3]

" The administration of Rutherford B. Hayes," wrote Cox, " was that of a *de facto* Executive." [4] It was a period of much political confusion. Henry Adams declared: " Politics are a good deal mixed. . . . Parties are broken up for the time." [5] Within the parties, internal conflicts raged. The Republicans found " stalwarts " pitted against " half-breeds," with reformers firing from the fringes. " Stalwarts " resented Hayes at the start and were further alienated by his lenient Southern policy and his appointments. Meanwhile, there was disharmony among the Democrats. In New York, intra-party strife had developed between Tilden men and Tammany. In economic matters, also, the Hayes years were difficult ones. Depression continued to plague the land. Unemployment was still widespread. Labor unrest periodically erupted into violent outbursts, as in the railroad strikes of 1877. [6]

Before Congress met in December 1877, Cox found time for another lecture tour. At Rochester, New York, he spoke in the same lecture series as Wendell Phillips, whom he had opposed so violently years before. During the fall, requests poured in from friends asking for government jobs. And he received notes of sympathy from other friends who blamed his defeat for the speakership on Tammany's adverse influence. One correspondent suggested that Cox had been " furnishing too much wit and humor in Congress all the time, which has detracted from your more solid merits in the eyes of the average dunce." [7]

When the Congress finally convened, the time-honored tariff debate was resumed. Early in the session Cox submitted a petition from New York importers asking tariff revision. Soon afterward he renewed his plea for free trade against the " thousand exploded sophistries of the protective school." In support of his opposition he cited the earlier experiment in reciprocal trade with Canada and the reciprocal trade arrangement with the Hawaiian Islands. With this plea, he spoke not only for the Free Trade Club, organized in New York in May 1877 by his friends, Abram Hewitt, Everett P. Wheeler, and publisher George S. Putnam, but also for the Democratic platform of 1876. All of his efforts failed, however. When the short session ended, he reported in correspondence with David A. Wells that he was still pressing for tariff reduction.[8]

Closely associated with the tariff was the currency question. The coinage act of 1873, called by inflationists " the crime of '73," had dropped the standard silver dollar from the roster of coins produced in United States mints. As the amount of silver from American mines increased during the 1870's and as the depression deepened, there was a corresponding pressure on politicians for the restoration of the free coinage of silver. Richard P. Bland's bill for more liberal coinage of silver at the old 16 to 1 ratio with gold passed the House in December 1876. In 1877 pressures on Congress became irresistible. In the special session called by Hayes in October 1877, the Bland bill again was pushed through the House, although Cox thought that the issue " should not be re-agitated." But when the vote came, his was in the affirmative. When this bill was followed by another calling for repeal of the 1875 Resumption Act, Cox protested that he would not vote for the repeal of the entire act but would favor postponing the date for resumption, in view of the continuing depression. Despite his hesitation, the bill passed, only to die in the Senate. On the silver question he appeared to have shifted ground. Earlier, he had fought against inflationary measures, and his present support of free silver coinage seemed to contradict his previous statements. Undoubtedly the continuing depression and the rise of the surprising Greenback-Labor party in 1876-1878 had much to do with his shift in position. Later, when Hayes vetoed the Bland-Allison Act, Cox called the veto message " a charge of fraud by a fraud " and joined in the vote that overrode the veto.[9]

On behalf of New York merchants and the New York Chamber of Commerce, he introduced, and eventually witnessed the passage of, a federal law leaving bankruptcy rules in the hands of the states.[10] The Western railroads came in for a large share of his ire. Having received tremendous land grants and generous advances of money from the federal government, these corporations had consistently failed to make interest payments to the government. By 1877 they owed a total of $65,000,000. Nor had they made provision for payment of the principal of their debt. Now a sinking fund bill was proposed by Senator Allen G. Thurman of Ohio. This bill provided for a systematic payment of the amount due the government, much to the dismay of railroad promoters Jay Gould and Collis P. Huntington. To the same end, Cox introduced a slightly different bill in the House. It was high time for such a measure, Cox asserted, since the railroads had been " stolen, watered, and gutted " by unscrupulous promoters. He demanded that " our railways should be managed in harmony with its [the country's] commercial, industrial, and public interests " and should not be subjected to the " dictation of railway kings." " It is a contest between the brawn of this country, aided at last by the honest brain, and those speculators who have failed in a great trust." Cox's bill passed the House by a wide 243-2 margin, only to be stymied by the Senate's insistence on Thurman's version of the bill." [11]

Cox continued to express his concern over the imprisonment of Irish-American Fenians by the English government. With a new Administration in power, he won approval for his resolution that called on the President to investigate and request the release of Edward Condon. Cox stated that the United States owed this action to Irish-Americans who had done so much to develop America.[12] As a result, Secretary of State William M. Evarts secured Condon's release.

Earlier, the Foreign Affairs Committee had examined the situation in Mexico where, in the past year, Porfirio Diaz had risen to power. Informing the House that " Mexico is our neighbor—' our sick man ' " and that " revolution seems to be her chronic condition," Cox contended that our policy had always been to recognize a *de facto* government. In Mexico, Diaz " has the capital; . . . has the archives; . . . has the army; . . . all the territory, all the insignia and paraphernalia of power which designate a *de facto* government." Hence, we should grant immediate recognition. On practical grounds, this would permit negotiation of commercial treaties. " The arts of peace should be especially cultivated toward our neighbor Mexico, with whom we ought and hope to trade." [13] Again Cox was looking after the commercial interests of New York.

The Mexican problem, however, remained troublesome. During 1877 Diaz continued to strengthen his position, liquidating opposition groups and promising concessions to American promoters in the hope of winning American recognition. When Mexican marauders raided across the border into American towns north of the Rio Grande, Secretary of State Evarts stated that a condition of recognition would be Diaz's cooperation in suppressing the border bandits. After this failed, Hayes ordered American troops to pursue Mexican bandits, even if pursuit carried them across the international boundary. Cox and the Foreign Affairs Committee held hearings, questioned Evarts and others, and continued to press the Administration to grant recognition. Finally in 1878 the Administration agreed, but a hitch developed, and Hayes' term ended before recognition became a fact.[14]

As the representative of a labor constituency, Cox presented numerous petitions, memorials, and resolutions calling for observance of the eight-hour-day regulation provided for by a federal statute in 1868.[15] This had been largely ignored by the Grant regime, especially in the navy yards and post offices, which of course employed a majority of government workers. In May 1878 Cox secured House adoption of a resolution to that effect, and he also expressed a hope for a uniform practice in dealing with government employees in such matters as vacations, leaves, and illness.[16] He secured passage of a bill providing for two grades within the letter carrier service with graduated pay, authorizing the Postmaster-General to establish a third grade for auxiliary letter carriers, and requiring carrier service in all cities of 50,000 population or more, such service to be made optional in cities of 20,000 to 50,000.[17] At last, a step had been taken toward securing some order, efficiency, and incentive in what was fast becoming the government's first career service.

Reform of the general civil service was desirable, but real reform, Cox said, was impossible under the Hayes Administration. He ridiculed the examination system established by Secretary of the Interior Carl Schurz. In a hypothetical examination, the candidate was asked: " Where is the State of Delaware? Answer: Can't say, couldn't see it. . . . What was the cause of the war of 1812? Free trade. Who is the president of the United States? This was answered by a tipsy applicant. The answer was: Rutherford B. Tilden. . . . This man passed. . . ." Cox accused the Hayes Administration of " corrupt and hypocritical practices " in using pleas of civil service reform to make whatever appointments it pleased. In 1877, when it was again proposed to have cabinet members appear in Congress, Cox protested, as he had in 1865, that such a proposal was unworkable under the American system of government since cabinet officers could not be ousted in case of an adverse vote by Congress.[18]

Always interested in books, he proposed a commission to consider plans to enlarge the Library of Congress. He pointed out that the Library, acquiring new books at the rate of 8,000 a year, was already housing 441,118 volumes in a space intended for 260,000. " It is not economy thus to allow our books to perish," he said.[19] In another matter of preservation, he sponsored a bill to repair the monument over Thomas Jefferson's grave at Monticello and seized the opportunity to extol the virtues of the founder of the Democratic party, " our greatest philosophic teacher, the overshadowing intellect of his time and country." The bill passed without difficulty.[20]

In the spring of 1878 the Democratic House revived the disputed election of 1876 by appointing the Clarkson Potter Commission to investigate charges of bribery connected with that election. Even though the investigation backfired on its originators, it uncovered much evidence of Republican pressure and promises of rewards for key election officials in the doubtful Southern states. This gave Cox another chance to castigate Hayes and reiterate the charge of fraud. A wrong had been committed against the American people by the electoral commission. " No washing will rinse out that spot. . . . No special pleading . . . no odor of sanctity over the deed can ever eradicate the damned spot." [21] It was this kind of talk that led one of Hayes's New York friends to write that Cox was a " miserable montebank " and that the " Erie railway " operating as " a Tammany machine " through Cox's friend, Hugh J. Jewett, was being " used to keep just such men as Cox in office." [22] Cox later recalled that it distressed him to charge Hayes with being a fraud, for he had known and liked " this President in his younger, happier, and better days in Cincinnati." But he felt strongly on the question—" I would never consent to quiet bad title, even though technically legal," he wrote Tilden.[23]

Cox's greatest oratorical effort of the session came on June 4, 1878, when he delivered a moving address on the Life-Saving Service. He was seeking a larger appropriation for the service and wished to prevent its proposed transfer from the Treasury to the Navy Department, where he feared it might fall into the hands of political spoilsmen. He traced the evolution of the service from the early, feeble, volunteer efforts up to the government's more systematic organization of 1872. Since that year 5,000 lives had been saved by the service, and loss from shipwrecks in 1877 had fallen to a new low of only $2\frac{1}{2}$ per cent of the total property involved. Although now organized into four districts, the service was also needed on the Texas and Great Lakes shores. The Life-Saving Service

> . . . is, in a high sense, divinely beautiful. Although it is limited to this country of ours, it is an incentive to the benevolent of all lands. It rescues the people of all nationalities. . . . These ancient mariners [the Greeks] appealed to Jupiter and Neptune, we appeal to the practical mechanics. We invoke the genius of chemistry, with its colored signals, its line, car, buoy, powder, and howitzer. We add electricity and steam to the dauntless heroism of the surfman. . . .

> Yet . . . there is a higher sanction than the Constitution or

humanity. It is that of Him who stilled the waves of Gallilee to save imperilled human life. . . . In the beauty of the lilies Christ was born across the sea and in the glory of his bosom he transfigured you and me. He died to make men holy, and for the salvation of human souls in desperate shipwrecks through sins. We may not imitate his example here, sir, except afar off, but by our voice and vote, we may do something by this measure to throw around our legislation a divine aureole and save human life so precious to Him who gave His life to save the lives of others. . . .

Ah, sir, there is a pathetic poetry belonging to the sea . . . a huge feline, licking your feet, purring at times pleasantly, but ready to crack your bones and eat you for all that, and then wipe the crimsoned foam from its jaws as if nothing had happened. . . . Nations vote pensions and decorations to the hero who first plants a flag on a parapet or rescues it from an enemy. How much nobler to decorate and pension the man, who seeing one of his own kind, though a stranger, in the struggle and despair of death, plunges into the very jaws of the unseen future amidst darkness and danger to reclaim his fellow being from a watery grave. We may construct upon the shore the image of Liberty holding up her torch to enlighten the world; . . . but no such light will attract the attention of good men of our kind like the serene and blessed illumination that radiates from our lifesaving statute and proclaims to all the world . . . that when overcome by the terrific disaster of the sea, they have at every perilous point along our coast, the heroic courage of men who are equipped and ready to leap into the surf, to launch their boats through its ' league-long ' rollers, to breast the tempest in its angry howling and to rescue those who are hanging upon the vast abyss and about to be swallowed up by the angry waters. It is said in the New Testament that a man shall give up his life for his friend. But these men, almost without pay, with a lion-hearted courage excelling that of the soldier . . . are ready in the pursuit of their high duty to glorify human nature by laying down their lives if need be for . . . even those who are aliens and strangers. . . .

Humanity and civilization should walk white-handed along with government. They strengthen and save society. . . . Let us do good deeds, pray hopefully that our vessel of state be free from leakage, collison, wreck, and loss. Send out the life-boat; fire the line over the imperilled vessel; free the hawser for the life-oar, and then with stout hearts and thankful souls lift up our prayer to Him who holds the sea in the hollow of His hand.[24]

An observer recorded that when Cox finished speaking, " A profound silence pervaded the House for an instant," but " in less time than I can describe it every member was on his way up the aisle toward him to extend congratulations." Cox himself was moved to tears. The New York *World* said it was " an eloquent and fervid speech . . . frequently interrupted with applause," and particularly stressed Cox's statement that most of his life in public service had " been like writing in water. . . . I would gladly lay down my commission and turn to other duties. . . . But what little I have accomplished in connection with this life-saving service is . . . its own exceeding great reward." [25] His proposal for increased appropriations for the service was adopted by an overwhelming majority. This session thereby ended with some satisfaction for Cox.

On June 17, 1878, while still in Washington, Cox wrote Tilden that he had been " rummaging over and burning up " some of his old letters and papers " accumulated through twenty years service " and was returning some material Tilden had given him years before. A fortnight later, he and General McClellan were guest speakers at the Monmouth battlefield centennial celebration in New Jersey where he eulogized his grandfather, General James Cox, who had fought at Monmouth and later served as a Jeffersonian Democrat in Congress.[26] Following this speech, he returned to New York to find politics in greater confusion than ever.

The earlier alliance between Tilden and Kelly in the Democratic party had broken down. "Honest John" felt that Tilden and his successor as governor had denied Tammany sufficient patronage rewards for the electoral strength supplied at the polls. "Cold, unyielding, precise," Kelly dominated the city machine "like a martinet," naming its tickets, selecting its appointees, and outlining its policies. Immigrants, who formed the mass of voters in lower Manhattan, were won over by Tammany aid in securing their naturalization papers, gifts of food, coal, and clothing. Such citizens naturally were quite willing to vote the straight ticket, as directed by Tammany henchmen. Ward heelers and district captains whipped up enthusiasm at street corner rallies, bonfire barbecues, and torchlight parades. The inevitable campaign wagon was described in *Puck*:

> As down the street it wildly steers
> And sounds its weird alarum,
> The horde of Tammany howls and cheers
> For Kelly and Refarrum.[27]

Party workers stood close to the polling places on election day and thrust the Tammany ballot into voters' hands. By such means Kelly gained virtually absolute control over city affairs. By 1878 he dominated the party's state machinery and blocked nomination of Tilden-backed candidates. Complications arose when some New York City Democrats combined with Irving Hall Democrats, revolted against Kelly and formed the County Democracy. Moreover, a Labor Reform party that had grown out of the labor disputes of 1877 entered the field, threatening to subtract many workers' votes from Tammany totals. Kelly's machine shook on its foundations.[28]

When congressional district conventions gathered in mid-

October, efforts were made for a compromise among the Tammany, Irving Hall, and County Democrats. In the Sixth District, The *World* reported that the convention, which met in " a bar-room at 173 Madison Street, adjourned to the hall back of the saloon, where Coroner Woltman put up the name of Cox for renomination." With no opposition, the nomination was approved by " cheers that lasted for five minutes." Cox then appeared to accept the " unanimous nomination " and to declare that " I shall always try to serve my country to the satisfaction of Republicans as well as Democrats." [29] In opposition, Labor Reformers named Isaac Bennett, while the Irving Hall Democracy put up Maurice DeVries. Election returns distributed the vote as follows: Cox 10,913, DeVries 6,378, Bennett 232. Though Cox won, the County Democracy beat Tammany in the city-wide election and sent Edward Cooper to the City Hall as mayor.[30]

A DEMOCRATIC CONGRESS, 1879-1880

While Democrats in New York were weakened by factional strife in 1878, nationally they showed surprising strength, maintaining control of the House and gaining a majority in the Senate. Because the expiring Congress failed to make appropriations for government operations, the President called the new Congress into a special session that ran from March 18 to July 1, 1879. It reconvened for its second session in December, to run until June 1880. In these sessions Cox continued as chairman of the Foreign Affairs Committee as well as Speaker *pro tem* on frequent occasions.[31]

Reports of Russian persecutions of Jews elicited from Cox a resolution calling for treaty negotiations with the Russian government in order to protect Jewish-American citizens who were in Russia on business. The House adopted this resolution. On May 21, 1881, Cox, asking the State Department for the correspondence concerning these negotiations, delivered a short speech on the subject. He described the anti-Semitic atrocities in Russia and expressed his hope for the eventual establishment of a Jewish national homeland. As for Russia, he declared: " We have become used to persecutions in that country. It is part of its barbarism," and, therefore, " it becomes us especially " to offer " asylum to these stricken people." [32] Lower East Side Jews in New York applauded. Applauding, too, were Irish constituents when Cox called for American aid to those suffering from famine in Ireland and when he won House approval of an invitation for Charles Stewart Parnell to address the House. Cox also pressed for an answer to the immigrant problem. Once again he pointed out that no care was being provided for the newcomers since, by Supreme Court edict, the states were no longer allowed to deal with the problem. He called for a $250,000 appropriation to provide immediate care for immigrants and " hospitality, and relief, too, from sharks." [33]

Of less direct political appeal, but certainly of great interest to New York shipping firms, was his work on behalf of a Panama isthmian canal. The French engineer, Ferdinand DeLessepps, had organized a company, which in 1879 began surveys with a view to building a canal at Panama. The American State Department and Congress became exercised over this encroachment on the Western Hemisphere. The House passed repeated resolutions denouncing the French company's action, and Cox's Foreign Affairs Committee conducted an investigation. Cox presented to the House the State Department's report on the steps taken by the French Panama company and pushed several resolutions requesting the President to declare the Clayton-Bulwer Treaty " finally and formally abrogated." These the House adopted.[34] But on the Cox committee-recommendation for United States naval stations on both sides of the Panama isthmus the Administration took no action.[35]

Together with his fellow Democrats, he fought to remove the last of the restrictive reconstruction measures from the statute books. In the 1878-79 session the Democratic House had refused to vote appropriations because the Republican Senate had rejected an appropriations bill rider eliminating federal control over elections. In the special session of 1879, with both Houses Democratic, a rider to the army appropriations bill provided repeal of the law authorizing the use of troops " to keep peace at the polls." When Hayes vetoed this, Congress resorted to making appropriations with the proviso that no moneys should be paid to United States marshals or federal troops who intervened in elections. Cox's attitude in these matters had been clearly expressed earlier, but he now added a few new touches. Especially, he fought the test-oath requirement for jurors, which barred ex-Confederate supporters from serving on federal juries. " What a farce," he exclaimed, " is all this amnesty business " so many years after the war. In a long speech on June 3, 1879, he called it " monstrous " that such an oath should remain. " It nullified a fair, intelligent jury trial " in the South. It was absurd since three federal judges would be unable to take the oath, nor could some twenty district attorneys, nor a number of congressmen, nor even a few cabinet officers. Those who had fought for the Union must take a " yard-long, iron-clad oath " while those Confederates who had been pardoned by Congress need take only a simple oath of loyalty. Thus, " the gallant gentleman from Virginia, General Joseph E. Johnston, and others . . . are only required to take the simple oath, " while the gallant band of Union

soldiers, led by . . . General Garfield" must take an oath
" swearing that they never, never, NEVER, did bear arms "
against the United States. Cox likened the practice of frequent oath-taking, which made it absurd and meaningless,
to the case of the Irishman who took the pledge to abstain
from liquor except for twelve specified drinks per day, which
occurred practically every hour of the day. "To those who
delight in pains, penalties, test oaths, bayonets, and force,"
and who would not substitute " love, gentleness, and forgiveness, my only curse upon such is, that God Almighty . . .
may forgive them, for ' they know not what they do.' " The
outcome of the fight was the repeal of the jurors' oath.[36]

During the debate over the river-harbor appropriation
bill of 1880, Roswell G. Horr, a corpulent representative
from Michigan, made disparaging remarks about Cox's small
size and stated that Cox's Foreign Affairs Committee was
engaged " mainly in the manufacture of witticisms." In
answer, Cox proceeded to give " the gentleman a lesson in
humor." Sending to Horr's desk a copy of his recently
published book, *Why We Laugh*, Cox explained that real
humor, to be effective, " should be ratiocinative " with a
" practical object." In view of this,

> . . . was it logical for my friend . . . to call the attention
> of the House to my body? Suppose I am little, was it logical,
> or parliamentary, or kind to say it? . . . It permeated every one
> of my two million pores. Suppose I had the gentleman's im-
> mensity of pores, where could not the laughter extend? . . .
> Was my size a subject for any gentleman's logical laughter?
> I never claimed, because of its smallness, exemption from the
> demands of courage or in the arena of debate. Laughter is
> health. It oils the joints and the countenance, causing it to
> shine. . . . Why should smallness, in such immensity of creation,
> and when everything may be reduced to atomies, be accounted
> contemptible? When one comes to consider all physical rela-

tions—the size of this dome and the goddess on it, much bigger, even than the gentleman, then of the mountains of the earth, then of the sun . . . and then of the constellations and systems far beyond . . . how contemptible a member of Congress seems! Therefore where is the humor of making a member of Congress out to be little, and laughing at his size? What is there to boast of in this enormity of flesh and size? . . . I endeavor to debate impersonally; never refuse to yield; never invade another's right; always consider my person almost an abstraction. I am not proud of my appearance as some men are who swell. . . . I argued against making Congress too big two years ago. Two hundred and fifty is enough. I should have labored for two hundred as our number. . . .

Then Cox concluded with an epitaph:

> Here lies the body of Congressman Horr
> 'Tis Greece, but living Greece no more.
> Requiescat.

This was followed by great laughter, after which Horr replied with more jibes at Cox's small size, declaring that he ought to be called "Dear Little Buttercup." He remarked that "Cox's friends had once asserted that had he been six inches taller, he would have been President," and he also concluded with an epitaph:

> Beneath this slab lies the great Sam Cox,
> Who was wise as an owl and brave as an ox;
> Think it not strange his turning to dust,
> For he swelled and he swelled till he finally bust.
> Just where he has gone, or just how he fares,
> Nobody knows and nobody cares.
> But wherever he is, be he angel or elf,
> Be sure, dear reader, he's puffing himself.

But Cox got in the last word on size by relating it to extravagance, "the canker which follows the war." He decried " the insane greed for wealth, the enormous growth of capital . . . shoddy display and superficial fashion, monopolizing corporations and family greed." He would not " contribute to this insane urge for making public works at every doorstep." [37]

In much the same vein, he urged cracking down on the transcontinental railroads, which are " our creatures and yet we are threatened here by them." The office of the Auditor of Railroad Accounts should be retained, he argued, " to ferret out the interests of the Government against these smart, provident, and unscrupulous agents " and help " the Government get back money due from the railroads." Unless the railroad lobbyists were checked, he said, " Congress will have to take charge of the railroads and make them amenable to the laws." [38]

As a member of the Joint Committee on the Census, he drafted the bill for the 1880 census and guided it through the House to passage. The proposed census was to be enlarged to include statistics on crop acreages in agriculture, professions and occupations at various age levels, corporations engaged in manufacturing, mining, and transportation, employed workers, hours of labor, and power used. The census would also provide the population basis for congressional reapportionment. Such statistics, he proclaimed, would " weigh and measure the individual elements that make up . . . [the nation's] collective force." It would lay a foundation for wise legislation.[39]

Once more he pushed for enforcement of the eight-hour law, still disregarded in many federal departments. Most department work, he contended, could be accomplished in less time than was currently consumed, because " a good many clerks, when not engaged in reading the newspapers," spent their time in " talking politics and spitting tobacco juice.

There is no man in all the world like an American clerk for splendid spitting. . . . Our American clerks can spit higher, spit farther, and spit more than any other people on the face of the earth—and get more pay for the performance! " Anticipating Franklin D. Roosevelt's New Deal by half a century, Cox declared that the federal government should serve as a model employer. " Let us set the example of a fair day's work and wages, and . . . the manufacturers and other employers . . . will follow in the wake." [40] For the night inspectors of customs at New York, he gained House approval for a pay raise, which he got Thomas F. Bayard to hustle through the Senate.[41]

To the Life-Saving Service Cox again turned his attention. He fought off proposals that would cut appropriations for this agency and reduce the salary of its superintendent, Sumner I. Kimball, who deserved instead great praise for " establishing, organizing, and disciplining the service." In addition, he proposed pensions for the families of twelve members of the service who had " died in the line of duty," but the House rejected the proposal.[42]

However, he won House approval for a centennial celebration to be held in New York commemorating the signing of the Treaty of Paris of 1783. By an interesting coincidence, his publishers, David F. Appleton and Fletcher Harper, were appointed commissioners for this exposition.[43]

Cox's ability as a speaker was again recognized when he was called upon by the House to deliver eulogies for three deceased congressmen and for the scientist Joseph Henry of the Smithsonian Institution. He praised the latter for his work with magnetic induction and called him " an apostle of this age of physical progress and grandeur." [44]

FAILURE AND SUCCESS, 1880-1883

Following Tammany's split with the Tilden-led state organization in New York, " Honest John " Kelly in 1879 again sought to regain state control. In 1880, unable to control New York's delegation to the Democratic National Convention, Kelly led his own contesting delegation to Cincinnati. Tilden, frequently mentioned as the logical candidate to retrieve the " great fraud " of 1876, withdrew his name from convention consideration. The nomination then went to Winfield Scott Hancock, who was hailed as a good soldier and as a judicious military governor in post-war Louisiana. Kelly was pleased, announced that he would bury the hatchet, and called upon all New York party men to back Hancock. The reconciliation was short-lived, however, for, once back in New York, he insisted upon a Tammany man as candidate for mayor in place of Edward Cooper.[45]

Meanwhile, the Republicans, unable to agree on Grant, Blaine, or John Sherman for President, nominated James A. Garfield, Cox's long-time antagonist in the House. The campaign, as far as Cox was concerned, had begun back in March when the Republicans had denounced Democratic disregard of the federal election law and Cox had responded by reminding Garfield and the Republicans about their own disregard of the fugitive slave law in the 1850's.[46] By 1880 the two parties " had achieved a remarkable state of equilibrium." A slight shift in public opinion could give one or the other victory. Republicans in the campaign tried to show that Hancock behaved like a coward in the Civil War, while Democrats sought to prove that Garfield was dishonest in the Crédit Mobilier scandal. Party platforms revealed little difference beyond a Democratic plank favoring " a tariff for revenue only." This might have been played into a real issue, but Hancock, with an eye on Pennsylvania's votes, asserted that " the manufacturing or industrial interests . . . [would] have as much protection" under Democrats as under Republicans and that the tariff was a " local issue," a statement that aroused much ridicule of the Democratic nominee.[47] If this remark cooled Cox's earlier enthusiasm, he gave no sign of it and entered into the campaign energetically. He tried to get William T. Sherman to speak for Hancock.[48] Visiting often at the candidate's headquarters on Governor's Island, he provided Hancock with a copy of his *Free Land and Free Trade*, which Hancock agreed to consult " for my own information." [49] Privately, Cox would have agreed with Henry Adams' judgment that Hancock was " not a first-rate choice." [50]

In his own New York bailiwick, Cox staged an active canvass for re-election. Tammany Hall and Irving Hall, although splitting the other congressional nominations, both endorsed Cox in the Sixth District. In late October he shared a platform with Hewitt on the steps of the federal sub-treasury building on Wall Street. As the afternoon was growing late when he arose to speak, Cox remarked, " I need not remind my friends that ' Sunset' is coming upon you, but I could talk all night." Declaring that he was " not much accustomed to Wall Street," he denounced " Republican misrule" while asserting that as he stood on the " sacred " spot where George Washington took his first oath of office, he could " not believe that we can be beaten out of our own again." [51]

Cox's prediction proved wrong, although only by a narrow margin. Hancock went down to defeat, but the popular majority was a scant 7,000 votes. The loss of New York, whether due to Hancock's inept remarks on the tariff or to the heavy Republican spending or to the splitting of Democratic strength through Kelly's maneuvers, sank Democratic hopes for success. The *World* believed that the election showed the " incompetency of the leaders " in New York.[52] Despite the general defeat, Cox enjoyed the personal satisfaction of being returned by a 10,000-vote majority in his district. He sent condolences to Hancock, who replied that " all the ' Bulldozing,' bribery, colonization, delays " had cost him the election in New York.[53]

Early in December Cox returned to Washington for the lame-duck session that held him there until March 1881. A month later he and his wife sailed for a European trip from which he returned barely in time for the opening of the first session of the Forty-seventh Congress. This was the Congress in which the Republicans controlled both Houses for the first time since 1875. The session lasted until August 1882. Following the campaign of 1882, Congress reconvened in December to run until March 1883. In the first of these sessions (1880-1881), Cox continued as chairman of the Foreign Affairs Committee. In the last two sessions, which were Republican-controlled, he served on the committees on Appropriations, the Census, and American Shipping, and represented the House officially on the Smithsonian Board of Regents.[54]

During the years 1880 to 1883, Cox's concern with American foreign affairs remained active and aggressive. In February 1881 he reiterated his earlier demand for abrogation of the Clayton-Bulwer Treaty, which he called " the diplomatic blunder of the century " and " a huge gorgon in our path," violating our own Monroe Doctrine and casting " a baleful shadow over the Isthmus." [55] In the following session, the problem of the Jews in Russia claimed much of his attention. For his earlier stand on this question, he had received wide acclaim. The American consul in Lyons, France, had sent congratulations for " your eloquent, timely, and statesman-like utterances " and added that he couldn't understand the attitude of " a large party " of Americans " who have a most absurd and ridiculous sentiment for Russia, who believed that she helped us in the time of our great Rebellion trial, forgetting . . . [that she] was inspired by her hatred of England." [56] Protesting Russian mistreatment of Jews as " part of my duty as a representative of a large Hebrew element," Cox described in detail the pogroms, " the horrors of 1881," some of which he had observed first hand during his recent trip abroad. He urged the President to protest firmly to the Russian government and to lend army tents for the care of Jews expelled from Russia.

Cox also continued his work for the release of Irishmen in British prisons. He called upon the State Department to secure the names of such individuals from Great Britain.[57] At a Cooper Union protest meeting he asked that James Russell Lowell, the " sycophantic" ambassador to Great Britain, be recalled for failing to protest vigorously enough.[58] In a letter to Carl Schurz, now an editor of the New York *Evening Post*, Cox tried to win the *Post*'s support for the cause of the Jews and the Irish.[59] For his work in regard to the Russian Jews, he received warm praise from the Jews in New York, both his constituents and others.[60] On the last of his under-dog causes, immigration, he urged the establishment of a federal board of immigration to examine immigrants and to bar paupers, convicts, and insane persons.[61]

The tariff issue was still alive and still cut across party lines. On the Democratic side of the House, Morrison, Hewitt, Roger Q. Mills, and Cox carried on the " gallant battle " against the protective tariff only to find some fellow Democrats like Randall voting with the Republicans for

protection. Most tariff speeches in these years were intoler-
ably dull, but Cox showed ingenuity in presenting the arguments against the tariff. He emphasized the need for foreign
markets and the adverse effects of the tariff on American
labor. On February 7, 1881, he offered a clear, concise,
logical statement of his views. He described the protectionist
doctrine as " a confused mass of contradictory assertions . . .
conflicting arguments . . . and the co-production of folly and
greed." The theory behind free trade was that " the individual is his own best judge of where and how he shall
trade." " Free trade is the natural condition. . . . The easiest,
cheapest, and best way for each locality " to get what it
needed was " to produce in abundance those things which it
can produce easiest, cheapest, and best, and exchange the
surplus production for the best fruits of other localities."
As for workingmen benefiting from the tariff, Cox maintained that twenty were injured for every one who received
any benefit. The United States was now in need of foreign
markets, which she could gain only by lowering duties on
imports from abroad.[62]

By 1882 the need for tariff revision was obvious for at
least four reasons: 1) the existing high rates impaired those
lines of manufacturing that depended on imported raw
materials; 2) the tariff bore heavily on consumers; 3) it
reduced export trade, and 4) it piled up an embarrassing
surplus in the federal treasury. After Garfield's assassination,
President Chester A. Arthur recommended and Congress
approved a commission to study the entire tariff problem.
At first, Cox opposed the creation of such a commission
" outside the Congress." When his amendment requiring
that commission members be congressmen was defeated, he
proposed a commission composed of " recognized representatives of agricultural interests . . . commerce . . . mechanical

and industrial interests." [63]   On May 23, 1882, he further
expanded his views, pointing to the growing government
surplus, which in 1881 reached $231,000,000 and in 1882
would amount to $280,000,000. Obviously, it was necessary
to curtail government revenues immediately in order to avoid
an embarrassment of riches. The tariff, adopted as a wartime measure, should have ended long ago:

> It destroyed commerce to build up at its expense manu-
> factures. . . . Even General Garfield cried aloud against its
> commercial despotism . . . until his voice was stifled in the
> smoke of torment which came from the furnaces of North-
> eastern Ohio. . . . My own district in New York City, that
> used to rejoice in ship-building, . . . is now deserted. . . . The
> tariff has done it all.[64]

The manufacturer's claim that protection increased wages
was nonsense, Cox argued, for wages were high not because
of the tariff but because of the scarcity of labor. Actually,
the tariff simply raised the cost of living, which since 1865
rose 21 per cent while wages increased only 6 per cent,
according to Carroll D. Wright's report on labor in Massachusetts. The tariff, " which hangs an incubus on labor,"
redounds to the benefit of " interested nabobs." Meanwhile,
nothing had been done to " lighten the burdens of the poor."
The result, according to Cox was that

> You force them [the workers] into unions, and then, with
> pretexts of mob and violence, with bayonet and bullet, drive
> them into desperation. You have legalized oil companies in a
> gigantic form of greed to grease the wheels of liveried coaches.
> . . . The men who raise your products, make your clothes, roll
> your iron, and build your houses are entitled to a fair share
> of the inheritance of the earth and the blessing of the govern-
> ment.

Referring again to " Pig Iron " Kelley of Pennsylvania, his

favorite target, Cox observed, " The gentleman's policy taxes little children, babies, even," through its tax on soap, castor oil, bowls, night shirts, combs, carpets, sugar, panties, fire crackers, and flags. In conclusion, he contended that the United States should take the lead in directing the world toward progress by reducing the tariff.

Despite his eloquent protests, the tariff commission was created, its nine members being avowed protectionists, its chairman being John L. Hayes, chief lobbyist of the Wool Manufacturers Association. After taking thousands of pages of testimony, the commission reported to Congress in December 1882, recommending an average reduction of 25 per cent.[65]

President Arthur added his own recommendation for " enlargement of the free list " and " simplification " of the complicated schedules of duties. When both houses began consideration of separate tariff bills, lobbyists descended " like a flock of buzzards " on Washington to buttonhole congressmen in the name of various interests. Despite the pressures, the Senate developed a bill that would reduce many duties more than the commission's recommendations called for. The House bill, however, advocated higher rates in many instances, but it was blocked by the obstructive, dilatory tactics of tariff reformers Cox, Morrison, John G. Carlisle, and Roger Q. Mills. Cox himself offered amendments calling for lower rates on such items as lead, drugs, shotguns, metals, lumber, sugar, starch, watches, glass, and tobacco. When the Republicans sought to raise the duty on castor beans and oil, Cox accused them of trying to destroy this " infant industry." [66]

Hewitt, who was ill in New York at the time, wrote Cox, encouraging him to continue his battle to secure " cheap food, cheap fuel, and cheap iron ore," which " are the

essential elements of growth and prosperity in any nation." [67]
By February 1883, the House protectionists faced a dilemma.
They had lost out on their own bill, and the Senate bill
provided for lower rates. The outcome was an amazing piece
of parliamentary legerdemain, engineered by Representative
Thomas B. Reed, whereby the House was forced into dis-
agreement with the Senate bill, which was then sent to a
conference composed only of staunch protectionist members.
With eighteen House Democrats led by Randall and one
Democratic senator in support, a "mongrel tariff" bill
reported from the conference committee was passed that
provided a general increase of duties in place of the reform
that had been intended when the discussions began.[68]

The revenue-reformist press wailed that the people had
been hoodwinked by the Republican majority in Congress.
Cox proclaimed to his opponents: "You fail on the tariff.
... You will be known as the great American Congressional
failure." Henry Adams agreed that "this last session of
Congress is just foul; . . . the worst Democratic administration would not be quite so revolting as this." Many Democrats urged that the next campaign be fought out on the
tariff issue.[69]

At the close of the first session of the Forty-seventh Congress, a joint committee had been established "to investigate
the causes for the decline of American shipping and shipbuilding" since the halcyon days of the fast Yankee clippers
and to recommend remedial measures. It was a satisfaction
to many shippers and shipbuilders to know that Cox had
been selected to be on this committee. Hewitt wrote Cox:
"You are the best man for the Shipping Committee, and
I am very glad the Speaker had sense enough to put you
on it." [70] The committee proceeded to send out questionnaires
to shipbuilders and shippers asking for information and

suggestions on policy. In November 1882, hearings in New York yielded three hundred pages of testimony. At the opening of Congress in December, the committee submitted its report. The majority recommended drawbacks for ship-builders on certain imported construction materials, limited liability for ship owners, abolition of the tonnage tax, lower consular fees for shipping services in foreign ports, higher mail contract subsidies, and the establishment of a bureau of commerce in the Treasury Department. While all committee members endorsed the majority's views, Cox and two other Democrats appended further recommendations to end tariff duties on all imported materials used in shipbuilding, to permit shippers to purchase foreign-built ships, to repeal the navigation acts that forbade the use of foreign-built ships in American domestic trade, and to revise the tariff so as to stimulate foreign trade.[71]

During December 1882, Cox devoted much time to pre-paring a speech on American shipping. He leaned heavily on the writings of others, and in a letter to economist David A. Wells he admitted being guilty of " petty and grand larcenies from your admirable treatise." [72] On January 6, 1883, Cox delivered his well-buttressed appeal for the revival of American shipbuilding and shipping. He deplored the sorry state of the American merchant marine and declared that " the remedy must be as heroic as the case is desperate." The difficulty, he said, lay primarily in the tariff and the navigation laws. The " repeal of the burdens on the naviga-tion " of American ships, " a reasonable compensation for mails," and freedom to buy materials and ships anywhere in the world would help greatly. " But the basic problem is the tariff which makes shipbuilding expensive and cuts down shipping." He saw little hope of reviving American shipping unless changes were made. Demonstrating how the tariff had killed shipbuilding by raising material costs by 20 to 67 per cent, Cox expressed the hope that America might return to her " old days of glory " at sea, and pleaded that the Republicans " assist us to take off the burdens from our navigation, and give us . . . the indispensable condition of civilization by commerce—liberty! "

Although Cox succeeded in getting House approval of his amendment to allow foreign construction materials to come in free of duty, the extended struggle over the tariff foreclosed any positive action on the shipping bill by the Senate.[73] Even from the beginning Cox had doubted " if we can pass any bill with any vitality to it," but he welcomed the opportunity to " present the liberalities as to ships." [74]

While favoring economy in government in general, Cox did not believe in skimping on the Life-Saving Service in particular. When the appropriation bill covering this agency was under consideration in 1882, he argued for liberal treatment. " The standard of civilization in any land," he asserted, " is its regard for the sanctity of human life." The service had 189 stations in 1882. In ten years it had saved 11,864 lives and $14,000,000 worth of property from shipwrecks. This record and Cox's eloquence won increased appropriations and a pension law for the Life-Saving Service employees.[75]

The murder of President Garfield by a frustrated officeseeker, which occurred while Cox was in Europe in 1881, highlighted the need for civil service reform, already much discussed. Finally in January 1883, the Pendleton civil service reform act passed Congress with virtually no opposition. Cox congratulated Republicans on their good sense in supporting civil service reform and in banning political assessments.[76]

In the New York political arena he watched while the

astute Daniel E. Manning molded a powerful organization that in 1882 swept the hitherto-unknown Grover Cleveland into the governor's chair at Albany. Cox hastened to forward his congratulations and received a nod of gratitude from the victorious candidate.[77] Throughout the country, the Republicans suffered major reversals in the 1882 elections. The " so-called tidal wave of 1874," commented *The Nation* on November 9, 1882, "was only a lively ripple compared with this overwhelming flood." The Democrats were assured of a majority of eighty in the next House. They had only three less than their rivals in the Senate. " The Republican party " is " now a burst bladder," observed Henry Adams.[78]

Outside of Congress and politics, other interests absorbed Cox's time and energies. In the spring of 1883 he purchased a large brick and stone house on New Hampshire Avenue in Washington. When Congress was not in session, he made lecture tours, which became almost annual affairs and helped provide him with a substantial income. He also added to his income as well as to his prestige by producing two travel volumes after his extensive trip abroad in 1881. In 1883 the Government Printing Office brought out an eighty-six-page volume of *Memorial Eulogies in the House of Representatives by Samuel S. Cox*, containing his tributes to Stephen Douglas, Samuel F. B. Morse, Michael Kerr, Benjamin H. Hill, and other leaders.

8

WORLD TRAVELER, DIPLOMAT, AND WRITER

Cox found time during his long career for what he called " other diversions," besides politics. He willingly cast aside his busy schedule of campaigning, politicking, and lecturing in order to enjoy life at home with his wife, Julia Ann; or to travel as far north as the North Cape, as far east as the plains of Russia, as far south as Aswan Dam on the Nile, and as far west as California; or to write some ten full-length books in addition to numerous magazine articles, speeches, and political tracts.

By the late seventies, he still seemed boyish in appearance, although he was fifty-odd years old. He was short and slender, with a large head planted on narrow shoulders. The thinning of his brown hair was offset by a bushy beard (the male trademark of his generation). Quick in manner and action, he seemed to be perpetually smiling, ever ready with a witty retort or a spontaneous joke. Punning, a favorite

Cox pastime, sometimes degenerated into an overstrained twist of sounds. Often, too, a mood of jollity was followed by melancholy and depression, as his correspondence so clearly reveals. His contemporaries, however, saw him most frequently in the gay, light-hearted, happy mood.

Julia Ann served as a balance wheel against his extremes of mood. She, too, was small and not especially handsome by the standards of her day. But she had an accommodating disposition, an ease of manner, and steady moods. There is no doubt that she enjoyed her husband's humor and his jokes, although she probably looked with less than approval upon his smoking and drinking habits. Extremely religious by nature, she expressed disappointment that she could not get her husband to go to church often.[1] Nevertheless, the Coxes were very close. Politics did not separate them. In fact, she was his confidante on many political matters, and his decisions were often influenced by her. The move from Columbus to New York, for example, was at least partially determined by her wishes.

In New York they shared their house with Julia Ann's sister, Elizabeth, and Elizabeth's husband, John A. Hardenburgh. For more than two decades they lived together harmoniously and the Coxes, who had no children, took great pleasure in watching the Hardenburgh's son grow up.

Cox made four trips abroad, prompted primarily by an intense curiosity to see what the rest of the world was like. His early Bible study had aroused a strong desire in him to visit the Holy Land, while his later reading of ancient and modern history stimulated an eagerness to see the places where history had been made.

The first trip came in 1851. It was more or less in the nature of a honeymoon for the Coxes, who had been married some months before. They were accompanied by Julia Ann's brother, Philo Buckingham, and a cousin. The eastern crossing of the Atlantic proved rough and made Cox wish that he had " a cast-iron stomach." It was almost enough, he said, to make him " a great free-soiler." Any kind of soil would do, just " let it be stable . . . rocky, but not rocking." [2] The Coxes found the countryside between Liverpool and London delightful—" a perfect succession of rural beauties " in " one sweet continuous garden," he wrote. In London the chief center of attention was the current world exposition in the Crystal Palace. The American exhibition was a great disappointment, since Hiram Powers's " Greek Slave " was the only American work on display that was worth much in Cox's opinion. On leaving the fair, the Coxes luckily caught a fleeting glimpse of Queen Victoria. A visit to the House of Commons gave Cox a chance to observe Lord John Russell, John Bright, and Disraeli in action. He made a note of " the brevity and pith of English speakers." [3]

Moving on to France, the Coxes visited the usual points of interest in Paris. Rural France impressed them with its " little tractlets " of land where the women, " vivaciously pretty " when young, " horribly ugly " when old, " do the greatest part of the field labor." They continued south to Marseilles, then by boat to Genoa. On board ship they met sculptor Powers whose statue they had admired so much at the London exposition. In Rome, Cox confessed he found St. Peter's disappointing. It inspired no such " holy awe " as he had felt at Westminister and Notre Dame. At Naples he philosophized over the failure of the revolutions of 1848, while his " senses ached with the continual beauty all around." [4]

The next leg of the journey was made aboard a French warship, carrying the Americans past Stromboli and Sicily. After a brief stop at Malta, they went on to Greece. In

Athens a Baptist missionary escorted them on a sightseeing tour. At Constantinople Cox found the city's setting the most glorious of any place he had visited, but its glamor faded " as soon as you began to thread its dirty, trashy, paved, narrow, doggy, donkeyfied, carriageless, up-and-down streets." A visit to the mosque of St. Sophia and a glimpse of the sultan made the stay in the Turkish capital more than rewarding. The hoped-for excursion to Palestine was cancelled because of a serious cholera epidemic there. The alternative was to take a ship back through the Aegean and up the Adriatic to Trieste and Venice. Cox marveled at the beauty of the Venetian architecture and painting. Moving west to Milan, the Coxes found much charm in the " trim and tidy " vineyards and mulberry groves.[5]

Through Switzerland, then north by rail to Heidelberg, Karlsruhe, Aix-la-Chapelle, Brussels, and back to Paris about which Cox wrote, " We have completed the round, . . . we felt like laying upon our oars and floating down the stream of Parisian life. . . . Youth at the prow and pleasure at the helm, we have floated between promenades and gardens, flowers and temples, colors and melodies." Crossing the Channel again, the Coxes returned to London. Side trips to Dublin and the Scottish highlands completed the tour. In September 1851, they sailed back to America, reflecting that Americans still had to devote themselves to developing the material resources of their own country before seeking to emulate the cultural attainments of Europe. Cox looked forward to the time when Americans might give greater attention to cultural pursuits.[6]

His next trip to Europe in 1869 was dictated by the need for rest in order to combat an attack of tuberculosis. He hoped to recover his health under the warm Mediterranean sun. It was, as he aptly phrased it, a " search for winter sunbeams." At Mentone on the French Riviera he relaxed for several months under the care of an English physician, Dr. Henry Bennett. Here in the shadow of the maritime Alps, he found " the air . . . so tempered with sunbeams; so mild and yet so bracing . . . that the despairing invalid may prolong his life; . . . the desponding receive genuine exhilaration, and the consumptive . . . receive cure." As his health improved, he was permitted to take side trips, such as one to nearby Monaco where he was impressed much more by the beautiful view of the sea than by the gambling casino.[7]

A little later, in company with Mrs. Cox and Dr. Bennett, he crossed over to Corsica where he examined Bonaparte's birthplace and climbed high into the mountains of the island's interior. Back to France and then across the Mediterranean to Algiers where, in his second contact with Moslem civilization, he found some of the natives industrious but most of them indolent and given to mumbo-jumbo orgies that he found repugnant. The natural scenery, especially Mt. Atlas, was impressive. Moving on to Spain, he traveled north to Alicante, Valencia, Granada, Madrid, Cordova, Toledo, Seville, and Malaga, noting the dryness of eastern Spain. Bullfighting left him " sick *ad nauseum*." At Granada, where the American minister, John P. Hale, joined him, he addressed a group of Spanish Republicans, warmly recommending to them the adoption of a federal republic to replace their decaying monarchy. In Madrid he listened to speeches in the Cortes and admired Spanish paintings, some of which he acquired for himself. By mid-summer the Coxes moved out of Spain back to France and once again into the general stream of travel.[8]

The third trip abroad came in 1881. Holland was first on the itinerary. Enchanted by the " red roofs and tall steeples," by the cleanliness, neatness, and industry of the people, Cox

recalled that it was the Dutch who had founded New York.
Passing rapidly through Germany and Denmark, the Coxes
arrived in Norway. From Oslo they went to Trondheim.
Boarding a fishing vessel here, they moved slowly up the
Norwegian coast. The mountains, which came down almost
to the water's edge, were awe-inspiring. Even the Alps
" were as nothing compared with these thousand miles of
majesty, with their waters and isles, glaciers and peaks, all
canopied with blue skies and fleecy clouds. . . ." At length
the climax of the journey was reached upon arrival at the
North Cape. This to Cox was the most impressive natural
beauty spot in all of Europe. It gave him a " feeling of
exultation and exaltation." Then came the supreme excitement of the entire trip as the hour of midnight came and the
sun remained shining. A cheer went up from the twenty
tourists standing in the prow of the little fishing schooner.
Even several thousand miles from home in the " land of
the midnight sun," Cox could not quite forget politics, however, for when the Fourth of July came, he delivered a speech
to the other passengers on the birthday of the United States,
a country " made up of all nations . . . but discovered first
by the Norwegians." [9]

Leaving the " weird and wonderful land " of Norway,
the Coxes continued east through Sweden and Finland to
St. Petersburg. Here the customs officers made a through
search of their luggage, " the first rigid search of the trip."
Cox attributed this to the recent assassination of Czar Alexander II. The only item seized from Cox's bags were the
New York newspapers he had brought from Stockholm in
the hope of getting time to read them along the way. " Our
papers were confiscated," Cox recorded. " The *Sun* would
not go down in this land; the *Tribune* was a voiceless oracle;
the *World* ceased to ' move after all '; the *Times* was out

of joint; and the *Express* came to a dead halt!" St. Petersburg struck Cox as a "city of beauty and bazaars, palaces and pigeons, monuments and minarets, domes and deviltry, ceremonies and cemeteries, armies and assassinations" on the banks of the Neva. Cox employed an Englishman named Pilley as a guide. At first Pilley was suspicious, thinking that Cox was Mark Twain traveling in disguise and fearing that he might become the butt of Mark Twain's jokes and pranks. Although Cox had let go with several impertinent jokes, he was finally able to convince Pilley that he was not Twain.[10]

Cox's observations on Russia have a special interest in the light of twentieth-century developments. Russian humor, he felt, was grim and almost savage. Vodka he discovered to be as potent as it was popular. Its effects made the Russian imbibers very affectionate! "They kiss, never kick or strike." The Russian system of higher education with scholarships open to all was good as far as it went, but Cox thought that much more should be done to educate the recently emancipated serfs. Russian mineral wealth impressed him, but he found their manufactured articles to be of inferior quality. At the Peterhoff he observed an oak tree bearing a brass plate stating that the tree was grown from an acorn that had been taken from the grave of George Washington. This might well serve as a reminder that the cause of popular freedom "was not altogether of hopeless growth in the Muscovite soil." [11]

On reaching Moscow, he visited the Kremlin, which mystified and intrigued him. The view of the city from the Kremlin tower revealed 385 churches by actual count, which made Brooklyn look tiny by comparison as "the city of churches." "But how can I describe the Kremlin, this home of sacerdotal dignitaries, fighting boyars, and 'terrible' kings, with its churches, gates, towers, and walls?" The city itself, as seen from the tower, "is like a spider web. Its streets radiate from and unite about the Kremlin battlements." Traveling south from Moscow, he was struck by the tremendous potentialities of the country, "an El Dorado for those who would work. What if American energy and its agricultural machines should take hold of these vast grain fields!" Cox felt that the government was the chief drawback to progress in Russia. Noting that there were already railroads "of our make" in Russia and some 800 steamers on the Volga "of the American kind," he thought that the transportation problem might eventually be overcome. "Then where is our vaunted supremacy?" But, he commented, "It will be a long time before Russia can compete in our grain market. . . . But the cooperation, skill, concentration and economy of the Americans cannot have a rival." [12]

As he moved toward Odessa, he admitted "a desire of leaving this realm." Not, he explained, because of any impoliteness or unkindness but because of a "feeling of insecurity," which arose from the fact that he was known to have denounced in Congress the Russian persecution of the Jews. Reaching Odessa, he recalled that, twenty years earlier, he had been offered the opportunity of going there to manage a grain elevator for his father-in-law, but he had turned it down; "What a business man Odessa lost, when I chose to be ' elevated ' otherwise and how little, alas! has politics gained." With a feeling of relief the Coxes sailed out of Odessa harbor on a Russian ship bound for Constantinople.[13]

Arriving at the Turkish capital, "the most monumental spot on either continent," they rediscovered memories of thirty years before. Lew Wallace, author of the widely-read novel *Ben Hur* and currently the American minister to

Turkey, persuaded them to stay at his house, twelve miles up the Bosphorus from Constantinople. Cox enjoyed the visit " in measureless content." He was charmed by the two " mystic goddesses " of the sultan's harem who came to call on Mrs. Wallace and Mrs. Cox, and was almost spellbound when the serving of tea forced the sultanas to remove their veils, thereby revealing their " Circassian faces, with their dreamy, beautiful eyes, and pure alabaster skin."

With Wallace, he visited Robert College, the American school founded some years before at Constantinople. Here he met Professor Edwin A. Grosvenor (father of Gilbert Grosvenor, later a director of the National Geographic Society in Washington).[14] The professor told him a very strange story. In 1872, during the Greeley presidential campaign, Grosvenor had attended a Greeley rally at Faneuil Hall in Boston. He moved to the Speaker's stand, gave his name to the presiding officer as " Sunset " Cox, delivered a strong speech calling for amnesty and brotherhood with the South and received " thundering applause " when he sat down. For a short time, he had actually believed that he was Cox. He had been teaching at Robert College for years and became Cox's guide on many excursions in the area. After attending a reception by the sultan, Cox thought Abdul Hamid II was an " able " ruler who " manages his own matters with adroitness." He noted that the Turks now had " convenient steamers, an underground railway, tramways . . . newspapers in a half dozen tongues, steam and light. . . ." He was impressed with the lack of race consciousness in the city where " blacks . . . mix in perfect equality with the white and brown of every line and station."

From Constantinople a Russian ship carried the Coxes on over the Aegean Sea and south past the isle of Rhodes. After two days and nights they arrived at Mersina. Here they received word of the death of President Garfield, a loss, Cox wrote, of " more than that of our Chief Magistrate. It is a personal affliction " since both were native Ohioans and had served together in the House for fourteen years. Cox noted with interest that one hundred Jews on board his ship, who were heading for Jerusalem from Polish Russia, had received financial help from American Hebrew congregations. He expressed the hope that " moral sentiment " in America would " bring pressure against the pogroms in Europe." [15]

At Beirut the Coxes left the steamer to travel inland to Damascus where they saw " the bazaars and Bedouins, mosques and muftis, gardens and guitars, and forges for swords and cutlery, houses decorated by rare arabesques." At Damascus, too, they visited the tomb of Henry T. Buckle, the famous English historian, who, declared Cox, " gave us, after Adam Smith, the best science of wealth, natural and social." The next move was to Palestine, " a strange phenomenon . . . almost treeless, riverless, and waterless, yet once the glory of the earth." Jerusalem, he found, consisted of " square, whitish houses with many domes " and with narrow, crowded streets. Side trips were taken to Golgotha, Calvary, and Bethlehem, where the place of the nativity with its three churches (Roman Catholic, Greek, and Armenian) was the main objective. Visits were also made to Olivet, Bethany, the Garden of Gethsemane, and the site of Solomon's temple.[16]

On leaving Palestine, the Coxes traveled to Alexandria and Cairo. The three great attractions of Egypt for Cox were its monuments, history, and climate. Summing up his impressions of the country, he put it this way:

> Arab towns of mud huts, long lines of loaded camels and donkeys, and their naked and half-naked drivers, and lazy

Arab boys and women begging for baksheesh; the fields of the Nile and the great river itself; the mosque and minaret; the hooded women, and turbaned, long-robed men; the accacia and palm; and in the two great cities luxury along with poverty; dirt with despotism; all the plagues including an abnormal government; sugarmills and palaces; and an equable temperature; with a sunset that never fails to allure and detain the eye.

On a trip inside the great pyramid of Cheops, Cox slipped on a wet stone and almost fell into a deep pool of water. Had it not been for his guide, " there would have been a vacancy in the Sixth Congressional District of New York." With a parting shot at the vanity of Egyptian kings, the Coxes returned by ship to New York.[17]

Cox's final trip abroad came in 1885-86 when he served as American minister to Turkey. Having traveled to Constantinople twice before by divergent routes, he proceeded this time via London, Paris, Vienna, the Danube River to the Black Sea and to the Bosphorus. Greeted by Gwynne Harris Heap, the American Consul-General, Cox and his wife moved into the summer legation at Therapia on the Bosphorus some twelve miles outside the capital (where they had previously stayed with Lew Wallace). Here, on the day of his arrival, Cox received a message of welcome from the sultan delivered by the foreign minister, Assim Pasha.[18] Although his health had been below par when he left the United States, now as he looked out over the Bosphorus and the terraced gardens of " roses, magnolias, heliotropes, jessamine," he felt that it was now " 65 per cent above and going up." After twenty-five years of congressional wrangling, he expected to enjoy " freedom in Turkey from political worry." [19]

The situation of Turkey, however, was not without its worries, for the Turks at least. All during the nineteenth century the empire had been crumbling. Russia, ever desirous of reaching the straits, had given the Turks the most recent push from the European side in the war of 1877 when a Russian army had driven to Adrianople, close to the Turkish capital. As a result, the Balkan peoples were crying for independence from Turkish rule. The provinces in Africa were dropping away. The Great Powers of Europe in 1881 forced Turkey to accept foreign control of her national debt to avert bankruptcy. The new sultan, Abdul Hamid II, who had at the beginning of his reign issued a liberal constitution and promised reform of a corrupt administration, had been sliding back toward reactionary despotic rule. He had built Yildiz, a powerful fortress-palace manned by antagonistic Mohammedan groups of Albanians, Kurds, and Arabs.[20]

It was to this palace that Cox went a month after his arrival for a formal reception by the sultan. He submitted his prepared speech in French to the Turkish foreign office for approval only to have an official seize upon the word *enchevetrement* that he had used for "entanglement." A minor diplomatic crisis ensued, finally to be ironed out after the meaning of the term was fully explained. Accompanied by Consul Heap, Professor Grosvenor of Robert College, and others of the legation, Cox was greeted at the palace by various Turkish officials who plied him with coffee, tobacco, and questions. At length he was conducted to the reception room on the second floor and there presented to the sultan, who was dressed in his finest garb. After making three low bows, Cox delivered his written speech orally in less than three minutes. The sultan then shook "me warmly by the hand," and all bowed out again.[21]

Shortly thereafter in a private interview with Abdul Hamid II, Cox presented the sultan with several albums of pictures, a gift from the President of the United States. Later the

sultan inquired about the growth of population and agricultural production in the United States, and Cox ordered
a complete set of the *Tenth Census* for him, plus a collection
of American fruit-bearing trees.[22]

Cox set about his duties with characteristic energy. In
Constantinople he found the legation in a run-down condition, and moved it from the dirty side alley to a more
respectable, main-street location. For this move he was
accused at home of changing from " a stingy Congressman
to an extravagant Minister," but he replied that the move
was made " principally at my own expense." He urged that
the Republican secretary of the legation, left behind by his
predecessor, Lew Wallace, be transferred, or if that could
not be done, that Cox be sent as minister to Austria.[23]

" The main business of the Diplomatic kind here," he
reported to the President, " is caring for the schools, missions,
etc.," operated by Americans in various parts of Turkey.
" Americans, especially Presbyterians, are the principal element in the regeneration of Asia Minor and Syria. Their
work is wonderful." Adding up the figures, he found the
total missionary investment ran to about $1,000,000 with an
annual expenditure of $360,000 in 394 different towns with
254 American and 1,049 Turkish employees engaged in the
missionary endeavors. The most prominent schools were
the American College in Beirut, Syria, Robert College, and
the American Home School for Girls in Constantinople. The
American legation was called on most frequently to protect
the mission schools against government efforts to close them.
According to earlier treaties, Turkey agreed to permit operation of American schools, subject to inspection of textbooks
and teaching by the board of censors of the government
department of public instruction. Cox acted on this treaty,
and in one case a bandit in Asia Minor was not only stopped

from interfering with missionary activity but was himself converted to Christianity.[24]

Cox negotiated with skill for naturalization and extradition treaties. During the lengthy negotiations the case of a naturalized American citizen, who had returned to Turkey where he had been arrested for non-payment of taxes, came up to embarrass Cox. He was instructed by the State Department to move quietly in this matter until treaty negotiations were completed.[25] Commercial and trade mark treaties were also up for discussion at the time. His work was made no easier when former minister Lew Wallace reappeared in Constantinople as the agent for an American torpedo manufacturer and " demoralized the Legation in a way no one can understand unless he were here." [26] After considerable labor, four treaties were consummated under Cox's guidance and sent to Washington.[27] Of this achievement, he was justly proud, considering the fact that these treaties had hung fire during the terms of his four predecessors.[28]

He noted that a number of American business firms already operated branch houses at Constantinople and in other parts of the empire. The square American oil can was to be seen everywhere, and was used for all kinds of purposes throughout the Near East. Cox thought that more American enterprises should market goods in Turkey and help develop Turkish resources. If Americans did not, others would, he wrote. The Russians, he observed, were already moving in, having taken the Caucasus oil region in the war of 1877. They were at the moment building a pipe line from the Caspian Sea. Indeed, Cox felt that Russia was the chief potential threat, and might very soon move to make the Black Sea " a Russian lake." [29]

The most serious crisis that threatened Turkey during his service in Constantinople developed in the fall of 1885.

The Treaty of Berlin of 1878 had created an autonomous Bulgaria, but the province of East Rumelia, lying south of Bulgaria, remained within the Turkish empire. In September 1885, a Bulgar-inspired revolt erupted in East Rumelia, which then announced its union with Bulgaria. Cox reported home on Turkish mobilization of 200,000 men on the border. About Serbian intervention, he declared that a general war of the Great Powers over the redistribution of Turkish territory in the Balkans seemed imminent.[30] When Russia called for the enforcement of the Treaty of Berlin, the ministers of the signatory powers conferred at Constantinople during the fall of 1885. Cox noted the meetings of his fellow diplomats at the house of the Italian minister. The outcome was an agreement among the powers allowing Bulgaria to retain East Rumelia. But Russia was far from satisfied and a year later, just as Cox was leaving Constantinople, a Russian-inspired revolt in Bulgaria sparked the Balkan powder keg again.

Looking back over the incident, Cox expressed concern over the American attitude. " It is fashionable for Americans," he wrote, " to praise Russia. The sympathy of our country with Russia was strengthened by the reforms projected . . . by Alexander II." But these reforms, Cox thought, were scarcely carried into actual effect. Indeed, he observed, the three freedoms—speech, press, and religion—were still not observed in Russia, and " if there has been any improvement in the liberalities of politics . . . of recent years, the world has yet to know it." He was sure that " our sympathies in America are misplaced." They might with better reason lie with Turkey, where at least religious toleration was a fact.[31]

As for other " diversions," Cox sandwiched in several trips between diplomatic duties. In February 1886 he traveled to Greece, there to enjoy a visit with the famous German archaeologist, Dr. Schliemann, who conducted him on a tour of the Acropolis, and he had a brief visit with King George, whom he pronounced a " most charming and elegant gentleman." From Athens Cox went on to Egypt and took an 800-mile cruise up the Nile to Aswan Dam. The summer months of 1886 were spent on the Isle of Princes, or Prinkipo, a few miles out in the Sea of Marmora from Constantinople. He returned to America in the fall of 1886, having served a little more than a year at the Turkish capital. Contemplating the Turkish situation, he remarked that " the sick man of Europe " was not going to die, as so many prophets had been predicting for so long. Salvation for Turkey lay in continuing to play the major powers off against each other, and in the sultan's " energizing and elevating his people by the revival of religion and education." This he hoped, would be accomplished within the next few decades.[32]

All of his travels found their way into his literary productions at one time or another. Having once been a newspaper man, he never got over the journalistic habit. During most of his travels he regularly sent back letters in which he described his journeys and the sights and scenes encountered en route. These letters were published in such papers as the New York *World*, the New York *Evening Post*, and the Columbus *Statesman*. The first of his travel books, as noted earlier, *A Buckeye Abroad*, describing his travels in 1851, was published when Cox was twenty-eight; the last, *The Isle of Princes, or the Pleasure of Prinkipo*, came out when he was sixty-four. During the thirty-six-year interval, he produced *A Search for Winter Sunbeams*, describing his trip of 1869 through France, Corsica, Algeria, and Spain; *Arctic Sunbeams* and *Orient Sunbeams* in 1882 which covered his journey via the North Cape and Russia to Turkey, the Near

East, and Egypt; *Diversions of a Diplomat in Turkey* in 1887, which was not only a travel book but also an account of diplomatic activities in the Ottoman empire. All of these were published by G. P. Putnam, with the exception of *Winter Sunbeams*, which Appleton brought out, and *Diversions of a Diplomat*, which Mark Twain's firm, Charles L. Webster and Company, handled. How well Cox's travelogues were received is not clear since the publishers' records of sales have long since perished. *A Buckeye Abroad*, however, must have sold well, for it went through eight editions in eight years. Mark Twain was especially anxious to get *Diversions of a Diplomat*, for which he offered Cox an 8 per cent royalty.[33] Even at this rate, the returns to Cox from his literary efforts must have been substantial during his lifetime.

From the time of his oft-quoted editorial, " A Great Old Sunset," Cox had practiced the craft of writing. He had a feeling for words, a facility in their use, and a large vocabulary. The journalistic style he developed in his early days was evident in his later writings and in his speeches as well. It gave a certain mobility to his style that made for rapid and pleasant reading. His sensitivity to colors, sounds, smells, to the ordinary sights as well as to the spectacular, plus a feeling for thoughts which had popular appeal, undoubtedly contributed much to his success as a writer. The fact that he wrote poetry (some of it pretty bad) and sketched and painted reveals an artistic flair that flavored his prose. His broad background in the arts, philosophy, history, law, religion, and science gave him a rare perspective for viewing the events and scenes he dealt with in his books.

However, he made no pretense, except in a few instances, of making a scientific analysis of the region, country, city, or people he visited. Indeed, he professed to no profundity

(and there is little in his writings). His purpose was merely
" to photograph " and record " impressions . . . taken upon
the spot." [34] The point of view was strictly personal. " My
humble task," he wrote in the introduction of *Arctic Sunbeams*, " is to invest the scenes there in pictures with the
interest which the author himself felt." [35] Cox was perhaps
at his best in the descriptive passages.

In describing the Dutch countryside, for example, he
wrote: " Everywhere you meet the shining steel and copper
of the kitchen, the rosy cheeks, yellow petticoats, stiff satin
robes and rich laces, brown cabinets and delicate china of
Jan Steen." [36] He describes the scene at Jaffa gate in
Jerusalem:

> Outside, two score of camels are kneeling at their food,
> amidst baskets and smokers, babies and porters, prestidigitators
> and shoemakers. . . . Every kind of article, animal, utensil, and
> fruit belonging to the needs of this generation, here is being
> sold, and every kind of person, from a Bedouin to a bishop,
> seems to be chaffering. Women in white, some of them muffled,
> being Moslems; others Christian and Hebrew, in white and
> Frank attire, without the provoking yashmaks to hide their
> features, pass and repass as in a masquerade, amidst the noisy
> cry of the dominant and dissonant Arab voice. . . . Here are
> Nubians, tall and straight, some of them eunuchs, and all of
> them black, which is impressive for its dead, dull, unshiny
> color. Here are sheiks, graceful in mien and bronzed in face,
> with . . . the long gun, decked with mother-of-pearl, slung over
> the shoulder.[37]

At Constantinople: " It is amusing . . . to see all the foot-
coverings of the world go by, from that of Adam up to the
latest fashion in Parisian boots—yellow Turkish babouches,
red Armenian, blue Greek, black Jewish shoes; sandals, great
boots from Turkestan, Albanian gaiters, low-cut slippers, leg
pieces in many colors, belonging to horsemen from Asia

Minor, gold-embroidered shoes, . . . shoes of satin, of rags, of wood." [38] His descriptions reveal a sense of alliteration and balance. As he says of the Dutch countryside, it suggested the " four c's—canals, commerce, cattle and cheese." [39] Norway was " a land of glaciers that are endless; . . . snows that never melt; waters that are forever tiding and rushing; clouds that never empty of snow and rain; and mountains by peaks, ranges, by thousands, and islands by thousands that are mountains." [40]

So much for the strong points in Cox's descriptive writings. The most common weakness, perhaps true of all travel works, is his wordiness and his repetitions. He seems called upon to use a hundred words where a score would suffice. The streets of Moscow are called a " spider web " in half a dozen places. The phrase " mosques and minarets " appears over and over again. Then, too, there is much straining to dramatize an incident, which often loses the desired effect. His reputation as a humorist grew (and he was regarded by some contemporaries to be in a class with Abraham Lincoln and Artemus Ward as a raconteur). But frequently his witty phrases are labored and his puns are too obviously manufactured. As a result, the reader is irritated rather than amused by Cox's exaggerated effort. As with many journalists, he was also given to oversimplification, fleeting impressions, and overstatement where his facts were based on isolated and sketchy observations.[41]

In addition to the travel works, he turned out four other books. First among these was his *Eight Years in Congress*, written at the end of his years as a Congressman from Ohio and published by Appleton in 1865. This work is mainly a collection of his more important speeches delivered in Congress between 1857 and 1865, with the addition of a few introductory remarks at the beginning of each chapter. Some of the speeches have been doctored from the original in the *Congressional Globe*. The next book was a post-war volume, intriguingly entitled *Why We Laugh*, published by Harper in 1876, with a second enlarged edition appearing four years later. Although it bore a general title, the book was primarily concerned with humor in Congress. Cox took his material from actual reports of congressional debates. He felt that wit started at a disadvantage in such a deliberative body as Congress because " it requires an effort to overcome ponderosity. To raise a laugh is to lift the weight of dignity—nay, to lift the weight off dignity." Nevertheless, he was convinced that wit was a necessary ingredient for the successful political leader: "All great wits are not great men, but all great men are witty." Items always good for a laugh in Congress (and Cox used these standbys regularly during his legislative days) were "references to whisky and Democracy; to party shibboleths and motions for adjournment; to the youth and age of members; . . . to the devil and the Lower House where he presides. . . ." He regretted the decline of eloquent oratory in Congress. "The finest feathers have been plucked from our bird of oratory," he wrote sadly. "He is fixed to earth." In analyzing laughter, he made a shrewd distinction between wit and humor. "Wit laughs at; humor with. Wit is the result of antipathy; humor of sympathy. Wit punishes pungently; humor cherishes cheerfully. Wit is the counterfeit detector of the issue of life; humor makes even the bogus coins ring merrily. Wit is lightning; it flashes and scathes. Humor is light, and radiates with pleasing flow." [42] In line with this reasoning and with the "sunshine" theme of his career, Cox himself was a humorist rather than a wit. Generally, he laughed with, rather than at; he was sympathetic, rather than antagonistic; he sought the best for humor, rather than the worst for wit.

In 1880 he produced a little volume of 126 pages, entitled *Free Land and Free Trade,* wherein he pointed up some of the facts of economic life as he saw them. " The thesis of this book," he explained, " is the necessity of enlarged foreign markets for the surplus productions from farm and factory in the United States." The United States was being forced " to the alternative of yielding the policy of selfishness (i. e., monopoly of the home market) or being choked with our own abundance." [43] The chapters that follow this initial statement are largely a summary and clarification of his views on the American economy which he had already expressed in his speeches in Congress. He reiterated that the United States might well learn the lesson inherent in the English repeal of the corn laws—that national prosperity and national self-sufficiency were incompatible and that in the long run national prosperity was actually lessened by the exercise of protection. No one nation could produce everything that it needed. Therefore, trade was not only desirable but necessary. The more that trade was stimulated rather than checked, the greater use of its resources a country could make, and thus the greater its prosperity. The tariff in America simply forced the " mass of the people to contribute to a peculiar class," the manufacturers, whom Cox called " the microscopic *insectivores* which are preying upon our generous body politic." [44]

The triumph of free trade, he held, would " eventually come and make it the interest and delectation of every nation to cultivate friendly relations with every other " and establish " that liberty which is the exaltation of individual and national life." [45]

In 1885 Cox brought out a 726-page voume, *Three Decades of Federal Legislation, 1855-1885.* This most ambitious production of his career was intended as a history of the period to help the younger generation understand the issues of the Civil War and the Reconstruction era. As he wrote, " I have endeavored . . . to show the rise of the Republican party in 1855 and its downfall in 1885." [46]

Despite its claim of objectivity, the book is a Democratic apology, as the division of the material clearly illustrates. The volume divides the era under consideration into three periods—the first decade from the rise of the Republican party to the end of the Civil War; the second decade from 1865 to the Democratic recovery of control of the House of Representatives in 1875; and the third decade from the " fraud " of the electoral commission to the inauguration of Grover Cleveland, " who will endeavor to avoid the excesses which gave the country so much unrest." [47] Cox's basic views include a belief in the inevitability of progress and the inherent virtue of the Democratic party. On the latter score, he makes no secret of his position, stating that he had always believed " what is now in 1885 apparent—that the party of Constitutional limitations, strict construction, state sovereignty, and federal unity would be found indispensable to honest and united government." [48] He also postulates the desirability of an agricultural-commercial economy. Moreover, a strong Christian viewpoint permeates his writing; chapters frequently close with brief moral lessons on the subject matter. " Although it is not so much the province of history to philosophize as to relate," he, nevertheless, thought it appropriate to comment with approval or censure upon the " men and measures of his Three Decades."

As to his sources and methods, he derived much material from the *Congressional Globe* and the *Congressional Record*, committee reports, executive documents, presidential messages, and newspaper and journal articles. His own speeches are quoted extensively, and frequently material from his speeches turns up in the text without quotation marks. " In case of conflicting testimony," he asserts, " the statements of witnesses or parties on each side have been considered or cited . . . accompanied by indisputable facts." One only wishes that he might have used footnotes or other references to indicate the sources of some of the questionable " facts " in the text. That he had read Blaine's *Twenty Years in Congress* is clear. In fact, *Three Decades* seems modelled on that work and Cox is at great pains in places to refute Blaine's assertions.

Early in the volume he explains the coming of the Civil War as the work of extremist groups North and South. The Northern abolitionists, he holds, were as much responsible as the Southern " fire-eaters." The secession crisis might have been averted had the reasonable Crittenden compromise been adopted. He blames its rejection entirely on the Republican party. The war is viewed as a great calamity not only because it split the Union but because it changed the American constitutional system. The war is held responsible for the demoralization of the public service, and the lessening of personal liberty is blamed on the abolitionists in league with " capital fattening on spoils and contracts," who pushed the war for their own purposes rather than for a simple restoration of the old Union. Radical reconstruction, in his eyes, merely carried out what the war had begun. It aimed " to secure permanent ascendancy of the Republican party by disqualifying Southern leaders on the one hand and creating Negro voters on the other." Lincoln, pictured as " the kind, and good and great Chief Magistrate " (words considerably different from those Cox used to characterize him in his wartime speeches), might have succeeded with his moderate plan of reconstruction. The entire Radical program, Cox held, was unconstitutional. He condemned the

Republicans for keeping the wounds of the war open. New issues of resumption, paper currency, and tariff should have been considered in the 1870's rather than the old issue of " the bloody shirt." The Civil War, having wrought a revolution in the central government and in the whole life of the South and of the North, was the central factor in shaping the America of the 1880's. With the elevation of Cleveland to the presidency, however, Cox saw hope for a better future. The work closes with a note of pride in the tremendous material advances made by the United States during the three decades.[49]

Cox's contract with his publisher called for a royalty of 50 cents for each copy sold after the first thousand.[50] The advertising blurbs carried comments from President Grover Cleveland, ex-President Rutherford B. Hayes, James G. Blaine, and Vice-President Thomas A. Hendricks. Cleveland declared that he could " conscientiously . . . commend it to my fellow-citizens " and that the " experience and ability of its author . . . make this volume a pleasing source of very valuable information." Hayes pronounced the book " valuable and trustworthy in matter, and scholarly and entertaining in style," while Blaine was impressed with the " clear and graphic style " and with the " personal incidents and anecdotes." [51]

This volume attracted wide attention among historians and literary men as well as politicians. James Ford Rhodes's review of it praised the author for his topical treatment of the subject and his " concise and brief " narrative, but objected to its lack of critical perspective, to Cox's habit of " saying a good word for nearly every public man," and to his failure to admit that he was wrong on the issues of the Civil War. Rhodes's remarks were perhaps less penetrating than those of Professor William A. Dunning who later observed in comparing Cox's work to Blaine's that " *Three Decades* . . . is no less partisan, and is even more inaccurate in details." [52]

One of its chief values was that it served as an antidote to the abolitionist-Republican picture of the period. Throughout the volume, Cox is critical of Republican leadership and policy, although he is less harsh here than he was in his congressional speeches. He does, however, provide much information not easily found elsewhere, interspersed with views of a strictly personal nature and delightful comments on his contemporaries. The defects are numerous and patent. The chief limitation is of course the partisanship that often results in highly emotional and questionable statements. The unfortunate omission of many important events makes for lack of balance. A larger amount of space is given the years before 1870 than to those after that date. There is, further, a tendency, perhaps natural, to exaggerate his own role in events. Some inaccuracies creep in, such as the statement that Greeley ran for President in 1868. The style is colorful, expressive, and often dramatic, with light touches of humor. On the whole, *Three Decades* makes good reading, despite emotional outbursts and lack of balance in spots.

There is no doubt that Cox took great pride in his literary production and in his association with literary men. His books gave him a sense of permanence. In them, he was leaving something of himself to posterity. His political labors, in contrast, had a seeming futility. But he could not isolate himself from politics even in literary refuge, for he dedicated *Eight Years in Congress* to his Ohio constituents, and *A Search For Winter Sunbeams* to his New York City constituents.

9

DEMOCRATS IN THE SADDLE AT LAST,
1883–1889

FIGHT FOR THE SPEAKERSHIP

Having been elected to Congress for the twelfth time in 1882, at the age of fifty-nine, Cox hoped to climax his long years of service by winning the speakership of the House. There could be no doubt as to his qualifications. Perhaps more than any other man in the House, he had represented the old Democratic principles of good government—states rights, lower tariff, frugal federal government, free exercise of civil liberties. He had entered the House earlier than any other present member. He had served competently as Speaker *pro tem* at various times and had missed by a hair being chosen permanent Speaker in 1876.

As early as January 1883, he was mentioned as the logical candidate for the position.[1] In February Abram Hewitt replied to Cox's solicitation for support: " I am not committed on the question of Speaker." But Hewitt explained that if he had once " preferred Randall to you," it was not " because

I did not like you as well as Randall." [2] By March the New York *Union* newspaper endorsed Cox for Speaker, as did several Ohio papers. Encouragement also came from upstate New York.[3]

In March when an attack of pneumonia slowed Cox down, he noted that Randall and John G. Carlisle of Kentucky had become his strongest rivals. He thought his tariff views "sounder" and "earlier taken than any one here." To editor Worthington C. Ford, he wrote, "I shall be presented by our New York Delegation for Speaker," and asked Ford to publish notices in the New York *Herald.* which would be favorable to his candidacy. Always optimistic, Cox said: "Mr. Carlisle will not get the Southern vote. Randall is after the New York and other Northern votes. . . . My chance, as it stands, is best." [4]

In June 1883 he gave a series of lectures in the South. While there, he tried to win the support of Southern congressmen. In July Thomas A. Hendricks wrote from Indiana: "I will do what I can to secure you a good vote from our delegation." Daniel W. Voorhees and William S. Holman of Indiana, Cox's colleagues in the House, also sent words of encouragement.[5] In August he received word from Carlisle who denied any attempt to lure the New York delegation away from him. Carlisle added that he personally preferred Cox to Randall, whom he confidentially considered "a stuffed shirt." [6] From Europe Hewitt wrote of his disgust with Randall and his hope that the Democrats would remain the "party of progress and reform." [7]

In the fall Cox campaigned in Ohio for his friend, George Hoadly, Democratic candidate for governor.[8] Carlisle "did not turn up" in the Ohio campaign, but Randall did. When the election carried Hoadly into office, Cox gloated: ". . . the gain [in Democratic votes] did occur where I spoke, and *vice versa* as to Randall." [9] As the fall progressed, he was happy over reports of " hosts of warm friends " in Detroit, but was dejected when the New York *Sun* came out for Randall.[10]

By mid-November Democratic leaders descended on Washington in anticipation of the opening of Congress. Carlisle arrived November 11, Cox a few days later, and Randall a week after that. Two weeks later Cox was sure that " Carlisle is my competitor. I fear him, as I believe Randall is gone." The Democratic caucus met in the Hall of Representatives on the evening of December 1. " At 7:30 General Rosecrans called the caucus to order." Cox awaited the result in the Foreign Affairs Committee room, Carlisle in the Appropriations room, and Randall in the Ways and Means room. Meanwhile, their names were presented respectively by Henry W. Slocum of New York, William R. Morrison of Illinois, and Andrew Curtin of Pennsylvania. Supporters of Randall failed to secure a secret ballot. As the voting closed, Morrison ran to the Appropriations Committee room shouting, " Carlisle has won! " Cox, hiding his disappointment, joined with Randall and Curtin to escort Carlisle before the caucus, and on December 3 Cox placed Carlisle's name before the House. Carlisle beat Thomas B. Reed of Maine and moved down the aisle to the Speaker's dais " with little Mr. Cox on one side and big Tom Reed on the other," and " Pig-iron " Kelley administered the oath of office. Cox observed: " I don't believe that my defeat as Speaker has helped revenue reform." [11]

The loss of the speakership rankled. Friends sent condolences, declaring " you were justly entitled to the place." [12] His defeat was due to the defection of his own New York delegation. A newspaper reporter registered astonishment that Cox was " so treacherously treated in the house of your friends " and " after thirty years of faithful service in the party." At first, Cox, still resentful, refused appointment as chairman of the Naval Affairs Committee, but later he accepted.[13]

In the Forty-eighth Congress (December 1883 to July 1884 and December 1884 to March 1885) the Democrats hoped in vain to revise the " mongrel tariff " of 1883. William R. Morrison, Carlisle's lieutenant, was placed at the head of the Ways and Means Committee to draft a new bill. By March 1884 Cox was worn down by his labors on the tariff and by his work as chairman of the Democratic caucus and of the Naval Affairs and Census Committees. Also, he complained that he was " half the time in the Speaker's chair " as Speaker *pro tem*. In early April he was " laid up from overwork." [14]

From the beginning of the session he worked for a new shipping bill, preparing to " tack on an amendment for free registration [of foreign ships] and free materials." Pleas and petitions from New York shippers, shipbuilders, and the Chamber of Commerce were numerous and urgent.[15] In the previous session he had presented the case for purchase of foreign-built ships and free importing of shipbuilding materials, but no action had been taken. When the bill reached the floor of the House, Cox wrote to W. C. Ford: " I laid for my chance, got in my oar, and carried the best amends I could." These " best amends " included exemption of shipbuilding materials from duty. Although delighted over his " not unexpected but rather marvelous success," Cox doubted that the Senate would accept the amendment and urged Ford to get the *Herald* to press for Senate adoption. The New York Free Trade Club sent tracts to every senator. Then Pennsylvania shipbuilders brought pressure against the amendment, and Cox lamented that " no one has been here to help me." When the Senate converted his amendment into a subsidy to shipbuilders, and when the Conference Committee, from which he was " left off," accepted the Senate version, he was completely disgusted, reporting that shipbuilders " are as high and dry on land as ever." [16] Nevertheless, during the following session, he was back again with further proposals to liberalize shipping legislation. With these, too, he was unsuccessful.

Closely related to the merchant marine question was the problem of developing a " new navy " and coastal fortification. In 1883 Congress had authorized the building of three light naval cruisers. There were complications: the American navy was hopelessly antiquated; also, modern shipbuilding facilities were lacking. No American mill had yet rolled steel for ship plates, and no vessel entirely of steel had been built in American shipyards. There was no agreement whether the new vessels should be built of wood or of steel. Cox pleaded for steel ships larger and " faster than the light cruisers " and for prompt action by Congress since " it takes time—about three years—to create the gunnery aboard." In addition, a larger merchant marine was necessary since " you cannot have American seamen unless you have a commercial marine . . . [with] more than 5 per cent of our seamen of American nativity." Thus tariff reduction would encourage development of American carrying trade and American merchant marine, " the nursery of seamen." [17]

As chairman of the Naval Affairs Committee, Cox hoped his words would carry weight. For national defense, however, " protection of harbors and coast . . . is the first necessity." Cox called for the building of batteries and fortifications along New York's harbor. Since defense, not aggression, was the primary object, coastal defenses, rather than a big navy, were essential. For New York's fortifications, he was not completely successful, since appropriations were made for the strengthening of only some of the harbor islands.[18]

Once again, he turned to the problem left over from the reconstruction period, the test oath. He offered a bill to remove the test oath for congressmen and jurors, and to allow ex-Confederates to serve in the United States army. He likened the oath to " whipping at the cat's tail, the thumb-screw, the rack, the disemboweling and quartering of the dead, and the burning of the live body." When the House finally adopted his bill, he said, " We are now approaching an era of good feeling." [19] In May the Senate accepted the bill with a slight modification, and the President signed it. Cox was jubilant over this long-fought-for triumph over proscription of ex-Confederates, although, the following year, he pointed out that " complete rehabilitation has not been accomplished. There are men yet living . . . who have not been restored to their citizenship." [20]

Labor continued to be of prime interest to him. He presented petitions from various unions against importation of foreign contract labor. The eight-hour law for federal employees, he again argued, should be strictly enforced. No effort had been made to enforce the law since 1877. " The laboring men," he asserted, ". . . have asked little and received less from legislation in our land than any other class. Yet they are the architects of our greatness. War fills a loftier niche in the Pantheon of nations, but labor, after all, is the conquering hero." The worker, therefore should be allowed time " for mental and moral recreation." Upon urging from Cox and others, the House early in 1884 adopted a measure forbidding the importation of foreign labor " under contract," and, in the following session, the Senate followed suit, with presidential approval coming soon after. This was a bill, Cox explained, " to protect labor without giving a bounty to those who employ it; therefore I am for it." [21] In June 1884 he secured passage of a bill providing a fifteen-day annual vacation with pay for letter carriers.[22] In recognition of this service, the letter carriers of New York City tendered " most earnest thanks " to Cox as " not only a true friend, but an eminent statesman and legislator " and presented to him " a magnificent gold watch." When the federal Bureau of Labor was established in 1885, Cox was pleased. " We cannot get too much information about labor," he announced, and " there could not have been selected . . . so competent . . . [a] head as Mr. Carroll D. Wright." [23]

With the recession of 1884, there were more than eleven thousand business failures and a sharp decline of exports. Cox again urged revival of reciprocal trade with Canada and a commercial treaty with Mexico to bolster the sagging American economy. At various times he also urged cultivation of better relations with Mexico, abrogation of the Clayton-Bulwer treaty, stronger protests to Russia regarding her treatment of American Jews, and federal aid to complete the pedestal for the Statue of Liberty, recently presented by France to the American people.[24]

VICTORY AND REWARD, 1884-1886

As the presidential election year of 1884 progressed, Henry Adams said, " Politics are meaner than ever. Arthur has lowered both parties to his moral standard. . . . Neither party shows a ray of capacity." [25] Cox commented on the confusion in early June: " Our people are in a quandary who to nominate for President . . . Tilden or not. . . . The New York Republicans seem to be coming to the front in opposition to Blaine." [26] The Democrats, as usual, turned toward New York. Tilden ruled himself out of the race because of poor health. Incumbent Governor Grover Cleveland, who was making a good record at Albany, was being built up by his New York supporters, Daniel E. Manning, William C. Whitney, and by Arthur P. Gorman of Maryland. But New York, as usual, was divided. "Honest John" Kelly's Tammany, which had lost much influence in the city government through a series of laws approved by Governor Cleveland, announced that Cleveland could not possibly carry New York. While Tammany secured twenty-four of the state's seventy-two delegates to the national convention, its influence was minimized by the binding force of the unit rule.[27]

After the Republicans nominated Blaine and the " Mugwumps " announced their intention to oppose him, Cleveland's " availability " became even more pronounced. The Democratic convention met in the Chicago Wigwam on July 8 and named Cleveland on the third ballot because, as one delegate put it, " we love him for the enemies he has made." [28] When Cleveland visited New York City soon after the convention, he was hailed by leading Democrats and Republican " Mugwumps " as the man to beat Blaine. As for Cox, he had been on friendly term with the Governor as early as 1882. He did not attend the 1884 convention, but served on the city welcoming committee to greet the Democratic nominee.[29]

Cox began the campaign before Congress adjourned. On June 9, speaking in the House, he delivered a ringing denunciation of the Republican party, " the defiled party of moral ideas and immoral deeds," responsible for " plutocratic usurpation of . . . Federal Government . . . unscrupulous fealty to corporate wealth, fast becoming the main, the only, and the all-sufficient qualification for the high offices of

State." A power behind the Republican party " has grown up within the last twenty-five years under national charters, cash subsidies, land grants . . . and the excessive profits of indirect tariff taxes " and " has now almost absolute control of the entire floating wealth of the nation . . . and the great bulk of the fixed wealth." Cox asserted that the cause of the Republican excesses was " plainly the continued extravagance of the war times, when the foundations of most of the present colossal fortunes were laid in great contracts and cemented with the blood, tears and cruel taxation of the people." [30]

The campaign grew progressively dirtier. Blaine was plagued again by the " Mulligan letters," which exposed his unsavory connection with railroad manipulators, while Cleveland was charged with the paternity of an illegitimate child. Because Blaine's past performance was suspected, many Republican journals refused him support.[31] Much to Cox's discouragement, however, the Democrats failed to make an issue of the tariff, the only marked point of difference between the party platforms.[32] Henry Adams found the campaign

> . . . funnier than words can express. Very great issues are involved. . . . A step toward free trade is inevitable if the Democrats come in. For the first time in twenty-eight years, a Democratic administration is almost inevitable. . . . We are all swearing at each other like demons. . . . No one talks about real interests. . . . Instead of this, the press is engaged in a most amusing dispute whether Mr. Cleveland has an illegitimate child! . . . whether Mr. Blaine got paid in railway bonds for services as Speaker." [33]

Undoubtedly the economic recession that in the past two years had brought a 25 per cent drop in wages and employment did much to turn voters against the party in power.[34]

In the fall of 1884 Cox spoke frequently for Cleveland

and lower tariffs.[35] In early October he delivered " a pleasant address" to the Thomas Jefferson Association of the Fourth Assembly District. When the wooden platform collapsed during the evening, he remarked that it " must have been made of Maine lumber," protected under the high tariff.[36] " Few men have such a reliable district," commented a friend, " or have such a grip upon it as you have." [37] Even though Cox was disappointed over the campaign " because of the economic questions having ' kerslumped,' " he would do his best to make " a respectable run." He solicited his friend Ford's help in winning the *Herald* to his support.[38]

Meanwhile, the split between Tammany and the County Democracy (the official title of the County Democrats) grew complicated. Hewitt, a leader of the County Democrats, assured Cox that he " did not wish to go back to Congress unless you were renominated." If the Sixth District failed to nominate Cox, Hewitt said, " I shall propose at once that you take my place in the Tenth District, as I can be spared much better from public life than you can." On this assurance Cox declared: " I have pleasant relations with everybody except the machine politicians." On October 5 he received the Tammany nomination. A week later he welcomed Grover Cleveland to a mass meeting held at the Academy of Music on East Fourteenth Street. In an address to the Polish Democratic Association, he condemned Blaine for " religious bigotry," for dining with monopolists like Jay Gould, and for favoring " concentration of power." He himself stood for a reduction of tariffs and taxes.[39] A huge businessmen's parade, numbering some 35,000, was staged on November 1 by Cleveland supporters. Cleveland stood on the reviewing stand at Madison Square for three hours.[40]

On November 5 the *Herald* announced that Cleveland had secured a thousand vote plurality in New York and with it the election. Cox won with a 15,000 majority. He jubilantly wrote to President-elect Cleveland " Accept my felicitations! . . . Twenty-seven years ago—I went to the Federal Capital and saw Buchanan nominated [i. e., inaugurated], and no Democratic President since till now." The long, lean years of waiting were finally over. Democrats were ready for the power, the glory, and the seats of the mighty. Cox wrote, " Thank God we lived to see, in measureless content, the old party of our love in the ascendant." [41] Congratulations reached him from as far away as Constantinople.[42]

Two weeks after the election, at a dinner meeting of the New York Chamber of Commerce at Delmonico's, Cox urged tariff revision, free ships, a stronger navy, and harbor fortifications at New York.[43] The reaction of Winfield Scott Hancock on reading the speech was that Cox " should be a minister of War or Peace . . . of the navy or the army or . . . [the Treasury]. I know that your ability and service entitle you to any like consideration! " [44]

Early in December, New York's Democratic leaders, eight hundred strong, including Cox, gathered at the Manhattan Club at 96 Fifth Avenue to greet Cleveland at a victory reception. Shortly afterward, Cox hopeful of reward under the new administration, wrote:

> Grover Cleveland is in his forty-eighth year . . . liberal in his thoughts . . . a man of democratic simplicity. . . . The keynote to his character is found in the moderation and frugality of his life. His firmness and courage, and his deliberate judicious action mark him as a man of . . . high capacity for leadership and administration.

He added " a revolution " had " dethroned the corrupt and effete party. . . . At length peace has come! Slavery, the *bête noir* of our politics, is no more." [45]

Cox hoped for an important appointment befitting his

years of long service in the Democratic party. The prospect was discouraging, however. In response to a plea for political favor, he wrote: " I do not know what my relation will be to the Administration or what influence I may have." [46] And at another point, in a letter to William F. Vilas, Cleveland's Postmaster-General, he observed: " I am left out of our politics." [47] Yet he did not give up hope of wielding some influence. He wrote Cleveland recommending Augustus H. Garland for a cabinet post and a New York judge, Aaron Vanderpoel, as one of " your advisors." He also offered advice on the inaugural address suggesting a passage dealing with Russian and German persecutions of the Jews.[48] The demands from job-starved Democrats were overwhelming. There were unceasing requests to Cox for aid in getting government appointments for " deserving Democrats." [49] However, when he, with ninety-four fellow Democrats in the House, urged Cleveland not to repudiate limited coinage of silver, the President-elect issued a letter through Manton Marble announcing his opposition to government silver purchases and coinage.[50]

As the lame-duck Congress came to a close in early 1885, George Jones, editor of the New York *Times*, urged Cox to secure a $13,500 pension for General Grant, who, now broke and in ill health, was laboriously preparing his *Memoirs* for publication in order to meet his debts.[51] Cox's support helped to influence the Democrats and to secure the pension. Grant sent his thanks " for your goodness," and Cox was gratified, for, as he wrote Cleveland, " your predecessor, dying of a mortal disease, has had the consolation of knowing that there is a generous amnesty toward him beyond all expression and in spite of all differences." [52]

March 1885 found Cox working diligently to complete his forthcoming memoirs, *Three Decades of Federal Legislation.*

He expressed the fear that the same forces that had secured " the usurpation of 1877 " were still operating in 1885. " We have the same timidity of wealth," he wrote,

> . . . the same cowardice of credit, and the same tenderness of trade, which then drowned the popular will by clamors for revival of business. The rich bartered political rectitude for contentment with their gains. But are we rid of the rich . . . bond-holder, . . . champagne revelers, . . . railroad kings, . . . sleek lobbies, . . . purchasable news-venders, . . . moneyed princes, . . . men of fashionable clubs and soft attire? These cannot be abolished. Their evil influence must be restrained. . . . For purposes of public conduct, we must turn to the principles and practices of the Union established by the fathers. . . . There must be more concern for the national character.

" The recent election " gave " hope of better days." Reviewing the past third of a century, Cox found the country " greatly changed . . . politically, socially, materially, nationally." He felt, however, that " it is only by guarding against the centralization of government that the great diversity of interests in a Union of such extent as ours can be harmonized, and individual rights secured." More emphasis was needed on " local independence and self-government." " The pendulum," he thought, " was again swinging toward decentralization." " The American Republic must become an exemplar for all future republics which may be created by the achievements of free men. . . . Let progress be in the paths of peace, humanity, and justice and toward the advancement of real liberty and mutual industry." [53]

Cleveland appointed Cox as minister to Turkey, a position he hesitated to accept, due to the illness of his eighty-four-year-old mother. After her death, Cox wrote to Cleveland, " thanking you again for giving a gleam to my darkened way, . . . I may now go to my mission—with a lighter heart as I do not drag . . . this chain of filial fear." [54] But he took the Constantinople appointment with reluctance. He wrote to a friend that the rise of new men, " as is natural, has pushed me to the rear. . . . I was not even able to command my old and favorite foreign committeeship, or my former Smithsonian regentship, always accorded to me even by Republicans." The discouragements of Congress, " the rolling, rolling, rolling up the stones . . . the foolish modes and rules, which few in control cared to correct—all this and more made me think that it was high time to seek " a change abroad. The Senate paid him the compliment of confirmation without referring his appointment to committee, an honor rarely accorded anyone who had not been a senator.[55]

Congratulations poured in from personal friends.[56] One asked: " In the sixth Congressional, who can fill your place? " [57] On April 4, 1885, *Harper's Weekly* ran his picture and noted: " His friends are legion, and his name at a political meeting is a tried target for cheers. It seems strange that he should be elsewhere than in his old seat in the House." Cleveland's other diplomatic appointments included Cox's old friends, " Gentleman George " Pendleton, Robert W. McLane, and Edward J. Phelps, who would go, respectively, to Berlin, Paris and London. Before Cox sailed, his Alma Mater, Brown University, awarded him an honorary LL. D. On June 8 New York friends gathered for a farewell dinner in his honor at Hoffman House to pay their respects, for " so long and so honorable a career in the public service." [58] Abram Hewitt presided at the dinner while such notables as ex-Mayor Edward Cooper, Everett P. Wheeler, and William Dorsheimer attended. Here Cox declared: " Politics . . . have been for a quarter of a century a great source of enjoyment and a great incentive to practical exertion." However, a change was desirable, and there would be " no longer for me the speaker's gavel, with its ' rap,' ' rap,' ' rap,' no longer the fierce debate and loud applause." [59] He was not convinced that his own appointment to Turkey was much of an honor. " It is a curious, strange experience for me that after I had reached my acme, and the ladder was all golden and beautiful like Jacob's, somebody jerks it from under me, and I have got to float serenely into an Oriental haven for Democratic virtue." [60]

Cox's work as minister to Turkey has been dealt with in the preceding chapter. His correspondence, however, reveals that, even while in Constantinople, his interest in American politics was unabated. He could not escape from a profession that had absorbed almost all his adult labors. Reminders kept coming from home. Word arrived of the deaths of General Grant, Vice-President Hendricks, Samuel Tilden, Horatio Seymour, and Winfield Scott Hancock. The news revived memories of early political battles. After three months in Constantinople he wrote Cleveland's secretary: " If I am needed . . . in the next Congress, I can return. . . . If I can help him [the President] return for another term . . . I will come home in time to do my part." [61]

News that Cox's recent book was " selling better than Blaine's " brought personal satisfaction as well as financial reward.[62] Comments and criticism of his book reached him from former colleagues, one of whom was William H. English of Indiana.[63] Another more recent colleague wrote that " the House met " and " you were not there. It was a shame. Everybody said so; everybody felt it." [64] Ex-Confederate Joseph E. Brown, now in Congress, sent " many thanks for your eloquent and statesmanlike effort, which resulted in the repeal of the ironclad oath. . . . The Southern States have great reason to honor your name. . . . You fully comprehend the theory and spirit of our Government . . .

[to] stand by the right and defend sound principles. . . . [We regret that] we do not hear your eloquent voice " in Congress.[65] When Cox learned of Joseph Pulitzer's resignation as congressman from New York's Ninth District, the longing for home grew so strong that by mid-summer 1886 he determined to return for the fall elections. " Call it home-sickness, or patriotism, or an inclination after old and fixed parliamentary habits," he wrote a friend.[66]

CONGRESS AGAIN, 1886-1887

Passing the newly erected Statue of Liberty on its recently completed pedestal, Cox and his wife arrived in New York in mid-October. They were accompanied by their Greek dragoman and their French maid from abroad, who remained as servants in the Cox household even after Cox's death.[67] Cox now submitted his resignation to Secretary of State Thomas Bayard asking that its acceptance be held up " for a little time until my trunk, boxes, etc." could come " through customs without delay or duty." [68] By the end of the month the resignation was accepted by the Department of State.[69]

Cox was on hand for the dedication of the Statue of Liberty. The statue had been projected some ten years before and was completed by Frederic A. Bartholdi in 1883, but at that time the pedestal on Bedloe's Island was scarcely started. Congress under Cox's prodding had appropriated $100,000, and another $100,000 was raised through the efforts of Joseph Pulitzer, editor of the *World*. Now on October 28, 1886, there was a mass parade in Manhattan, after which a flotilla of gaily-bedecked boats made its way to Bedloe's Island. Many people of importance were present at the dedication, including Bartholdi, President Cleveland and his cabinet, city and state officials. Cox listened to the dedicatory speeches of William Evarts and Chauncey Depew and cheered with the crowd as the whistles blew and the guns roared in salute to the 300-foot Goddess of Liberty who was beginning her reign over New York harbor.[70]

The complexion of New York politics had changed considerably since Cox had left the country sixteen months before. Governor David B. Hill led the state Democratic party after Cleveland went to Washington, while John Kelly handed on the Tammany reins to the able Richard Croker. Although Tammany's relations with the Hill organization were cordial and the hostility of the County Democrats had lessened, nevertheless Tammany worried over the coming mayoralty election. The depression of the mid-eighties had increased labor's discontent. The Knights of Labor, a growing organization, had entered New York politics and named " single taxer " Henry George for mayor. This threatened to cut heavily into the normally large Democratic vote.[71] Tammany leaders knew that to win they would need a strong candidate with labor appeal. Cox was mentioned as the most available candidate. When he declined, Tammany, reuniting all Democratic factions, named Abram Hewitt to oppose George and the young Republican Theodore Roosevelt.[72]

Although unwilling to run for mayor, Cox eagerly accepted the nomination tendered by the Democrats of the Ninth Congressional District. This was a double nomination— for the unexpired term left by the resignation of Joseph Pulitzer the previous April and for the new Congress to begin in 1887. The Ninth District lay on the lower East Side of Manhattan with a population similar to that of Cox's old Sixth District. It was usually called the " Administration district " because of its reliably Democratic majorities. Cox campaigned enthusiastically for his own and Hewitt's election. At a Democratic rally, reported by the New York *World* on October 15 and 16, 1886, he appeared with Hewitt, Pulitzer, and August Belmont to praise President Cleveland, Governor Hill, and the Democratic Congress for meeting "nearly every demand of . . . the Knights of Labor." Congress had passed an arbitration law and had supported enforcement of the eight-hour law.[73]

The National Tariff Reform League under David Wells and the Young Men's Democratic Club gave Cox strong support, and he sailed through to an easy victory. Hewitt, too, was elected, although by a slim margin, over Henry George. One contemporary observed: "So far as I have been able to determine, Mr. Cox is the only man who had been twice elected to the same Congress."[74]

When Congress met on December 6, 1886, "Cox was given an ovation as he entered on the arm of his colleague, Mr. Hewitt," who continued in Congress until his inauguration as mayor. "Friends gathered around him," the *World* correspondent reported on December 7, "and there was much shaking of hands." The President's message pleased Cox, especially its references to the "successful exertions" of "our late minister to Turkey" for the "improved treatment of American missionaries." Cox found the President's words on the surplus and the tariff "not only politic; but wise and cogent." He hoped this session would bring the long-awaited tariff changes.[75]

Despite his auspicious entrance, Cox was to be disappointed again in this session. He helped defeat a bill authorizing a railroad to run to newly-found mines in Yellowstone National Park. He believed that this was "not in the interest of the people" but solely for the "self-aggrandizement" of the railroad promoters. He asked Congress to "vote it down and preserve this marvelous scenery for our people

today and for posterity." [76] The failure of the Morrison
tariff reduction bill, defeated in the previous session and
beaten again with the aid of some forty Randallite Democrats, led President Cleveland to write Cox that he felt " very
intensely as to his disappointment." By mid-January serious
illness forced Cox to absent himself for the remainder of
the session.[77]

Laid up in his room at the Riggs House, he mused over
the vicissitudes of politics. He was low in spirits because
" nobody at the White House was ever sent over to inquire "
about him. To the President he wrote numerous letters,
recommending J. Proctor Knott, long-time congressman, for
a federal appointment; thanking Cleveland for naming L. A.
Gingerich, " a protege of mine, as internal revenue collector
in New York "; and lamenting " the ever lasting ' ding
dong ' about patronage." In a few of his letters, he complained, " I am left somewhat alone in my relation to
politics." He made a personal visit to Cleveland in November, during which he reported on New York City politics
and urged appointment of a friend for " Inspector of the
Steamboat Service in New York " and for shipping commissioner in the metropolis.[78]

Because Cox had only limited success in securing patronage, he turned his attention again to writing. He had been
on intimate terms with Mark Twain for some years, having
visited often in the latter's Hartford home. Now that Twain
had his own publishing house, Cox sent proposals for a new
book. Having " no doubts as to the readableness of your
book," Twain was sure that it would contain " slathers of
religion and fun," which, he thought, was the recipe for
literary success. To a manager in the firm, he wrote: " Yes,
we do certainly want Cox's book," and in the fall, Charles L.

Webster Company (Mark Twain's firm) published Cox's *Diversions of a Diplomat in Turkey.*[79]

SUNSET OF A LONG CAREER, 1887-1889

By December 1887, Cox was back in Washington for the new session of Congress, which lasted until the following October and proved extremely tiring for him. The House awarded him some honors befitting his standing as one of its senior members. He received the much hoped-for appointment as house regent of the Smithsonian Institution. His chairmanship of the Census Committee and membership in the Committee on Territories, although pleasing, did not make up for the failure to achieve appointments to the more important committees, such as Rules and Foreign Affairs, on which he had formerly served. Nevertheless, he was chosen to serve as Speaker *pro tem* during Carlisle's frequent absences.[80] These duties often caused him " not to get home before 6 or 7 " and to miss more than one dinner invitation to the White House.[81] Toward the end of the session, poor health again forced his absence for several weeks.[82]

The principal struggle in the Fiftieth Congress came over the tariff. Since the early 1880's federal revenue had been producing an annual surplus of about $100,000,000. Various proposals had been made to dispose of this money, and the pressure from the revenue reformers continued to increase.[83] President Cleveland delighted the reformers in December 1887 by devoting his entire congressional message to urging tariff reform and reduction. Calling the tariff " a burden upon those with moderate means and the poor, the unemployed and the employed, the sick and the well," the President recommended that " our present tariff laws, the vicious, inequitable and illogical source of unnecessary taxation, ought to be at once revised and amended." [84] Cox was overjoyed that a chief executive had finally come around to his own point of view. The sequel, however, was to prove discouraging.

The Mills Bill, providing for a modest 7 per cent reduction of duties on finished goods, while seeking free or cheap raw materials such as wool, lumber, flax, jute, and copper ore, was reported to the House on April 17. Three months of bitter, strenuous debate followed, inspiring the strongest oratorical and parliamentary efforts of Roger Mills, Carlisle, Cox, Randall, Thomas B. Reed, and William McKinley. As early as March, Cox, who had already spent a lifetime studying the subject, began preparing a speech for this debate, which he delivered on May 17.[85] It was a long speech filling some sixteen pages of the *Congressional Record* and asserting that the decision on the tariff should be a " matter of sound business judgment" and not " mere party discussion" and " personal recrimination." [86] Cox thought the proposals for reduction were moderate indeed. He would prefer elimination of more of the restrictions on trade, but for the present he would gladly support the proposed measure. Tariff duties were like a road:

> Twenty per cent duty is like a bad road; 30 per cent is a corduroy road; . . . 40 per cent is like a broad, deep rapid, unbridged river; and 50 per cent like a swamp flanking the river on both sides, while 80 or 100 per cent, such as is levied upon steel rails, blankets, and windowglass, is a band of brigands who strip the merchant of nearly all he possesses. He should be grateful to God that he escapes with his life.[87]

As usual, he was rewarded with laughter and applause. He reiterated arguments he had previously advanced, and concluded with a plea for the freedom of labor—" for freedom to work as we please and to dispose of our products as we please." [88] Revenue reformers cheered. David Wells sent Cox warm congratulations on a job well done,[89] and Cox himself thought the speech good enough to have 50,000 copies printed and sent to leading Democrats, " throughout the country."

When the House finally passed the Mills Bill on July 21 by a vote of 162 to 149, he felt that his long years of labor over the tariff had not been entirely lost.[90] His satisfaction was short-lived, however, for Senate amendments, pushed by lobbyists, distorted the bill beyond recognition and choked it to death in the Conference Committee, much to the disgust of both Cox and Cleveland.[91]

Early in April Cox presented a bill to authorize the taking of the eleventh census and to re-establish the Bureau of the Census which had been abolished in 1885. He explained that the new census would be similar to that of 1880 with expanded statistics on nationality, ages, physical conditions, marital status, the national economy, and the mortality of the population. He proudly announced the estimated increases in population and production as the centenary of the national government approached.[92] The Cox bill passed the House and the Senate in the following session.[93]

On April 24, hoping to increase the number of Life-Saving Service stations, he made a dramatic plea for the Service. He sketched its origin, growth, and impressive record. It had saved more than 35,000 lives and more than $45,000,000 worth of property in its seventeen years of existence. Referring to his recent serious illness when he lay near death he recalled a picture on the wall in his room of a life boat making a rescue at sea. " In my poor sick fancy I grasped the tiller of the life boat. I clung to it with the tenacity that overcame the sinking heart of an emaciated body. . . . [It] inspired me with a fresh hope and a new life, gave me smiling assurance that I might still survive . . . to plead for the Lifesaving Service in many Congresses." Although the bill for enlarging the Service did not pass this session, a threatened reduction in appropriations was forestalled.[94]

Always the friend of the postal employees, he presented bills for creating additional classes of letter carriers and for classifying post office clerks and railway mail service workers. In May 1888 he secured passage of the eight-hour law for postal employees and a law providing a fifteen-day annual leave with pay. The New York Letter Carriers Association celebrated this event by holding a mass meeting at the Academy of Music to adopt resolutions of thanks for Cox's labors. When the Post Office Department sought to evade the effect of the eight-hour law by requiring the week's fifty-six hours to be served in fewer than seven days, Cox advised the letter carriers to fight for strict interpretation of the law, a view sustained by the Supreme Court in 1892 when it ordered the payment to postal employees of three and a quarter million dollars for overtime beyond the legal eight-hour day.[95]

The presidential campaign of 1888 was taking shape at the same time that the Mills bill was being debated in Congress. In June the Democrats renominated Grover Cleveland while the Republicans responded by naming Benjamin Harrison of Indiana. The chief differences between the parties lay again in their respective stands on the tariff. Although plagued by ill health during most of the summer, Cox nevertheless determined to do all he physically could to insure Cleveland's re-election.[96] In late September he began commuting between Washington and New York in order to give a series of lectures on Turkey at Cooper Union.[97] In New York Cleveland's position was weakened by David B. Hill's candidacy for re-election as governor. Hill's reputation as a machine politician alienated many Republican " Mugwumps " who had supported Cleveland four years before. It also drove away prohibitionist support. Tammany remained loyal to Cleveland, as did Hewitt's County Democrats, but some of the minor city Democratic groups were less trustworthy.[98]

By mid-October Cox was busy with his own campaign. He wrote the President's secretary asking that Cleveland say a word in his behalf, since he had defended " the President's policies throughout . . . the only Democratic member for New York City to do so." The County Democracy did not give him its nomination, but Tammany and the United German group in his district gave their blessing.[99] A busy three weeks followed. He reported again early in November that he was " more or less worried with the campaign," for he had been making two or more speeches a day and was not in good health. " I don't believe it will come easily," he said. This, he announced to the President, " is my last and likely your last campaign." [100]

The election returns were something of a surprise. In the country at large, Harrison won the presidency even though Cleveland amassed 100,000 more votes. New York's record for political paradoxes ran true to form. Hill was elected governor with a 19,000-vote margin, while Cleveland lost the state by 13,000. Cox, as usual, won—his fifteenth congressional victory.[101] But for the Democrats, the prospects were not bright: they had lost no only the presidency but both Houses in the next Congress.

The lame duck session, beginning on December 3, 1888, was the last in which Cox served. Once more, he championed New York's commercial interests. In the first few weeks he called for appropriations to improve the harbor channels whereby " this magnificent port " handled two-thirds of the nation's total imports and customs revenues, one-half of its exports, three-fourths of the passengers traveling to and from the United States, and three-fifths of its immigrants. He predicted, with surprising vision, that in fifty years New York's population would be eight million and that the whole waterfront would be covered with wharves. Because of larger vessels, the main harbor channel had been deepened in 1880 to twenty-six feet, but a depth of thirty feet would soon be required. It was only fair that New York, which supplied so many services to the country, should receive congressional attention.[102]

The question of building an isthmian canal was once more raised by Cox, who called attention to the French failure at Panama and to the advantages of a canal. He therefore presented a bill to incorporate the Maritime Canal Company of Nicaragua that had been organized in the early 1880's by a group of New York promoters. Finally, in February 1889, Congress gave its assent to the incorporation.[103] In one other business matter Cox presented the view of those New York book publishers who had profitably published unauthorized editions of the works of English writers. He offered their petition against the proposed international copyright bill, which would, if passed, prohibit book pirating. In this he was seconded by Mark Twain who wrote Cox that " only about three authors in a century would profit by it— that is, their heirs would." [104]

Ever since the Kansas struggle during his first session in the House, Cox had been interested in the establishment of new Western states. Now in his last session, on a bill to admit Dakota as a state, Cox offered an amendment to divide Dakota into two states and to provide also for the admission of Montana and Washington. On January 15, 1889, he made a powerful plea for the adoption of this "omnibus" bill. Dakota's size, population, and transportation facilities "indicate a prosperous community" and fully justified the creation of two states. The whole process of American admission of new American states to equal footing with old states stood in sharp contrast to European colonial systems. It was "ennobling to contemplate the quiet and yet immense expansion of our members and our realm" that produced a "glowing pride" in the West with its "bustle, motion, and struggle." Westerners, he declared, "live in the future, rather than in the present. . . . Before this all-pervading spirit governments become mere incidents in the advancement of the race." Cox's arguments were apparently convincing, and the enabling act went through late in February.[105]

With the last session of the Fiftieth Congress over and with his health still poor, Cox eagerly accepted the invitation of grateful Dakota leaders to visit their section. Before setting out on the Western trip, he delivered a speech to the Knights of St. Patrick.[106] Accompanied by his wife, he left early in June. On July 4, he delivered an address at Huron, Dakota Territory. One enthusiastic newspaper reported:

> Mr. Cox stood in the midst of the assembled thousands of his fellow citizens at Huron. . . . No more imposing or grander ovation was ever given to an American citizen. . . . The prairies, the towns, and the villages for miles around were deserted, for their inhabitants would look upon their great deliverer. These people would hear the voice of the eminent statesman who in the House of Representatives had raised his voice for fair play. . . . He was their hero. They pressed him, for they deemed him something nobler than a mere orator. . . .[107]

Cox was even more eloquent than usual that day. He began: "Standing on the threshold of these young states, and in the morning of another century, may we not have glimpses of the far future of their destiny?" This destiny "may not be that of a Paradise regained . . ." but here "may be found the shining nucleus . . . [of] the concentrated genius of the most miraculous progress known to human society." The Dakota celebration "combines Jefferson and the Declaration, . . . Jefferson and Louisiana, . . . France with her revolution, and our own . . . all imbound in the golden rigol of republican institutions and human felicity." He concluded with: "All hail! Sisters of the Northwest! . . . I welcome you to the enjoyment of the privileges, advantages, immunities, and guarantees which protect property, reputation, person, liberty, religion, and life" in the United States.[108]

After their return to New York, the Coxes went to their usual vacation place at Manhattan Beach on Staten Island. "Hither have I hied myself," Cox wrote a friend, "to the salt sea beach where I correct my abnormal condition of health." On August 25, 1889, he described the pleasures of the seashore and his hotel, "this gorgeous marine hospital," where he sat writing while his ears were "dinned with the music of the band." After a few days he returned to his New York home on East 12th Street. Although suffering from a bad cold, on August 30 he attended the "grand annual summer night's festival of the New York Letter Carriers' Association" at the Empire City Colosseum and Washington Park. This was his last public appearance.

A week later acute peritonitis developed, and recovery was impossible. At 8:40 in the evening of September 10 the sun set for the last time for Samuel Cox.[109]

Messages of sympathy poured in on the widow from relatives, political party groups, letter carriers' associations, and friends like ex-President Cleveland, Levi P. Morton, General Sherman, John Hay, and Governor Hill. Cleveland spoke of

" your husband's honorable career " and " his useful life."
John Hay wanted Mrs. Cox to know " how high a place
Mr. Cox held in the esteem and affection of his fellow
legislators. Few men have even lived more universally loved
and admired; few have ever died more sincerely mourned." [110]
On September 12 the funeral was held at the First Pres-
byterian Church just a few doors from Cox's home. The
New York Letter Carriers' Association sent a large floral
display like an envelope, with a post mark in flowers in the
upper right hand corner reading " New York, 9-10-89, 8:30
P. M." The Life-Saving Service sent a life belt and a muffled
oar with the inscription " Our Champion." Honorary pall-
bearers included Grover Cleveland, Levi P. Morton, William T. Sherman, George Hoadly (ex-Governor of Ohio),
Thomas Ewing, Jr., and Milton H. Northrup, while the
House of Representatives sent Democrats Carlisle, Randall,
and Holman, and Republicans William McKinley, Joseph
Cannon, and Thomas B. Reed. Relatives from Zanesville
joined the widow in the procession. Services were conducted
by the blind chaplain of the House, Dr. William H. Milburn,
and the famous Dr. T. DeWitt Talmage of the Brooklyn
Tabernacle, who described Cox as " firm as a rock, brilliant
as a star, artless as a child " and declared, " We shall not
see his like again." Interment was at Greenwood Cemetery
in Brooklyn.[111]

The obituaries were filled with high praise for the departed
representative. " A national loss," said the New York *Times*,
which declared that " it was probably due to his independence
more than to any other cause that he did not attain the
high position in his party to which his abilities entitled him.
His kind, brilliant, and winning presence will be greatly
missed in the House." *Harper's Weekly* carried a large picture of Cox and a column-long notice, calling him " one

of the most useful legislators of his time " and " one of the best-liked and most misunderstood of our public men. . . . Very few Congressmen have been able to so readily secure the passage of their bills as Mr. Cox." The Philadelphia *Public Ledger* spoke of his " brilliant mind," " sterling ability," " elevated sense of humor," asserting that " he played many parts, and played them all well . . . lawyer, . . . journalist, . . . author, . . . diplomat, . . . politician, . . . statesman . . . a man of signal intellectual force and mental worth . . . a conspicuously useful man in Congress . . . most beloved among his associates." [112]

On October 10, at a German-American memorial meeting in Cox's honor, Grover Cleveland praised Cox as a " wise and generous man," who " was never actuated by a corrupt or selfish interest " but whose " zeal was born of public spirit and the motive of his labor was the public good." J. Proctor Knott, ex-congressman from Kentucky, eulogized Cox for " the varied faculties of his extraordinary intellect," " his illimitable stores of information," his widespread knowledge, his broad services and his exemplary conduct. Knott concluded that " no man was ever more widely known or more lovingly revered among his countrymen." [113]

Cox's will, probated on November 20, bequeathed his estate, real and personal, to his wife. A search of the records of the New York County Surrogate Court failed to reveal any accompanying inventory of his property but showed only a pencilled notation to the effect that the net value of the personal property was $5,000.[114] This would seem to indicate that Cox had already turned over to his wife the bulk of the proceeds from royalties on his books, some of which had had large sales.

When the next Congress met, the day of April 19, 1890 was set aside by the House for eulogies of the late member from New York. Of the thirty members who delivered eulogies, the most prominent were Nathaniel P. Banks of Massachusetts, who had served many years in the House with Cox, Roger Q. Mills, and Richard P. Bland. On July 8, 1890, the Senate heard praise for the departed congressman expressed by John Sherman, William Evarts, Daniel W. Voorhees, and others.[115]

Most tangible remembrance of Cox came from the two groups he had done most to benefit. On the day following his death the New York Letter Carriers Association resolved to raise a fund to erect a statue of their "friend." Other local associations pitched in and, within two years, some $10,000 had been collected. On July 4, 1891, an eight-foot bronze statue of Cox, "The Letter Carriers' Friend," was unveiled with appropriate ceremonies in Astor Place in lower Manhattan, just a few blocks from Cox's home. Thomas Ewing, Jr., son of the famous Ohio Whig statesman, made the dedicatory address. After some thirty years, in November 1924, the statue was relocated at Tompkins Square Park, Avenue A and 7th Street, within the boundaries of Cox's old district.[116] The New York Letter Carriers Association also have continued to the present day to conduct a yearly Memorial Day pilgrimage to Cox's grave in Greenwood Cemetery.[117] The Life-Saving Service presented to Mrs. Cox a two-foot memorial vase, appropriately inscribed in memory of Cox's labors.[118]

10

SUNDOWN

A SUMMARY

The story of Samuel Sullivan Cox's career, spanning most of the latter half of the nineteenth century, forms a chapter in the larger story of American politics. During his adult years American party politics witnessed the spectacular rise of the Republican party to a quarter century of power, with the simultaneous split in 1860 and subsequent eclipse of the Democratic party which had exercised control in Washington for almost three generations. There followed the slow revival and recovery of the Democratic party during the lean years of Civil War and reconstruction. In the late 1870's the Democrats were able to battle evenly with the Republicans, and finally in the mid-1880's they regained control of the White House and Congress.

In this milieu, Cox had three decades of active leadership. An examination of the assumptions on which he operated may shed light upon his political beliefs and ideas which, on the surface, appear to be contradictory. If he is classifiable at all, he may perhaps be best described as a conservative in the Jeffersonian tradition. His was a belief in a simple, modest, frugal federal government of strictly limited powers, as defined in the Constitution, coupled with respect for states rights and local government where the decisions could be made by the people most directly affected. On occasion, however, the argument for states rights became a matter of political expediency rather than a matter of genuine principle. It served Cox, as it had served Jefferson, as a weapon for opposing and limiting the party in power. But no doubt it was on the basis of principle that he protested against the increase of federal powers which would lead to centralization of government. It was not merely for political reasons that he opposed the reconstruction legislation. Viewing the Civil War and reconstruction policies as destructive of the federal arrangement of dividing governmental powers between central and state governments, he frequently pushed resolutions in Congress for the perservation of those powers reserved to the states. He had a deep-seated democratic conviction that government must reflect the popular will and that this could best be achieved by having most public policy matters determined at the local level.

His influence upon the course of American politics from the 1850's to the late 1880's is difficult to measure. The most that can be said is that the course of American public affairs might have moved along different lines had Cox not lived during the period. He tried to forestall the breach in the Union and the secession of the Southern states in 1860-61. He did everything that a congressman could do to satisfy Southern demands without surrendering completely to Southern "fire-eaters." While his work did not halt secession nor prevent Northerners and Southerners from taking up arms against each other, he served his purpose as a man of compromise whose chief aim was to save the Union.

His desire to maintain the Union at any cost arose doubtless from his upbringing in the tradition of Jacksonian Democratic politics, handed down to him by his father and his grandfather. The Union was to Cox in 1861 what it was to Jackson in 1832: inviolable. This was the fixed star by which he set his course. No arguments against the evils of slavery, not even the appeal to states rights, could shake his belief. When, despite his compromise efforts, the break in the Union came, he supported the Lincoln Administration in its military efforts, even though he deplored the use of armed might to pull the Union together again. It was a great tragedy that Americans should kill each other over a dispute which Cox believed might well have been settled by the time-honored, practical, political means of discussion, compromise, and adjustment of interests. As he understood it, the politicians's function was to harmonize and adjust conflicting and competing interests. The pre-Civil War generation of politicians had failed to fulfill this function. Granting their failure, Cox, feeling the need to act, supported the war to restore the states to the Union. But he resisted the changed purpose of the war. The original intent had been to restore the Union, not to free the slaves or to perpetuate Republican party power. Hence, when Lincoln issued the Emancipation Proclamation, Cox denounced it as a corruption of the war's original purpose and as a deception upon those who were fighting. He maintained that the original intent had not been to destroy slavery and to create a social revolution in the domestic affairs of the South. But when Cox became convinced that emancipation was not an obstacle to the restoration of the Union, he moved to support it. Even though much of his action was dictated by partisan policy, restoration of the Union was his first consideration.

Closely tied to his concern for preservation of the Union with state powers undiminished was his concern for individual liberties. Recognizing that prosecution of the Civil War required an all-out Union military effort, he contended that such an effort should not mean a suspension of the values that the American democratic system was designed to protect. One of the prime values that he saw endangered was the freedom of the individual to think, say, and publish what he believed. On the principle of freedom, he condemned the wartime disregard of individual liberties—suspension of *habeas corpus*, arbitrary arrests of persons who questioned the wisdom of the war, censorship, and the suspension of opposition newspapers. He reiterated time and again that American liberty was endangered whenever the constitutional safeguards of that liberty were ignored. In general, he rejected Lincoln's justification of arbitrary measures, believing that the means should not destroy the chief end of government, that a war to preserve the Union should not kill respect for individual liberty.

It is difficult to determine how much of Cox's action in these matters was dictated by a regard for principle and how much by political expediency. In the Kansas crisis of 1857-58, for example, there is little doubt that he was interested in preserving Democratic ascendancy, but he was also concerned with the principle of popular sovereignty as the best means of permitting the people of any particular territory to decide the fate of slavery in that territory. Clearly, it was to the advantage of the Democratic party to banish the slavery dispute from the halls of Congress, where it was rapidly tearing the party apart, and to put it on the plains of Kansas, where, for a time at least, it would not embarrass the Democratic party. This policy was simply a postponement of the issue, but it promised a period of relative quiet, free of agitation, in Congress, during which tempers could cool and calmer political heads could work out a more permanent answer to the question without resorting to arms and bloodshed.

A similar mixture of political expediency and principle was apparent in Cox's action in relation to the reconstruction of the South. His tenacious opposition to the radical reconstruction program stemmed in large part from his understandable desire to see Southern Democrats back in control of their states, thereby making possible a resurrection of Democratic power at the national level. Yet, here too, he expressed, as he had in the secession crisis, the principle of brotherhood and moderation, advocating forgiveness and decent treatment of Southerners, even though they had made a serious mistake in leaving the Union in the first place. He urged amnesty to all as quickly as possible. This would allow the Southerners to recover their political rights, permit Southern states to resume their proper place in the Union, and remove such special punishments as the " iron-clad " oath which barred Southerners from political participation. His work was undoubtedly designed to bring Southern Democrats back to the party, but if the words " malice toward none " and the oft-expressed desire for reunion and forgiveness meant anything at all, it made sense to allow Southerners to return to full, participating citizenship as soon as they had abandoned the Confederate cause. Here was the plea of a man of moderation, a plea for mildness, leniency, and justice that went almost unheard in the tumult and violence of the early reconstruction years. It took more than a decade after Appomattox for moderation to prevail.

Cox's strong belief in social justice sometimes supple-

mented his theory of limited popular government and sometimes conflicted with it. He championed the cause of many
minority groups—the Indians in the West, the newly arrived
immigrants in the Eastern cities, the Irish insurgents in British
jails, Jews suffering under Russian pogroms. And he urged
the United States government to take action to prevent or
remedy injustices to these groups. But for the injustices to
the Negro, Cox had a blind spot.

A conservative in most respects, he looked back to the
pre-1860 years as to an ideal. Yet even here his views and
actions were mixed. He believed that agriculture and commerce could continue to be the principal and most significant
of pursuits for Americans, even as they had been in the early
nineteenth century. The small farm and the self-sufficient
farmer, who produced some surplus that entered into the
stream of commerce, were representative of the Jeffersonian
ideal way of life for Cox. Hence, he opposed protective
tariffs and championed a low tariff policy, which would
assist the American farmer to sell his surplus abroad while
encouraging American shippers and merchants.

Although he looked backward to an agrarian way of
life, he was constantly confronted by the new pattern of
large-scale manufacturing in the country. He often spoke
of American development in terms of progress. Yet the
rapid advance of an urban-industrial era troubled him. When
it was clear to him that progress required industrial growth,
he came to accept industrialization as inevitable. In fact,
with his opposition to a high tariff, he looked ahead to a
future age as well as back to an earlier day. A low tariff
would not only benefit agriculture and commerce but would
open new markets abroad. Since the country's increasing
productive capacity indicated a need for new markets, a
revision of the American protective tariff policy would be

needed (as twentieth century Americans were to learn). Cox seems to have caught a glimpse of this future necessity and voiced it often in his speeches.

While he was anxious to assist economic progress, his views on government subsidy varied with the object of the aid. He supported subsidies for shippers and shipbuilders in the form of mail contracts, and he urged reduction or elimination of duties on materials required in shipbuilding. But he opposed government aid for railroads and even supported the move for governmental regulation of railroads through the Interstate Commerce Commission, created in 1887. This inconsistency reflects his partisan views as well as his desire to represent New York City's commercial interests.

When Cox championed measures for the betterment of workers, principle and expediency once more went hand in hand. Thus his efforts to improve the lot of letter carriers— by providing higher pay, a shorter work week, and regular vacations—reflected his position as representative of a working-class constituency as well as his sincere interest in obtaining a regular career service for postal employees. His post office measures, his drive for an eight-hour work day for employees of the government, and his efforts to establish the Life-Saving Service, all indicated a forward-looking kind of statesmanship and foreshadowed a twentieth-century concern for social welfare. As a member and chairman of the congressional committees on the United States census of 1870 and 1880, and as regent of the Smithsonian Institution he was instrumental in providing large amounts of factual data for public use in reaching rational decisions. By having the Ways and Means Committee divided into an Appropriations Committee and a Banking and Currency Committee, he laid a foundation for a more efficient handling of the government's increasingly complex financial problems.

In his views on world affairs and American foreign policy, he was typical of his generation. A vigorous proponent of Manifest Destiny, he wished the United States to annex Cuba, by force if necessary, and he suggested the acquisition of Canada. He supported the McLane-Ocampo Treaty in the late 1850's in the hope that the United States would secure a foothold in northern Mexico as well as in the Tehuantepec Isthmus. When he urged American domination of the Western Hemisphere, through expansion of the Monroe Doctrine, his speeches rang with jingoism. An ardent champion of American maritime rights, he proposed acceptance of the Declaration of Paris of 1856, provided the European signatories would accept American qualifications. In relation to Europe, he asked that the United States take a strong stand against English imprisonment of Irish Republicans and against Russian persecution of Jews. The stimulation of American foreign trade formed the over-all consideration in his thinking on foreign affairs.

As a parliamentary leader in Congress, there was no question of his skill and shrewdness. Fellow Democrats chose him as their party floor leader in six sessions, and he was often Speaker *pro-tem* of the House. Despite this recognition, he often felt his efforts to be futile. He believed that his physical size placed him at a disadvantage. Never weighing more than one hundred and forty pounds, he found that other men, while recognizing the power of his intellect, counted physique of importance in the political arena. Had he been six inches taller, a friend remarked, he might have been President.

With a thorough understanding of the rough and tumble of politics, Cox loved a verbal fight, but more as debater than pugilist. His intentions were not to overpower but to win his opponent to his own way of thinking. He showed little meanness of spirit or permanent hostility; rather, an innate friendliness ran through his relations with other men. With his bubbling good humor, effervescent wit, and kindly nature, he won the affections of many people but failed to command the allegiance of certain hard-headed political realists. Because he could not restrain his impulse to pun and joke, the real meat of his message often disappeared in bursts of laughter from his listeners. One long-time observer of Congress was sure that if Cox "could have suppressed his natural tendency in this direction, he might have gone a rung or two higher." [1] His genial disposition, so aptly characterized by the " sunbeams " of his constant allusions, led him to step aside too easily for more determined competitors. As Henry Adams phrased it, " It is the curse of politics that what one man gains, another man loses." [2] " He always smiles," Garfield, speaking of Cox, said with condescension.[3] Cox's connection with Tammany, while it helped to win elections, tended to arouse suspicion and to cast a shadow over his career. A colleague remarked that although " Mr. Cox was the best equipped and ablest politician of his party," yet he was " never fully trusted." " He did not attain the position " to which his talents entitled him because he appeared to " lack courage and conviction— a politician in search of mere majorities." [4]

Despite many failures, Cox successfully fulfilled the function of opposition party leader. His cutting attacks on the party in power were effective in keeping that party from engaging in further excesses. During the war President Lincoln took into account Cox's views on prisoner exchange, free speech, *habeas corpus*, and personal liberty. During reconstruction his steady insistence on general amnesty for ex-Confederates kept that issue in the political forefront. Cox, in opposition, also offered alternatives, such as his proposal for continued negotiation in the secession crisis, his proposal for a speedy end to the war through negotiation, and his proposal for tariff reduction and free trade. That these were not adopted did not lesson their validity or wisdom. Furthermore, he kept alive the spirit of constitutional, democratic government when it seemed threatened with extinction under the attacks of the Radicals during the Civil War and reconstruction.

Personally, Cox bore the marks of a successful politician. He possessed talent as a speaker, humor, tact, sympathy, a capacity for friendship, and a desire to help others. He often coined catch phrases and slogans that gained wide currency. He exhibited showmanship, courage, pugnacity, and good sense. As spokesman for the opposition, guardian of minorities, and pleader for the old order, he made his contribution to American politics.

Although a thorough partisan, he nevertheless maintained a certain independence of attitude, envied by other congressmen, which perhaps cost him important positions that went to lesser men.[5] His uncanny parliamentary skill was noted by " Czar " Reed, no mean parliamentarian himself: " Mr. Cox was not an orator . . . perhaps not a wit; but in action he was a whole skirmish line, and has covered more movements of the Democratic party, and led it out of more parliamentary pitfalls than any one of its orators and all its leaders put together." [6] As to Cox's place in American political history, he belongs on the second rung of the ladder. Never quite able to climb to the top by reaching the White House, nevertheless, for a generation he stood among the top three or four leaders of his party.

His career illustrates the problem of a political leader in a democratic government, who must discover the means of reconciling the demands of his constituents with his own beliefs and principles while keeping in mind the public interest. If democratic government is to function properly, the public service must have men of Cox's character, strong intellect, and broad experience. William M. Evarts best stated Cox's case: he was " a scholar . . . an editor . . . a diplomat . . . a wit; . . . and yet the warp and woof of his life was that of a member of Congress." Evarts added that " through thirty years among the eminent men of the Democratic party in the state of New York " there had been " no one that can be fairly considered as having been more engaged, and more usefully engaged, and more constantly engaged in public affairs than Mr. Cox." [7] It is only on the shoulders of such skillful, conscientious, energetic political leaders as Samuel Sullivan Cox—the man who hitched his wagon to a sunset—that democratic government in America can rest securely.

Chapter I

YEARS OF PREPARATION

1. H. J. Cox, article in Zanesville *Signal*, June 4, 1875.
2. William V. Cox and Milton H. Northrup, *Life of Samuel Sullivan Cox* (Syracuse, N. Y., 1899), pp. 17-21 (hereafter cited as Cox and Northrup, *Cox*); *Congressional Record*, 44 Cong., 1 sess., p. 987 (hereafter cited as *Cong. Rec.*).
3. Cox and Northrup, *Cox*, pp. 22-29.
4. William T. Utter, *The Frontier State*, 1803-1825 (Columbus, 1942), pp. 198, 200, 211-213, 317; Francis P. Weisenberger, *The Passing of the Frontier, 1825-1850* (Columbus, 1941), pp. 15-16; 104; Norris F. Schneider, *Y Bridge City* (Cleveland, 1950), pp. 78-115.
5. Ms minutes of the Board of Deacons and Trustees, Market Street Baptist Church, Zanesville, O., still surive for the years after 1844. These show that Ezekiel Cox was very active and held many church offices.
6. Cox and Northrup, *Cox*, pp. 38-39.
7. Records in registrar's and alumni offices, Ohio University, Athens, Ohio; *General Catalogues of the Ohio University, 1804-1857* (Athens, O., 1857), pp. 12-13.
8. Ohio University Alumni office has a photograph of Cox's mural. According to the late Professor Thomas N. Hoover of Ohio University, the original remains behind the wood panelled wall of the office of the dean of women.
9. Cox and Northrup, *Cox*, pp. 43-46.
10. *Ibid.*, pp. 45-56.
11. Ms records of the Athenian Literary Society, Ohio University Library; letter to Cox from Calvin D. Case, Hogo, Kansas, n. d., recalls days as fellow student at Ohio University: in the Cox Papers, Brown University Library (hereafter cited as Cox Papers, Brown.)
12. Cox and Northrup, *Cox*, pp. 43-44.
13. Letter to the author from Eugene B. White, secretary of Beta Chapter (Brown University) of Delta Phi fraternity, November 14, 1949.
14. Cox and Northrup, *Cox*, pp. 54-56.
15. *Ibid.*, pp. 48-51.
16. Samuel Sullivan Cox, "The Moravian and Gnattenhutten Massacre," *Knickerbocker Magazine*, XXVII (1846), 204-214.

17. James Buckingham, compiler, *The Ancestors of Ebenezer Buckingham . . . and His Descendants* (Chicago, 1892), pp. 96-98.

18. Samuel Sullivan Cox, *The Scholar as the True Progressive and Conservative* (Columbus, 1852).

19. Letter to G. P. Putnam from Cox, Columbus, October 17, 1853: in the Cox Papers, New York Public Library (hereafter cited as Cox Papers, NYPL).

20. *Columbus Dispatch*, June 9, 1933.

21. *Ohio Statesman*, May 19, 1853.

22. *Columbus Dispatch*, June 9, 1933.

23. Cox and Northrup, *Cox*, pp. 74-75.

24. Eugene H. Roseboom, *The Civil War Era, 1850-1873* (Columbus, 1944), pp. 4-10 (hereafter cited as Roseboom, *Civil War Era*).

25. Frederick J. Turner, *The United States, 1830-1850*, ed. Avery Craven (New York, 1935), Chapter VII.

26. Henry C. Hubbart, *The Older Middle West, 1840-1880* (New York, 1936), pp. 11-13, 47 (hereafter cited as Hubbart, *Older Middle West*).

27. Ralph H. Gabriel, *The Course of American Democratic Thought* (New York, 1940), pp. 14-25.

28. Hubbart, *Older Middle West*, pp. 11-13.

29. Roseboom, *Civil War Era*, p. 262.

30. *Ohio Statesman*, December 14, 1853.

31. Cox and Northrup, *Cox*, p. 77.

32. *Ohio State Journal*, March 3, 4, 1854.

33. Letter to Stephen A. Douglas from Cox, Columbus, March 24, 1854: in the Douglas Papers, University of Chicago Library (hereafter cited as Douglas Papers, U of C).

34. David H. Bradford, "The Background and Formation of the Republican Party in Ohio, 1844-1861" (doctoral dissertation, University of Chicago, 1947), pp. 122-126.

35. *Ohio State Journal*, July 14, 1854.

36. Roseboom, *Civil War Era*, pp. 286-293.

37. Cox and Northrup, *Cox*, p. 77.

38. John W. Forney, *Anecdotes of Public Men* (2 vols.; New York, 1873), I, 283.

39. Letter to (name illegible) from Cox, Columbus, March 18, April 19, 1856: in the Cox Papers, NYPL.

40. *Ohio Statesman*, February 28, 1856.

41. *Ibid.*, June 22, 1856.

42. Cleveland *Plain Dealer*, July 16, 23, 1856, quoted in Roseboom, *Civil War Era*, p. 319.

43. Letters to Cox from Charles J. Foster (Democratic national committee-man) Washington, August 21, 1856; and from William Bell, Newark, O., May 20, 1856: in the Cox Papers, Brown.
44. Cox and Northrup, *Cox*, pp. 223-224.
45. *Ohio Statesman*, September 21, 23, October 4, 1856.
46. *Ohio State Journal*, October 11, 1856.

Chapter II

A FLEDGLING CONGRESSMAN

1. *National Intelligencer*, September 8, 1857, quoted in Allan Nevins, *Ordeal of the Union* (2 vols.; New York, 1947), I, 47.
2. Letter to Franklin Pierce from Cox, Columbus, September 3, 1857: in the Franklin Pierce Papers, Library of Congress (Library of Congress will hereafter be cited as LC).
3. *Ohio State Journal*, November 4, 5, 11, 1857.
4. Roy F. Nichols, *The Disruption of American Democracy* (New York, 1948), pp. 132-137, 140-142 (hereafter cited as Nichols, *Disruption*).
5. Letters to Cox from George W. Houk, Dayton, Ohio, December 10, 1857; and from Charles J. Foster, Columbus, December 10, 1857: in the Douglas Papers, U of C.
6. Samuel Sullivan Cox, *Eight Years in Congress* (New York, 1865), p. 14 (hereafter cited as Cox, *Eight Years*); S. S. Cox, *Why We Laugh* (New York, 1880), p. 353.
7. *Congressional Globe*, 35 Cong., 1 sess., pp. 53-57 (hereafter cited as *Cong. Globe*).
8. *Ohio Statesman*, December 18, 19, 22, 1857.
9. Quoted in *ibid.*, December 29, 1857.
10. *Ohio State Journal*, December 17, 19, 21, 1857.
11. *Ohio Statesman*, February 21, 1858.
12. *House Report* No. 648, 36 Cong., 1 sess., pp. 282-285 (Covode Committee, Report on Kansas).
13. *Ohio Statesman*, March 13, 1858.
14. *Cong. Globe*, 35 Cong., 1 sess., pp. 261-263; S. S. Cox, *Three Decades of Federal Legislation* (Providence, 1885), pp. 75-76 (hereafter cited as Cox, *Three Decades*).
15. Letter to James Buchanan from Cox, Washington, December 21, 1857: in the James Buchanan Papers, Historical Society of Pennsylvania Library (hereafter cited as Buchanan Papers, HSPL).
16. *House Report* No. 648, 36 Cong., 1 sess., pp. 133-136.

17. Cox, *Eight Years*, p. 14.
18. Letter to Cox from Charles J. Foster, Columbus, February 2, 1858: in the Douglas Papers, U of C.
19. *House Report* No. 648, 36 Cong., 1 sess., pp. 229-230, 304-305, 309-310.
20. *Cong. Globe*, 35 Cong., 1 sess., pp. 1880-82.
21. Letters to Buchanan from Cox, Washington, May 18, 1858; and n. p., n. d., probably June, 1858: in the Buchanan Papers, HSPL; *House Report* No. 648, 36 Cong., 1 sess., p. 230.
22. Cox, *Eight Years*, p. 15; Cox, *Three Decades*, pp. 56-58.
23. *Ohio State Journal*, March 8, May 1, 1858.
24. *Cong. Globe*, 35 Cong., 1 sess., pp. 515-517.
25. *Ibid.*, p. 3026.
26. *Ibid.*, pp. 794-797, 2514.
27. *Cong. Rec.*, 47 Cong., 1 sess., p. 6743.
28. *Cong. Globe*, 35 Cong., 2 sess., pp. 1047, 1068.
29. Quoted in *Ohio Statesman*, July 6, 1858.
30. Letters to Cox from William Bell, Newark, O., May 5, 1857; from H. Beach, Washington, D. C., May 27, 1857; from Alex Walsh, Cincinnati, May 27, 1857; and from E. C. Granger, Fort Bliss, Texas, December 7, 1857: in the Cox Papers, Brown.
31. Letter to Cox from T. J. Andrews, Newark, O., February 23, 1858: in the Cox Papers, Brown.
32. *Ohio Statesman*, July 30, 1858.
33. *Scioto Gazette* (Chillicothe, O.), August 5, 1858.
34. Letters to Cox from T. S. Haskins, Pancoastburg, O., June 8, 1858; and from C. P. Brister, n. p., June 26, 1858: in the Cox Papers, Brown.
35. *Ohio State Journal*, August 18, 26, 30, September 1, 1858.
36. Cox, *Eight Years*, p. 15; Cox, *Three Decades*, pp. 57-58.
37. Cox, *Why We Laugh*, pp. 353-361.
38. *Ohio State Journal*, October 20, 1858.
39. Cox, *Why We Laugh*, p. 362.
40. *Ibid.*, p. 353.
41. Letters to Douglas from Cox, Chicago, August 26, 1859; Columbus, December 17, 1859, September 23, 1859: in the Douglas Papers, U of C.
42. Letters to Douglas from Fred Rife, Columbus, October 24, 1859; and from J. B. Marshall, Cincinnati, November 11, 1859: in the Douglas Papers, U of C.
43. Ms Minutes of Board of Deacons, Market Street Baptist Church, Zanesville, O., May 4, 13, 19, June 6, 1859; Zanesville *City Times*, June 16, 1859.
44. Letter to Buchanan from Cox, October 19, 30, 1859: in the Buchanan Papers, HSPL.

45. Letter to Cox from Buchanan, Washington, November 1, 1859; letter to Lewis Cass from Cox, Columbus, July 5, 1860: in the Buchanan Papers, HSPL.
46. J. Fred Rippy, *America and the Strife of Europe* (Chicago, 1938), pp. 55-76.
47. *Cong. Globe*, 35 Cong., 1 sess., pp. 420-435.
48. *Ibid.*, 36 Cong., 1 sess., pp. 1239-43.
49. *Ibid.*, 35 Cong., 2 sess., pp. 396-397.
50. *Ohio State Journal*, September 27, 1859.
51. Nichols, *Disruption*, pp. 232-242.
52. Avery Craven, *The Coming of the Civil War* (New York, 1942), pp. 407-412.
53. *Cong. Globe*, 36 Cong., 1 sess., pp. 74-80.
54. *Ibid.*, 36 Cong., 1 sess., pp. 581, 619.
55. Cox, *Three Decades*, p. 95.
56. *Ibid.*, pp. 59-61.
57. Letter to Lewis Cass from Cox, Columbus, July 5, 1860: in the Buchanan Papers, HSPL.
58. *Ohio Statesman*, July 6, 31, August 2, September 26, 1860.
59. *Ohio State Journal*, October 16, 1860.
60. Kenneth M. Stampp, *And the War Came: The North and the Secession Crisis, 1860-1861* (Baton Rouge, 1950), pp. 13-25.
61. *Cong. Globe*, 36 Cong., 2 sess., p. 36; 37 Cong., 3 sess., p. 1410.
62. Nichols, *Disruption*, pp. 440-441; Cox, *Three Decades*, p. 28.
63. James F. Rhodes, *The United States from the Compromise of 1850* (9 vols.; New York, 1902-1919), III, 254, 262-263 (hereafter cited as Rhodes, *History*).
64. Letter of Cox to George L. Converse, printed in the *Ohio Statesman*, January 31, 1861.
65. *Cong. Globe*, 36 Cong., 2 sess., pp. 372-377.

Chapter III

LEADER OF THE LOYAL OPPOSITION IN WAR TIME

1. Cox, *Three Decades*, pp. 64-80.
2. *Ohio Statesman*, January 31, 1861.
3. *New York Tribune*, November 9, 16, 30, 1860.
4. *Ohio State Journal*, November 28, 1860, March 27, 1861; Cincinnati *Commercial*, February 1, 1861.
5. Wood Gray, *The Hidden Civil War* (New York, 1942), pp. 36-39; Mary Scrugham, *The Peaceable Americans, 1860-1861* (Columbia Uni-

versity Studies in History, Economics, and Public Law, No. 96, New York, 1921), pp. 13-14; Elbert J. Benton, *The Movement for Peace Without Victory During the Civil War* (Western Reserve Historical Society, Collections No. 99, Cleveland, 1918), p. 3; George H. Porter, *Ohio Politics During the Civil War Period* (Columbia University Studies in History, Economics, and Public Law, No. 40, New York, 1911), p. 49.

6. *Ohio Statesman*, January 2, 1861; Cincinnati *Enquirer*, January 9, 10, 1861.

7. Gray, *The Hidden Civil War*, pp. 33-34.

8. Letter of Stephen A. Douglas to G. H. Lanphier, quoted in Allen Johnson, *Stephen A. Douglas* (New York, 1908), pp. 447-448.

9. Cox, *Three Decades*, p. 100.

10. Cox, *Eight Years*, p. 7.

11. James G. Randall, *The Civil War and Reconstruction* (New York, 1937), pp. 232-244 (hereafter cited as Randall, *Civil War*).

12. Quoted in Gray, *The Hidden Civil War*, p. 49; Cox, *Three Decades*, pp. 78-80.

13. *The Crisis*, April 18, 1861; *Ohio Statesman*, April 18, 1861; Cincinnati *Enquirer*, April 18, 1861.

14. *Cong. Globe*, 36 Cong., 2 sess., p. 137.

15. Gray, *The Hidden Civil War*, pp. 33-34, 39.

16. Cox and Northrup, *Cox*, p. 88.

17. Gray, *The Hidden Civil War*, p. 38; Albert L. Kohlmeier, *The Old Northwest as the Keystone of the Arch of the American Federal Union* (Bloomington, 1839), pp. 228-231.

18. Letters to Cox from Thomas G. Addison, July 11, 1861; from W. Fenwick, July 12, 1861; and from Charles M. Gould, March 3, July 17, 1861: in the Cox Papers, Brown.

19. *Ohio Statesman*, April 25, 1861; Cincinnati *Enquirer*, April 28, May 22, 1861.

20. Gray, *The Hidden Civil War*, pp. 46-51.

21. Clement L. Vallandigham, *Speeches, Arguments, Addresses and Letters of Clement L. Vallandigham* (New York, 1864), pp. 324-325.

22. *Cong. Globe*, 37 Cong., 1 sess., pp. 4-5, 95-96, 226.

23. *Ibid.*, pp. 331, 448, 458; Edward McPherson, *The Political History of the United States During the Great Rebellion* (Washington, 1865), p. 286 (hereafter cited as McPherson, *History of Rebellion*).

24. *Cong. Globe*, 37 Cong., 1 sess., pp. 35-37.

25. Letter to William H. English from Cox, Columbus, October 23, 1861: in English Papers, Indiana Historical Society Library.

26. Letter to Andrew Johnson from Cox, Washington, October 26, 1861: in the Johnson Papers, LC.

27. *Cincinnati Enquirer*, October 3, 19, November 1, August 4, 1861; *The Crisis*, August 29, September 1, 1861.
28. *Cong. Globe*, 37 Cong., 2 sess., p. 229.
29. Cox, *Three Decades*, pp. 243-244.
30. Randall, *Civil War*, p. 437.
31. Ben Perley Poore, *Perley's Reminiscences of Sixty Years in the Nation's Metropolis* (2 vols.; Philadelphia, 1886), I, 103.
32. *Cong. Globe*, 37 Cong., 2 sess., pp. 569-574, 242-249; Cox, *Eight Years*, pp. 216-236.
33. Letters to Cox from George L. Converse, Columbus, February 28, 1862; from Robert Harryman, Newark, O., January 26, 1862; from Charles Follett, Newark, O., February 4, 1862; from William H. English, Lexington, Ind., February 18, 1862; and from Murat Halstead, Cincinnati, February 26, 1862: in the Cox Papers, Brown.
34. Letter to Franklin Pierce from Cox, Washington, February 24, 1862: in the Pierce Papers, LC.
35. *Cong. Globe*, 37 Cong., 2 sess., p. 1649.
36. Randall, *Civil War*, pp. 371-373, 482-484.
37. *Cong. Globe*, 37 Cong., 2 sess., Appendix, pp. 242-249; Cox, *Eight Years*, pp. 236-258; *The Crisis*, June 18, 1862.
38. Letters to Cox from John G. Thompson, Columbus, March 26, 1862; from W. M. Anderson Seven Oaks [Va.?], May 5, 1862; from William D. Barrick, Fredonia, O., April 21, 1862; and from Murat Halstead, Cincinnati, February 26, 1862: in Cox Papers, Brown.
39. Letters to Cox from George L. Converse, Columbus, December 17, 1861; and from Willa G. Boggs, Springfield, O., March 25, 1862; from George L. Converse, March 15, 1862; and from Wayne Griswold, Columbus, April 15, 1863: in the Cox Papers, Brown.
40. Porter, *Ohio Politics During the Civil War Period*, pp. 96, 98-100.
41. *Ohio State Journal*, June 30, 1862.
42. *Cong. Globe*, 37 Cong., 2 Sess., App. p. 248.
43. *Ohio State Journal*, July 8, 1862.
44. *Ibid.*, August 9, September 12, 1862; Cox, *Three Decades*, p. 190.
45. Letter to John J. Crittenden from Cox, Springfield, O., September 23, 1862: in the Crittenden Papers, LC.
46. Cox, *Three Decades*, p. 190; Cox and Northrup, *Cox*, p. 90.
47. Abraham Lincoln, *Complete Works*, ed. John G. Nicolay and John Hay (10 vols.; New York, 1905), II, 239.
48. *Ohio Statesman*, October 17, 1862; *Ohio State Journal*, October 17, 20, 1862, December 6, 1862, January 5, 1863.
49. *The Crisis*, October 8, 15, 22, 1862.
50. Randall, *Civil War*, pp. 387-394; Cox, *Three Decades*, pp. 223-236.

51. Cox, *Three Decades*, p. 221.
52. *Cong. Globe*, 37 Cong., 3 sess., p. 2.
53. Letter to Manton Marble from Cox, December 5, 1862: in the Marble Papers, LC.
54. *Cong. Globe*, 37 Cong., 3 sess., pp. 21, 165.
55. Letter to Abraham Lincoln from Cox, Washington, December 5, 1862: in the R. T. Lincoln collection of Lincoln Papers, LC.
56. *Cong. Globe*, 37 Cong., 3 sess., pp. 94-100; *The Crisis*, December 24, 1862; Cox, *Eight Years*, pp. 259-261.
57. *Cong. Globe*, 37 Cong., 3 sess., pp. 281, 626, 916.
58. Randall, *Civil War*, p. 400.
59. Theodore C. Smith, *The Life and Letters of James A. Garfield* (2 vols.; New Haven, 1925), I, 362.
60. Cox, *Eight Years*, pp. 281-300; *The Crisis*, January 21, 1863.
61. *Cong. Globe*, 37 Cong., 3 sess., pp. 917-918, 921-923.
62. Letter to Manton Marble from Cox, Washington, March 11, 1863: in the Marble Papers, LC; letter to Cox from Erastus Corning, Albany, March 13, 1863: in the Cox Papers, Brown.
63. *Ohio Statesman*, March 8, 1863.
64. *The Crisis*, April 8, 15, 1863.
65. McPherson, *History of Rebellion*, p. 162.
66. *The Crisis*, May 2, 1863; J. L. Vallandigham, *The Life of Clement L. Vallandigham* (Baltimore, 1872), pp. 248-258.
67. The official testimony of the trial appears in Vallandigham, *Life*, pp. 263-283 and in *Official Records of the War of the Rebellion*, Ser. 1, Vol. XXIII, 12; Ser. 2, Vol. V, 485, 555-567, 633-646, 665-666, 705-706, 958-969; Vol. VII, 4-10, 16 (hereafter cited as *O. R.*)
68. *O. R.*, Ser. 2, Vol. V, 654.
69. Cox, *Three Decades*, p. 84.
70. Cox, *Eight Years*, pp. 327-334.
71. Cox, *Three Decades*, p. 236.
72. Cox, *Eight Years*, pp. 335-336.
73. Letter to Manton Marble from Cox, Columbus, June 14, 1863: in the Marble Papers, LC; Cox, *Three Decades*, pp. 227-232.
74. Letter to Lincoln from Cox, Columbus, June 14, 1863: in the R. T. Lincoln Collection of Abraham Lincoln Papers, LC.
75. Letter to Manton Marble from Cox, Chicago, June 27, 1863: in the Marble Papers, LC.
76. Letter to William H. Seward from Cox, Columbus, June 15, 1863: in the R. T. Lincoln Collection of Abraham Lincoln Papers, LC.
77. Letter to Manton Marble from Cox, Columbus, June 1, 1863: in the Marble Papers, LC.

78. *Ohio Statesman*, October 21, 1863; Cincinnati *Enquirer*, October 20, 1863; letter to Manton Marble from Cox, October 21, 1863: in the Marble Papers, LC.

79. *Cong. Globe*, 37 Cong., 1 sess., pp. 31, 117, 124; 2 sess., pp. 2292, 2621.

80. Letter to Cox from George L. Converse, Columbus, December 17, 1861: in the Cox Papers, Brown.

81. *Cong. Globe*, 37 Cong., 2 sess., pp. 119-122.

82. Cox, *Three Decades*, pp. 291-292.

83. Letter to Franklin Pierce from Cox, Washington, February 24, 1862: in the Pierce Papers, LC.

84. Cox, *Eight Years*, pp. 169-187.

85. Letter to Cox from George L. Converse, Columbus, January 25, 1862: in the Cox Papers, Brown.

86. Cox, *Three Decades*, p. 273.

87. Letters to Cox from David Fales, Biddeford, Maine, February 8, 1862; from William H. Seward, Washington, February 27, 1862; and from David Hoadly, New York March 24, 1862; in the Cox Papers, Brown.

88. Ms " Journal of Proceedings of Joint Commissioners Under the Convention Between the United States of America and the Republic of New Granada of the 10th of September 1857 ": in the National Archives of the United States.

89. S. S. Cox, *Before the New Granadian Claims Commission, in the Case of the Panama Railroad Company* (Washington, 1861).

90. S. S. Cox, *United States and Colombian Commission, Claim of Pacific Steamship Company* (Washington, 1866); also Mss in the National Archives of the United States, Claim No. 186 of Panama Railroad Co.; S. S. Cox, *Cases of Panama Railroad Company, Pacific Mail Steamship Company, and the United States Mail Steamship Company* (Washington, 1866).

91. Ms " Journal of Proceedings of Joint Commissioners ": in the National Archives of the U. S.

92. Tyler Dennett, *John Hay* (New York, 1934), p. 62; *Cong. Globe*, 38 Cong., 1 sess., p. 1166.

93. *Cong. Globe*, 37 Cong., 2 sess., p. 884.

94. *Ibid.*, 38 Cong., 2 sess., pp. 54-55.

95. *Ibid.*, pp. 48-53.

Chapter IV

DEFEAT IN 1864 AND REMOVAL TO NEW YORK

1. Letter to Cox from E. M. Etheridge, Washington, July 2, 1863: in the Cox Papers, Brown; *Cong. Globe*, 38 Cong., 2 sess., pp. 3, 1207, 1255.
2. Letter to Charles Lannan from Cox, Columbus, August 16, 1863: in the Charles Lannan Papers, LC.
3. Letter to David Todd from Cox, Columbus, November 2, 1863: Ms letter recently purchased from Parke-Bernet Galleries, New York; letter to Manton Marble from Cox, November 6, 1863: in the Marble Papers, LC.
4. Letter to Charles Lannan from Cox, November 23, 1863: in the Lannan Papers, LC; letter to Manton Marble from Cox, Washington, November 28, 1863: in the Marble Papers, LC.
5. *Cong. Globe*, 38 Cong., 1 sess., pp. 6-7, 33.
6. Cox, *Why We Laugh*, p. 128.
7. Carl Sandburg, *Abraham Lincoln: The War Years* (4 vols.; New York, 1936), II, 492.
8. *Cong. Globe*, 38 Cong., 1 sess., pp. 12, 34, 94, 259, 843, 970, 1428, 2880, 3521.
9. *Ibid.*, pp. 12, 34-35, 70-72, 189.
10. *Ibid.*, pp. 263-264.
11. *Ibid.*, pp. 99, 259, 871; letter to Franklin Pierce from Cox, Washington, March 17, 1864: in the Pierce Papers, LC.
12. George S. Boutwell, *Reminiscences of Sixty Years in Public Affairs* (2 vols.; New York, 1902), II, 8-9.
13. *Cong. Globe*, 38 Cong., 1 sess., pp. 1506-1512; Cox, *Eight Years*, pp. 98-113.
14. Letters to Cox from James Adams, Boston, Mass., April 16, 1864; and from James Atkins, Akron, O., January 29, 1864: in the Cox Papers, Brown.
15. *Cong. Globe*, 38 Cong., 1 sess., pp. 1626, 1634-1635; *The Crisis*, April 20, 1864; letter to Manton Marble from Cox, Washington, April 12, 1864: in the Marble Papers, LC.
16. *Ohio State Journal*, April 12, 1864.
17. Jacob D. Cox, *Military Reminiscences of the Civil War* (2 vols.; New York, 1900), II, 470.
18. *The Crisis*, December 16, 1863. This splinter group returned to the Methodist fold after the end of the war.
19. Quoted in Randall, *Civil War*, p. 620.
20. Letter to Cox from W. Borchard, Warren, O., March 10, 1864: in

the Cox Papers, Brown; letter to Manton Marble from Cox, Washington, May 2, 14, June 4, 1864: in the Marble Papers, LC; letter to George B. McClellan from Cox, Washington, June 9, 1864: in the McClellan Papers, LC; letter to Cox from George B. McClellan, Saratoga, June 20 [1864]: in the Madigan Collection of McClellan-Cox correspondence, New York Public Library (hereafter cited as Madigan Coll., NYPL).

21. Letter to Manton Marble from Cox, July 25, 1864: in the Marble Papers, LC; letters to Cox from McClellan, Orange, N. J., July 14, [1864]: in the Madigan Coll., NYPL.
22. *The Crisis*, August 3, 1864.
23. F. W. Chapman, *The Buckingham Family* (Hartford, Conn., 1872), p. 260.
24. Letter to Cox from Col. Durbin Ward, Atlanta, August 2, 1864: in the Cox Papers, Brown.
25. *The Crisis*, August 21, September 7, 1864.
26. Charles R. Wilson, "McClellan's Changing Views on the Peace Plank of 1864," *American Historical Reviews*, XXXVIII (April, 1933), 498-505.
27. Randall, *Civil War*, pp. 553-554, 621.
28. Letter to Cox from McClellan (n. p.), September 15 [1864]: in the Madigan Coll., NYPL; letter to Manton Marble from Cox, Columbus, September 6, 1864: in the Marble Papers, LC.
29. Letters to Cox from August Belmont, New York, September 2, 1864; and from Samuel L. M. Barlow, New York, October 7, 1864: in the Cox Papers, Brown.
30. Letter to Manton Marble from Cox, Columbus, September 20, 23, October 9, 1864: in the Marble Papers, LC; letter to Cox from McClellan, Orange, September 24 [1864]: in the Madigan Coll., NYPL; *Cong. Rec.*, 46 Cong., 1 sess., pp. 1936-1939; Sandburg, *Lincoln*, III, 569.
31. Letter to Cox from Samuel L. M. Barlow, New York, October 15, 1864: in the Cox Papers, Brown.
32. Letter to Manton Marble from Cox, Columbus, October 12, 1864: in the Marble Papers, LC; letter to Cox from McClellan, Orange, October 20 [1864]: in the Madigan Coll., NYPL.
33. Letter to Cox from Winfield Scott Hancock, Washington, December 17, 1864: in the Cox Papers, University of Chicago Library (hereafter cited as Cox Papers, U of C.).
34. *Cong. Globe*, 38 Cong., 2 sess., pp. 124-126, 275, 617, 665, 734-735, 776, 1123.
35. *Ibid.*, pp. 437-444; Cox, *Eight Years*, pp. 61-64.
36. Letter to Cox from Abraham Lincoln, Washington, January 31, 1864: Ms letter in possession of the Benjamin Book Shop, New York.

37. *Cong. Globe*, 38 Cong., 2 sess., pp. 1311-13, 1317; Cox, *Eight Years*, pp. 61-65.

38. Ohio General Assembly, *House Journal*, 1862, App., p. 33; 1863, p. 476.

39. *Ohio Statesman*, February 4, 1861.

40. *Cong. Globe*, 37 Cong., 2 sess., pp. 56, 60.

41. *Ibid.*, 37 Cong., 3 sess., pp. 598-600, 633, 637.

42. *Ibid.*, 38 Cong., 1 sess., pp. 708-713; Cox, *Eight Years*, pp. 350-370.

43. *Cong. Globe*, 38 Cong., 1 sess., pp. 1766-67, 2095, 2107-08; Cox, *Eight Years*, pp. 370-390.

44. Letters to Manton Marble from Cox, Washington, December 7, 21, 1864, January 13, 17, 1865: in the Marble Papers, LC.

45. Cox, *Eight Years*, p. 397; Edward C. Kirkland, *The Peacemakers of 1864* (New York, 1927), *passim*.

46. *Cong. Globe*, 38 Cong., 2 sess., pp. 237-242; letter to Cox from James Guthrie, Louisville, January 22, 1865: in the Cox Papers, Brown; Cox, *Eight Years*, pp. 398-416; Cox, *Three Decades*, pp. 327-328.

47. Letter to Manton Marble from Cox, Washington, January 18, 26, 1865: in the Marble Papers, LC.

48. A speech by William H. Seward delivered at Auburn, N. Y., October 31, 1868, quoted in Cox, *Three Decades*, p. 274.

49. W. J. Rhees, *The Smithsonian Institution, Documents Relative to Its Origin and History, 1835-1899* (2 vols.; Washington, 1901), I, 279; G. Brown Goode, "The Origin of National Scientific and Educational Institutions in the United States," *American Historical Association, Annual Report*, 1889, p. 124.

50. Letter to Manton Marble from Cox, Washington, March 12, 1865: in the Marble Papers, LC.

51. Gray, *The Hidden Civil War*, p. 220.

52. Everett P. Wheeler, *Sixty Years of American Life* (New York, 1917), p. 155.

53. James Buckingham, *The Ancestors of Ebenezer Buckingham*, p. 39.

54. Cox and Northrup, *Cox*, p. 96.

Chapter V

RETURN TO POLITICS

1. James G. Blaine, *Twenty Years of Congress* (2 vols.; Norwich, 1884-1886), II, 434.

2. Letters to the Secretary of State from Cox, New York, June 19, 25,

1866; June 14, August 20, December 18, 1867: in the Department of State, Miscellaneous Letters, United States National Archives.

3. Cox, *Three Decades*, p. 240.

4. Letter to Manton Marble from Cox, Washington, February 20, 1866: in the Marble Papers, LC; letter to Andrew Johnson from Cox, New York, June 2, 1866: in the Johnson Papers, LC.

5. Letters to Cox from R. W. Grundy, New York, February 15, 1866; from J. F. Driggs, Washington, March 7, 1866; from L. W. Emerson, February 15, 1866; and from F. Hassaurech, Cincinnati, March 25, 1886: in the Cox Papers, Brown.

6. Letters to Cox from M. L. Bryan, London, O., January 9, 1866; and from T. H. Sites, Newark, O., July 22, 1866: in the Cox Papers, Brown.

7. Letters to Manton Marble from Cox, New York, September 18, 1866; Washington, September 21, 1866; New York, October 7, 1866: in the Marble Papers, LC.

8. Letter to Andrew Johnson from Cox, November 24, 1866: in the Johnson Papers, LC; letter to William H. Seward from Cox, New York, December 24, 1866: in the Cox Papers, Ohio State Historical Society Library; Cox and Northrup, *Cox*, p. 21.

9. Letters to Manton Marble from Cox, New York, September 22, 1867; Zanesville, O., October 4, 1867: in the Marble Papers, LC; letters to Cox from William Bell, Newark, O., January 12, 1867: in the Cox Papers, Brown; *Memorial Addresses on the Life and Character of Samuel Sullivan Cox* (Washington, 1890), pp. 243-244.

10. Letter to Manton Marble from Cox, New York, November 11, 1867: in the Marble Papers, LC.

11. Letter to Manton Marble from Cox, Washington, December 16, 1867: in the Marble Papers, LC; letter to Cox from Edward Cooper, Washington, December 18, 1867: in the Cox Papers, Brown.

12. Letter to Andrew Johnson from Cox, Washington, January 31, 1868: in the Cox Papers, NYPL; letter to Manton Marble from Cox, Washington, February 2, 1868: in the Marble Papers, LC; Cox, *Three Decades*, p. 591.

13. Letter to Commissioner of Pensions from Cox, Washington, February 19, 1868: in the Cox Papers, LC; letter to Cox from F. A. Aiken, Washington, June 22, 1868: in the Cox Papers, Brown.

14. Howard K. Beale, *The Critical Year* (New York, 1930), *passim.*

15. Cox, *Three Decades*, p. 245.

16. *Ibid.*, p. 589.

17. *Ibid.*, pp. 581, 593-594; Claude G. Bowers, *The Tragic Era* (Cambridge, 1929), pp. 194-197.

18. Howard K. Beale, "The Tariff and Reconstruction," and "On Rewriting Reconstruction History," *American Historical Review*, XLIV (1939), 276-294; XLV (1940), 807-827.

19. Letter to J. W. Schuckers (Chase's secretary) from Cox, New York, May 11, 1868: in the Chase Papers, Historical Society of Pennsylvania Library.

20. Charles H. Coleman, *The Election of 1868*, Columbia University Studies in History, Economics, and Public Law No. 392 (New York, 1933), pp. 102-114.

21. *Official Proceedings of the Democratic National Convention* (New York, 1868), p. 216.

22. Gustavus Myers, *The History of Tammany Hall* (2nd ed.; New York, 1916), p. 216.

23. Coleman, *Election 1868*, pp. 200-201, 213-214, 239-246; Cox, *Three Decades*, p. 614.

24. Letter to Andrew Johnson from Cox, New York, July 23, 1868: in the Johnson Papers, LC; letter to Manton Marble from Cox, New York, July 26, 1868: in the Marble Papers, LC; letter to Samuel J. Tilden from Cox, New York, August 27, 1868: in the Tilden Papers, NYPL.

25. Letter to Cox from George B. McClellan, Orange, October 26, [1868]: in the Madigan Coll., NYPL.

26. New York *Tribune* (semi-weekly ed.), October 13, 30, 1868; letter to Manton Marble from Cox, New York, October 28, November 23, 1868: in the Marble Papers, LC.

27. New York *Tribune* (semi-weekly ed.), November 3, 1868.

28. *Ibid.*, November 20, 1868; *Congressional Directory*, 41 Cong., 1 sess., p. 67; *Harper's Weekly*, November 28, 1868; letter to Cox from George B. McClellan, n. p., November 7, [1868]: in the Madigan Coll., NYPL.

29. *Congressional Directory*, 41 Cong., 1 sess., p. 67; *Manual of the Corporation of the City of New York* (New York, 1869).

30. *Ninth Census of the United States, 1870* (Washington, 1872), I, 213.

31. Letters to Manton Marble from Cox, New York, November (no day), 1868; November 23, 1868: in the Marble Papers, LC; Cox and Northrup, *Cox*, p. 98.

32. Letters to Cox from George Wilks, Paris, December 23, 1868: in the Cox Papers, Brown; letters to Hugh McCulloch from Cox, Nice, France, January 9, March 23, 1869: in the Cox Papers, LC; Cox and Northrup, *Cox*, p. 99; letters to Manton Marble from Cox, Nice, France, January 10, March 23, 1869; Mentone, France, February 13, 1869; Ajaccio, Corsica, March 10, 1869: in the Marble Papers, LC.

33. Ellis P. Oberholtzer, *A History of the United States Since the Civil War*

(5 vols.; New York, 1926-1931), II, 198 (hereafter cited as Oberholtzer, *History*).

34. Worthington C. Ford, ed., *Letters of Henry Adams, 1858-1891* (Boston, 1930), p. 149.

35. *The Nation*, September 21, 1869.

36. New York *Tribune* (semi-weekly ed.), November 6, 1868; Coleman, *Election 1868*, p. 365.

37. *Cong. Globe*, 41 Cong., 2 sess., pp. 9-10; *Harper's Weekly*, December 18, 1869.

38. *Cong. Globe*, 41 Cong., 2 sess., p. 978.

39. Shelby M. Cullom, *Fifty Years of Public Service* (Chicago, 1911), pp. 141-142.

40. Letter to Manton Marble from Cox, Washington, December 17, 1869: in the Marble Papers, LC.

41. New York *Tribune* (semi-weekly ed.), May 29, 1869.

42. Ida M. Tarbell, *The Tariff in Our Times* (New York, 1911), pp. 56-59.

43. *Cong. Globe*, 41 Cong., 2 sess., pp. 110, 263, 893, 1125, 1316, 1474, 2209, 3998; 102, 916, 978, 3724; App., pp. 193, 272-273; New York *Tribune* (semi-weekly ed.), December 21, 1869.

44. *Cong. Globe*, 41 Cong., 2 sess., App., pp. 2239-2250.

45. *The Nation*, May 5, 1870.

46. *Cong. Globe*, 41 Cong., 2 sess., pp. 2506-13, 2254, 2589, 2690, 2760-61, 2972, 3788, 4107.

47. *The Nation*, July 21, 1870.

48. *Cong. Globe*, 41 Cong., 2 sess., pp. 75, 99, 190-191, 241, 4474, 5066.

49. *Ibid.*, pp. 4437-43, 4966, 4970.

50. *House Report*, No. 31, 41 Cong., 2 sess., p. 289.

51. Letter to Manton Marble from Cox, Washington, February 27, 1870: in the Marble Papers, LC.

52. *Cong. Globe*, 41 Cong., 2 sess., pp. 497-500; Edward McPherson, *The Political History of the United States During Reconstruction* (Washington, 1870), pp. 572-576 (hereafter cited as McPherson, *Reconstruction*).

53. McPherson, *Reconstruction*, pp. 576-579.

54. *Cong. Globe*, 41 Cong., 2 sess., pp. 281-283, 1766.

55. William A. Russ, Jr., "Congressional Disfranchisement, 1866-1898," (doctoral dissertation, University of Chicago, 1933), pp. 183-190.

56. *Cong. Globe*, 41 Cong., 2 sess., pp. 103, 1466, 3032-33, 3150, 3494-95; Edward McPherson, *Handbook of Politics, 1870* (Washington, 1871), pp. 582-583 (hereafter cited as McPherson, *Handbook*).

57. *Cong. Globe,* 41 Cong., 2 sess., App., pp. 397-401, 3809, 3884.

58. *Cong. Globe*, 41 Cong., 2 sess., pp. 795-797, 1010-12, 1305; New York

Tribune (semi-weekly ed.), December 17, 1869; *Harper's Weekly*, December 11, 1869.

59. Letters to Secretary of State from Cox, December 18, 1869, January 5, December 10, 1870: in the Department of State, Miscellaneous Letters, National Archives of the United States.

60. *Cong. Globe*, 41 Cong., 2 sess., pp. 70, 3955, 128-129, 4322, 5601, 4846-47.

61. *Ibid.*, pp. 522, 3690, 3725, 2777, 4110, 4736, 5351, 5250.

62. *Ibid.*, p. 3774.

63. New York *World*, October 7, 14, 1870.

64. *The Nation*, July 7, 1870.

65. New York *World*, October 11, 18, 21, 28, November 5, 1870; New York *Tribune* (semi-weekly ed.), October 25, 28, November 1, 4, 8, 11, 25, 1870.

66. Letter to Manton Marble from Cox, Washington, December 12, 1870: in the Marble Papers, LC.

67. *Cong. Globe*, 42 Cong., 2 sess., pp. 1217, 2017-18, 3035, 3209, 3234, 3305, 3341, 3450, 3514; Frederick W. Taussig, *The Tariff History of the United States* (New York, 1923), pp. 185-189 (hereafter cited as Taussig, *Tariff*).

68. *Cong. Globe*, 41 Cong., 3 sess., pp. 25, 119, 332; 42 Cong., 2 sess., pp. 1301-06, 1692, 1722, 1813, 1867, 2696-98.

69. *Ibid.*, 41 Cong., 3 sess., pp. 108-109, 138, 174, App., pp. 137-142; Cox, *Three Decades*, p. 595; *The Nation*, December 29, 1870; letter to Manton Marble from Cox, Washington, December 17, 1870: in the Marble Papers, LC.

70. *Cong. Globe*, 41 Cong., 2 sess., p. 886; App., pp. 302-305; Cox, *Three Decades*, p. 604; McPherson, *Handbook, 1872*, pp. 28-29.

71. James D. Richardson, comp., *Messages and Papers of the Presidents* (10 vols.; Washington, 1898), VII, 153 (hereafter cited as Richardson, *Messages*).

72. *Cong. Globe,* 42 Cong., 2 sess., pp. 2783, 3381, 3744-45, 3796.

73. *Ibid.*, 41 Cong., 2 sess., pp. 3809; 41 Cong., 3 sess., App., pp. 127-132; 42 Cong., 1 sess., pp. 451-454; Cox, *Three Decades*, pp. 476-479.

74. James McGurrin, *Bourke Cockran, A Free Lance in American Politics* (New York, 1948), p. 23 (hereafter cited as McGurrin, *Cockran*).

75. *Cong. Globe*, 42 Cong., 2 sess., pp. 1120-21; *House Report*, No. 22, 42 Cong., 2 sess., pp. 1-100, 289, 588; Cox, *Three Decades*, p. 475.

76. Fred H. Harrington, *Fighting Politician: Major-General N. P. Banks* (Philadelphia, 1948), pp. 189-192 (hereafter cited as Harrington, *Banks*).

77. *Cong. Globe*, 41 Cong., 3 sess., pp. 66-67, 408, 416, 696-698, App., p. 129; New York *Tribune* (semi-weekly ed.), December 13, 1870.

78. *Cong. Globe*, 41 Cong., 2 sess., pp. 4443-45; 42 Cong., 2 sess., p. 301; App., pp. 55-56, 309; Cox and Northrup, *Cox*, pp. 167-169.

79. *Cong. Globe*, 41 Cong., 3 sess., pp. 32-33.

80. *The United States Coast Guard—Its History, Vessels, and Doctrine* (Washington, c. 1945), pp. 30-32; *Cong. Globe*, 41 Cong., 3 sess., pp. 1607-08; 42 Cong., 1 sess., p. 641; 2 sess., pp. 1341; Cox and Northrup, *Cox*, pp. 201-202, 212.

81. Letter to Manton Marble from Cox, Washington, February 25, 1871: in the Marble Papers, LC; Bruce R. Trimble, *Chief Justice Waite* (Princeton, 1938), p. 129; letter to E. B. Washburne from Cox, New York, June 5, 1871: in the Washburne Papers, LC; *Cong. Globe*, 42 Cong., 2 sess., pp. 370, 1959.

82. Letter to the author from Victor H. O'Neill, executive secretary, Delta Phi fraternity, New York, June 1, 1950.

83. *Cong. Globe*, 42 Cong., 2 sess., pp. 108-110, 1033; 21 Cong., 3 sess., pp. 566, 1920; App., pp. 127-132; Horace Merrill, *The Bourbon Democracy of the Upper Mississippi Valley, 1865-1900* (Baton Rouge, 1953), pp. 64-65.

84. Myers, *The History of Tammany Hall*, pp. 229, 237, 245-247; DeAlva S. Alexander, *A Political History of the State of New York* (3 vols.; New York, 1909-23), III, 247, 266, 272-275 (hereafter cited as Alexander, *Political History*).

85. *Cong. Globe*, 42 Cong., 2 sess., pp. 771-772.

86. Rhodes, *History*, VI, 417-483, 430.

87. *Official Proceedings of the Democratic National Convention*, 1872 (Baltimore, 1872), pp. 31, 58; New York *World*, July 4, 5, 9, 10, 11, 1872.

88. *Harper's Weekly*, February 10, 1872.

89. New York *World*, August 19, September 6, 1872.

90. Rhodes, *History*, VI, 431; *The Nation*, July 11, 1872; Oberholtzer, *History*, III, 65; Cox, *Three Decades*, p. 627.

91. S. S. Cox, *Grant or Greeley?* (New York, 1872).

92. Letter to Parke Godwin from Cox, New York, September 19, 1872: in the Bryant-Godwin Papers, NYPL.

93. New York *Tribune* (semi-weekly ed.), October 8, 25, 29, November 7, 1872; New York *World*, October 29, November 5, 1872.

94. Letter to Cox from James W. Bates, Ft. Wood, New York, November 7, 1872: in the Cox Papers, Brown.

95. Letter to Cox from Lyman Tremaine, Albany, November 11, 1872: in the Cox Papers, Brown.

96. New York *Tribune* (semi-weekly ed.), November 8, 26, 1872; New

York *World*, November 6, 1872; Cox, *Three Decades*, pp. 627-628; Cox and Northrup, *Cox*, pp. 104-105.

97. *Cong. Globe*, 42 Cong., 3 sess., pp. 10, 226, 2111.

98. *Ibid.*, pp. 11, 357; *Appleton Annual Cyclopedia, 1873* (New York, 1874), p. 188.

99. *Cong. Globe*, 42 Cong., 3 sess., p. 1833.

100. *Ibid.*, 2 sess., pp. 19, 46, 55, 234, 420, 754-758, 1475; App., pp. 117-120.

101. *Ibid.*, pp. 1903-05; New York *Tribune* (semi-weekly ed.), March 7, 1873; Cox and Northrup, *Cox*, pp. 106-107.

Chapter VI

DEMOCRATIC REVIVAL, 1873-1878

1. Letter to Manton Marble from Cox, Washington, January 9, 1873: in the Marble Papers, LC; Cox and Northrup, *Cox*, p. 108; *Manual of the Corporation of the City of New York*, p. 223.

2. *Ninth Census of the United States, 1870*, I, 213, 439, 599.

3. Frank Weitenkampf, *Manhattan Kaleidoscope* (New York, 1947), pp. 1-9, 14-16.

4. Alexander, *Political History*, III, 308-310, 325.

5. New York *World*, September 19, 20, 27, 1873; Rhodes, *History*, VII, 43-48; Horace Merrill, "Bourbon Democracy of the Upper Middle West, 1865-1896," (doctoral dissertation, University of Wisconsin, 1943), pp. 105, 129-130.

6. Ralph R. Tingley, "American Cobden Clubs" (master's thesis, University of Chicago, 1947), p. 97.

7. New York *World*, August 19, September 1, October 2, 3, 24, 25, 30, 31, 1873; New York *Tribune* (semi-weekly ed.), March 11, May 20, June 20, 1873; letter to Manton Marble from Cox, New York, October 13, 1873: in the Marble Papers, LC.

8. November 5, 7, 1873.

9. New York *World*, December 2, 19, 1873; *Cong. Rec.*, 43 Cong., 1 sess., pp. 6, 74, 2083, 3939.

10. Letter to Manton Marble from Cox, Washington, December 7, 1873: in the Marble Papers, LC.

11. *Cong. Rec.*, 43 Cong., 1 sess., pp. 1076-77, 2364, 2835, 2876-82; John Sherman, *Recollections of Forty Years* (2 vols.; New York, 1893), I, 508; Rhodes, *History*, VII, 53-64.

12. New York *Tribune* (semi-weekly ed.), November 11, 18, 1873; *The*

Nation, November 20, 27, 1873; Rhodes, *History*, VII, 31-32; *Cong. Rec.*, 43 Cong., 1 sess., pp. 62, 181, 3172; 1160, 1241-43, 2198-2200, 3126-28, 3778-4107, 985, 1131, 2033; Chester L. Barrows, *William M. Evarts* (Chapel Hill, 1941), pp. 224-225; Allan Nevins, *Hamilton Fish* (New York, 1936), pp. 667-675.

13. Letter to N. P. Banks from Cox, November 17, 1874, quoted in Harrington, *Banks*, p. 203.

14. New York *World*, April 7, 1874, September 10, 1874; Alexander, *Political History*, p. 310.

15. New York *Tribune*, (semi-weekly ed.), October 16, 1874; Alexander, *Political History*, pp. 314-318; New York *World*, October 15, 16, 28, 1874.

16. New York *World*, November 4, 13, 1874; Alexander *Political History*, p. 319.

17. Letter to Manton Marble from Cox, Washington, February 25, 1874: in the Marble Papers, LC; *Cong. Rec.*, 43 Cong., 2 sess., pp. 19, 344, 381, 436, 643, 1125-28.

18. *Cong. Rec.*, 44 Cong., 2 sess., pp. 208-219; Richardson, *Messages*, VII, 286; Sherman, *Recollections of Forty Years*, II, 520-521; letter to Samuel J. Tilden from Cox, Washington, December 12, 1874: in the Tilden Papers, LC.

19. *Cong. Rec.*, 44 Cong., 2 sess., pp. 260, 287, 378, 903, 1511-13; Cox and Northrup, *Cox*, p. 109; David S. Muzzey, *James G. Blaine* (New York, 1934), p. 72.

20. Letter to Cox from Mark Twain, Hartford, February 4, 1875: Ms letter in possession of Sidney L. Kraus of Philadelphia.

21. Letter to James M. Comly from Cox, New York, March 23, 1875: in the Comly Papers, Ohio Historical Society Library.

22. Cox and Northrup, *Cox*, p. 242.

23. New York *Tribune*, November 23, 30, December 7, 1875.

24. Cox and Northrup, *Cox*, p. 237; *Cong. Rec.*, 44 Cong., 1 sess., pp. 10, 250-251, 1146-53; 3042, 3655, 3880.

25. *Cong. Rec.*, 44 Cong., 1 sess., p. 167; letter to Thomas F. Bayard from Fernando Wood, Washington, December 10, 1875: in the Bayard Papers, LC.

26. *Cong. Rec.*, 44 Cong., 1 sess., pp. 320-325, 405-407, 420; Blaine, *Twenty Years of Congress*, II, 554; Muzzey, *James G. Blaine*, p. 79; New York *World*, January 11, 1876.

27. *Cong. Rec.*, 44 Cong., 1 sess., pp. 208, 769, 801, 1681, 4707.

28. *Ibid.*, pp. 1302, 1312, 3746-48, 4556, 4563, 5218, 5232.

29. *Ibid.*, p. 1590; letter to Secretary of State from Cox, Washington, Febru-

ary 5, 1876: in the Department of State, Miscellaneous Letters, United States National Archives.

30. *Cong Rec.*, 44 Cong., 1 sess., pp. 2699, 2817, 4431; App., pp. 178-184, 2067, 2617, 2232-42, 2669, 4476, 1812.

31. *Cong. Rec.*, 44 Cong., 1 sess., pp. 414, 1540, 1892, 2502, 4708, 4716, 5331-34, 5642; Champ Clark, *My Quarter Century of American Politics* (2 vols.; New York, 1920), I, 165.

32. Letter to Manton Marble from Cox, February 7, 28, 1876: in the Marble Papers, LC.

33. Cox and Northrup, *Cox,* p. 112; *Cong. Rec.*, 44 Cong., 1 sess., pp. 4708, 4716.

34. Matthew Josephson, *The Politicos, 1865-1896* (New York, 1938), pp. 219-220; Denis T. Lynch, *The Wild Seventies* (New York, 1911), pp. 362-364; New York *World,* June 20, 23, 26, 28, 1876.

35. New York *World,* June 29, 30, 1876; *Official Proceedings of the Democratic National Convention* (St. Louis, 1876), pp. 69-74.

36. Allan Nevins, *Abram S. Hewitt, with Some Account of Peter Cooper* (New York, 1935), pp. 305-308 (hereafter cited as Nevins, *Hewitt*).

37. Paul L. Haworth, *The Hayes-Tilden Disputed Election of 1876* (Cleveland, 1906), pp. 16, 38 (hereafter cited as Haworth, *Election of 1876*); Josephson, *The Politicos, 1865-1896*, pp. 220-223.

38. Letters to Samuel J. Tilden from Cox, Washington, July 28, 1876; and from Francis Kernan, Utica, New York, September 1, 1876: in the Tilden Papers, NYPL; New York *World,* October 14, 28, 31, 1876.

39. New York *World,* November 8, 9, 1876; Nevins, *Hewitt*, pp. 328-329; Haworth, *Election of 1876*, pp. 63-115.

40. Letter to M. Ashe from Cox, New York, November 16, 1876: in the Hayes Memorial Library, Fremont, Ohio.

41. Haworth, *Election of 1876*, pp. 63-155; Nevins, *Hewitt*, pp. 328-329; New York *World,* November 10, 15, 22, 29, 1876.

42. The Tilden Papers in NYPL contain hundreds of congratulatory letters and telegrams; letter to Tilden from Cox, New York, November 15, 1876; letter to (unknown) from Cox, November 15, 1876: in the Tilden Papers, NYPL.

43. Letter to Billy Florence from Cox, New York, November 9, 1876: in the Cox Papers, New York Historical Society Library; New York *World,* November 9, 1876.

44. New York *World,* November 2, 5, 1876; Don C. Seitz, *The Dreadful Decade* (Indianapolis, 1926), pp. 293-294; *Cong. Rec.*, 44 Cong., 2 sess., p. 6.

45. Cox, *Three Decades,* pp. 636-637, 639.

46. Letter to William E. Dodge from Abram S. Hewitt, Washington, December 17, 1876: in the Cooper-Hewitt Papers, Cooper Union Library.
47. Lynch, *The Wild Seventies*, p. 426; M. H. Northrup, " A Grave Crisis in American History," *Century Magazine* LXII (1901), 923-924; *Cong. Rec.*, 44 Cong., 2 sess., pp. 197-99, 930-939.
48. *Cong. Rec.*, 44 Cong., 2 sess., pp. 231-234, 671; Cox, *Three Decades*, pp. 649-650; Herman V. Ames, " Proposed Amendments to the Constitution of the United States during the First Century of its History," *American Historical Association Report, 1896* (2 vols.; Washington, 1896), II, 397.
49. New York *World*, January 25, 28, 29, 30, 1877.
50. Cox, *Three Decades*, pp. 652, 659-660.
51. *Cong. Rec.*, 44 Cong., 2 sess., pp. 1477-1506, 1685, 1690, 2011; Haworth, *Election of 1876*, pp. 224-233; Cox and Northrup, *Cox*, pp. 159-162; Nevins, *Hewitt*, pp. 371-373.
52. *Cong. Rec.*, 44 Cong., 2 sess., pp. 1487-1503.
53. *Cong. Rec.*, 44 Cong., 2 sess., pp. 2034, 2049, 2067-68; C. Vann Woodward, *Reunion and Reaction* (Boston, 1951), pp. 51-67, 101-149.
54. *Cong. Rec.*, 44 Cong., 2 sess., pp. 201, 240-241, 1154, 1394-99, 1644-50; 249-250; 205-207.
55. Charles R. Williams, ed., *Diary and Letters of Rutherford B. Hayes* (5 vols.; Columbus, 1924), II, 426.
56. Cox and Northrup, *Cox*, pp. 241-242.
57. Cox, *Three Decades*, pp. 93, 95.
58. Letter to R. B. Hayes from Cox, Aiken, South Carolina, March 20, 1877: in the Hayes Papers, Hayes Memorial Library; letter to Manton Marble from Cox, Cincinnati, May 7, 1877: in the Marble Papers, LC.

Chapter VII

CONGRESSIONAL UPS AND DOWNS

1. Ms letters in possession of Carnegie Book Shop, 140 E. 58th Street, New York.
2. James Bryce, *The American Commonwealth* (2 vols.; New York, 1891), I, 143; Cox, *Why We Laugh*, pp. 153, 184-185.
3. Nevins, *Hewitt*, p. 401.
4. Cox, *Three Decades*, p. 669.
5. Worthington C. Ford, ed., *Letters of Henry Adams, 1858-1891* (Boston, 1930), pp. 303-304 (hereafter cited as Ford, *Adams Letters*).

6. Josephson, *Politicos, 1865-1896*, pp. 251-252.
7. Letters to Cox from Edward McPherson, Washington, October 3, 1877; from Aaron Sheady, Gettysburg, November 16, 1877; from Patrick Mahon, Rochester, N. Y., October 28, 1877; from H. J. Hewitt, New York, October 10, 1877; from Amasa J. Parker, Albany, October 12, 1877; from William T. Grace, Washington, December 18, 1877; from George L. Converse, Columbus, Ohio, October 18, 1877; and from J. T. Irvine, Zanesville, Ohio, November 7, 1877: in the Cox Papers, Brown.
8. *Cong. Rec.*, 45 Cong., 2 sess., pp. 350, 814, 2402, 2154, 4384; App., p. 86; Wheeler, *Sixty Years of American Life*, p. 150; letter to D. A. Wells from Cox, Washington, April 2, 1878: in the Wells Papers, NYPL.
9. Oberholtzer, *History*, IV, 20-33; Cox, *Three Decades*, pp. 670-672; *Cong. Rec.*, 45 Cong., 1 sess., pp. 228-229, 232, 465; 2 sess., pp. 1419-20.
10. *Cong. Rec.*, 45 Cong., 1 sess., pp. 166, 262.
11. *Ibid.*, 2 sess., pp. 2778-90.
12. *Ibid.*, pp. 4569-71, 4591, 4687.
13. *Ibid.*, pp. 103, 1664, 2642, 4311, 4402, 4585.
14. *House Report*, No. 701, 45 Cong., 2 sess.; Barrows, *William M. Evarts*, pp. 351-362.
15. *Cong. Globe*, 40 Cong., 1 sess., p. 425.
16. *Cong. Rec.*, 45 Cong., 1 sess., pp. 133, 172, 243, 306, 370; 2 sess., pp. 1574, 3322-25.
17. *Ibid.*, 1 sess., pp. 4881-82.
18. *Ibid.*, pp. 1707-13.
19. *Ibid.*, pp. 2034-35.
20. *Ibid.*, pp. 2493-94, 2918.
21. *Ibid.*, pp. 2798-99, 1707-09.
22. Letter to R. B. Hayes from John Livingston, New York, March 17, 1878, enclosing clippings of Cox's statements from the New York *Sun* and the Cincinnati *Enquirer*: in the Hayes Papers, Hayes Memorial Library; Cox, *Three Decades*, pp. 630-633, 667-668.
23. Letter to Samuel J. Tilden from Cox, Washington, June 17, 1878: in the Tilden Papers, NYPL.
24. *Cong. Rec.*, 45 Cong., 2 sess., pp. 2086, 2094.
25. New York *World*, June 5, 1878.
26. New York *World*, June 29, 1878; Cox and Northrup, *Cox*, pp. 11-14.
27. Quoted in Weitenkampf, *Manhattan Kaleidoscope*, p. 17.
28. Alexander, *Political History*, pp. 378-384, 389-396; Matthew J. Breen, *Thirty Years of New York Politics* (New York, 1899), pp. 234-242; *Appleton's Annual Cyclopedia, 1878*, pp. 624-625; Nevins, *Hewitt*, pp. 432-433.
29. New York *World*, October 22, 1878.

30. *Ibid.*, October 17, 24, 26, November 6, 1878; Alexander, *Political History*, p. 397.
31. DeAlva S. Alexander, *History and Procedure of the House of Representatives* (Boston, 1916), p. 398 (hereafter cited as Alexander, *House History*).
32. *Cong. Rec.*, 46 Cong., 1 sess., pp. 1725, 1988; 2 sess., pp. 3431; Cox and Northrup, *Cox*, pp. 177-188; Barrows, *William M. Evarts*, p. 404.
33. *Cong. Rec.*, 46 Cong., 2 sess., pp. 393, 1433, 2262-63.
34. *Ibid.*, pp. 2689, 4251; *House Report*, No. 1121, 46 Cong., 2 sess.
35. Barrows, *William M. Evarts*, pp. 363-367.
36. *Cong. Rec.*, 46 Cong., 1 sess., pp. 1051, 1191, 1262, 1745-55; 2 sess., p. 4446; New York *Tribune*, June 3, 4, 6, 1879; Russ, "Disfranchisement," pp. 229-232; Oberholtzer, *History*, IV, 48-51.
37. *Cong. Rec.*, 46 Cong., 2 sess., pp. 117-118, 727-736, 484-481, 3438-39; New York *World*, January 24, 1880; Cox and Northrup, *Cox*, pp. 243-246.
38. *Cong. Rec.*, 45 Cong., 3 sess., pp. 832, 1417, 1860.
39. *Ibid.*, pp. 365, 1237-39, 1534-44, 1951-81; New York *World*, February 19, 1879; Carroll D. Wright, *The History and Growth of the United States Census* (Washington, 1900), pp. 56-69 (hereafter cited as Wright, *Census*).
40. *Cong. Rec.*, 46 Cong., 1 sess., pp. 742, 1133-36, 1158-61.
41. *Ibid.*, 2 sess., pp. 27, 319, 4199-4204; letter to T. F. Bayard from Cox, Washington, April 5, 6, 1880: in the Bayard Papers, LC.
42. *Cong. Rec.*, 45 Cong., 3 sess., App., pp. 68-71.
43. *Ibid.*, 46 Cong., 2 sess., pp. 1938, 2533.
44. *Ibid.*, 45 Cong., 3 sess., pp. 1287-89, 1509, App., pp. 280-283.
45. New York *World*, June 19, 21, 25, 1880; Alexander, *Political History*, III, 411, 418-427, 447-459; Nevins, *Hewitt*, pp. 434-437; *The Nation*, July 1, 1880.
46. Robert G. Caldwell, *James A. Garfield* (New York, 1939), pp. 300-303; *Cong. Rec.*, 46 Cong., 2 sess., p. 1708.
47. Josephson, *Politicos, 1865-1896*, pp. 287-289.
48. Letter to William T. Sherman from Cox, New York, September 12, 1880: in possession of Parke-Bernet Galleries, New York, on January 15, 1950.
49. Letter to Cox from W. S. Hancock, Governor's Island, N. Y., July 3, 28, 1880: in the Cox Papers, U of C.
50. Ford, *Adams Letters*, p. 324.
51. New York *World*, October 11, 13, 22, 1880; Cox, *Three Decades*, p. 673.

52. Josephson, *Politicos, 1865-1896*, p. 300; Alexander, *Political History*, III, 462-463; New York *World*, November 3, 5, 1880.

53. Letters to Cox from W. S. Hancock, Governor's Island, December 4, 1880: in the Cox Papers, U of C; and from J. A. Garfield, Washington, December 6, 1880: Ms letter in possession of John Heise, Syracuse, N. Y.

54. Cox and Northrup, *Cox*, pp. 114, 126; *Cong. Rec.*, 46 Cong., 3 sess., pp. 790, 833; 47 Cong., 1 sess., pp. 238, 299.

55. *Ibid.*, 46 Cong., 3 sess., App., pp. 177-179.

56. Letter to Cox from B. F. Peixotto, Lyons, France, August 18, 1880: in the Cox Papers, Brown.

57. *Cong. Rec.*, 47 Cong., 1 sess., App., pp. 651-658, 165, 645, 569, 4692, 5106, 6711.

58. New York *World*, April 4, 1882.

59. Letter to C. Schurz from Cox, Washington, January 29, 1882: in the Carl Schurz Papers, LC.

60. Letter to Philip Cowen from Emma Lazarus, New York, September 30, 1882: in the Lazarus Papers, NYPL.

61. *Cong. Rec.*, 47 Cong., 1 sess., p. 5106.

62. *Ibid.*, 46 Cong., 3 sess., App., pp. 147-151.

63. *Ibid.*, 47 Cong., 1 sess., pp. 3668-71, 2574-76.

64. *Ibid.*, pp. 3575-85.

65. *Ibid.*, pp. 3581-85, 3668; Ida M. Tarbell, *The Tariff in Our Times* (New York, 1911), p. 101; Edward Stanwood, *American Tariff Controversies in the Nineteenth Century* (Boston, 1903), pp. 202-206.

66. *Cong. Rec.*, 47 Cong., 2 sess., pp. 1811, 1921, 1996, 2168, 2591.

67. Letter to Cox from A. S. Hewitt, New York, January 29, February 9, 15, 23, 25, 1883: in the Cooper-Hewitt Papers, Cooper Union Lib.

68. *Cong. Rec.*, 47 Cong., 2 sess., pp. 2665, 2725; letter to W. C. Ford from Cox, Washington, February 14, 1883: in the Cox Papers, NYPL; James A. Barnes, *John G. Carlisle* (New York, 1931), p. 57; New York *Tribune*, January 17, 1883; Tarbell, *The Tariff in Our Times*, pp. 118-137; Stanwood, *American Tariff Controversies in the Nineteenth Century*, pp. 209-220.

69. *Cong. Rec.*, 47 Cong., 2 sess., p. 3737; Ford, *Adams Letters*, p. 348. H. C. Thomas, *Return of the Democratic Party to Power in 1884* (New York, 1919), p. 117.

70. Letter to Cox from A. S. Hewitt, New York, August 23, 1882: in the Cooper-Hewitt Papers, Cooper Union Lib.

71. *House Report* No. 1827, 47 Cong., 2 sess.

72. Letter to D. A. Wells from Cox, Washington, December 28 [1882]: in the David Wells Papers, NYPL.

73. *Cong. Rec.*, 47 Cong., 2 sess., pp. 929-34, 1074-77, 1124.

74. Letter to W. C. Ford from Cox, Washington, January 5, 1883: in the Cox Papers, NYPL.

75. *Cong. Rec.*, 47 Cong., 1 sess., pp. 164, 1311-13, 2264-75; New York *Tribune*, February 13, 1882; letter to Cox from Hancock, Governor's Island, May 29, 1882: in the Cox Papers, U of C.

76. *Cong. Rec.*, 47 Cong., 2 sess., pp. 20-21; *Harper's Weekly*, January 6, 1883.

77. Letter to Carl Schurz from Cox, Washington, May 21, 1882: in the Schurz Papers, LC; letter to Cox from Grover Cleveland, Buffalo, November 19, 1882: Ms letter in possession of J. Heise, Syracuse, N. Y.

78. Ford, *Adams Letters*, p. 343.

Chapter VIII

WORLD TRAVELER, DIPLOMAT, AND WRITER

1. Interview of the author with Mrs. James A. Bailey of Zanesville, O., who lived for a time during her girlhood in the home of her aunt, Mrs. S. S. Cox.

2. S. S. Cox, *A Buckeye Abroad* (New York, 1852), pp. 12-13.

3. *Ibid.*, pp. 25, 29-38, 40-41, 51-55.

4. *Ibid.*, pp. 77-79, 81-83, 105, 123-126, 170, 181-182.

5. *Ibid.*, pp. 186, 190, 194-208, 214-218, 265-273, 275-279.

6. *Ibid.*, pp. 329-345, 347, 366, 393-395, 403, 434-444.

7. S. S. Cox, *A Search for Winter Sunbeams* (New York, 1869), pp. 23, 26, 41-45.

8. *Ibid.*, pp. 67-71, 118-123, 215-217, 247-250, 259-261, 293-298, 362, 406-410.

9. S. S. Cox, *Arctic Sunbeams* (New York, 1882), pp. 24-41, 49-63, 81-83, 100-112, 132.

10. *Ibid.*, pp. 188-192, 204-207, 223-225.

11. *Ibid.*, pp. 225, 231, 234, 266-267, 271, 284.

12. *Ibid.*, pp. 289-292, 313-317, 326-327.

13. *Ibid.*, pp. 334-336.

14. Letter to the author from Gilbert Grosvenor, December 9, 1954; S. S. Cox, *Orient Sunbeams* (New York, 1882), pp. 1, 4, 6-7.

15. Cox, *Orient Sunbeams*, pp. 23-27, 45-50, 107-118, 133-146, 155, 174, 176, 183-185.

16. *Ibid.*, pp. 242, 259, 291-292, 299, 314, 316-320, 342.

17. *Ibid.*, pp. 362-366, 378, 387, 399, 406.

18. S. S. Cox, *Diversions of a Diplomat in Turkey* (New York, 1887), pp. 2-4 (hereafter cited as Cox, *Diversions*).

19. *Ibid.*, pp. 5-6; Cox and Northrup, *Cox*, p. 134.

20. Cox, *Diversions*, pp. 633-634, 660-661.

21. *Ibid.*, pp. 12-23.

22. *Ibid.*, pp. 36-42, 60, 64; letters to Grover Cleveland from Cox, Constantinople, June 19, August 18, 1885: in the Cleveland Papers, LC; Nevins, *Hewitt*, pp. 450-451.

23. Cox, *Diversions*, pp. 70-71; letters to Daniel Lamont from Cox, Constantinople, October 20, 27, 1885; letters to G. Cleveland from Cox, Constantinople, October 6, 1885, January 1, 1886: in the Cleveland Papers, LC.

24. Cox, *Diversions*, pp. 7-9, 291-303, 379; letter to G. Cleveland from Cox, October 6, 1885; letter to D. Lamont from Cox, Constantinople, October 20, 1885: in the Cleveland Papers, LC.

25. Letters to Dept. of State from Cox, Constantinople, Dispatch No. 35, October 23, 1885; No. 116, January 30, 1886; No. 123, February 2, 1886; No. 125, February 6, 1886; letters to Cox from Secretary of State, Washington, Dispatch No. 49, November 28, 1885; No. 72, January 18, 1886; No. 82, February 5, 1886; No. 105, March 22, 1886: in the Dept. of State Papers, U. S. National Archives.

25. Letter to G. Cleveland from Cox, Constantinople, January 1, 1886: in the Cleveland Papers, LC.

26. Letter to G. Cleveland from Cox, Constantinople, January 1, 1886: in the Cleveland Papers, LC.

27. Letters to Dept. of State from Cox, Constantinople, Dispatch No. 26, October 13, 1885; No. 59, November 20, 1885; No. 67, November, 1885; No. 151, April 13, 1886; letters to Cox from State Dept., Washington, Dispatch No. 36, October 28, 1885; No. 60, December 29, 1885; No. 122, May 6, 1886: in the Dept. of State Papers, U. S. National Archives.

28. Letter to G. Cleveland from Cox, New York, October 22, 1886: in the Cleveland Papers, LC; Cox, *Diversions*, p. 677; L. J. Gordon, *American Relations with Turkey, 1830-1930* (Philadelphia, 1932), pp. 208, 333.

29. Cox, *Diversions*, pp. 154-174.

30. Letters to G. Cleveland from Cox, Constantinople, October 6, 1885, January 1, 1886: in the Cleveland Papers, LC.

31. New York *Herald*, October 1, 1885; Cox, *Diversions*, pp. 636-641, 660-665.

32. Cox, *Diversions*, pp. 152-153, 654-656, 678, 683-684; letter to W. H. French from Cox, Athens, Greece, March 23, 1886: in the Cox Papers, NYPL.

33. Letter to Fred Hall from Mark Twain, Elmira, N. Y., July 9, 1887,

quoted in Samuel S. Webster, *Mark Twain, Business Man* (Boston, 1946), p. 384.

34. Cox, *A Buckeye Abroad*, pp. 5-6.
35. Cox, *Arctic Sunbeams*, p. 11.
36. *Ibid.*, p. 28.
37. Cox, *Orient Sunbeams*, p. 11.
38. Cox, *Diversions*, p. 388.
39. Cox, *Arctic Sunbeams*, p. 9.
40. *Ibid.*, p. 187.
41. Cox, *A Buckeye Abroad*, p. 6.
42. Cox, *Why We Laugh*, p. 110, 127, 347, 388.
43. Cox, *Free Land and Free Trade* (New York, 1880), p. 1.
44. *Ibid.*, pp. 78, 112-113.
45. *Ibid.*, pp. 124-126.
46. S. S. Cox, *Three Decades of Federal Legislation* (Providence, 1885), p. 6.
47. *Ibid.*, p. 677.
48. *Ibid.*, p. 5.
49. *Ibid.*, pp. 63, 73-80, 81-83, 124-125, 223-229, 240, 250-257, 344-374, 622-697.
50. Copy of contract beween Cox and publishers James A. Reid and Robert A. Reid, dated January 21, 1885: in the Cox Papers, Brown.
51. Letter to Cox from J. H. Jewett, Providence, July 9, 1887: in the Cox Papers, Brown.
52. James F. Rhodes, "Review of Cox's *Three Decades*," *Magazine of Western History*, III (1886), 356-366; William A. Dunning, *Reconstruction, Political and Economic, 1865-1877* (New York, 1907), pp. 407-408.

Chapter IX

DEMOCRATS IN THE SADDLE AT LAST, 1883-1889

1. New York *Tribune*, January 17, March 30, April 3, 1883.
2. Letter to Cox from A. S. Hewitt, New York, February 23, 1883; letter to Hewitt from Cox, New York, April 7, 1883: in the Cooper-Hewitt Papers, Cooper Union Lib.
3. Letters to Cox from W. D. Hill, Defiance, O., February 4, 1883; from H. S. Greenleaf, Rochester, N. Y., February 6, 1883; and from C. H. Bauer, New York, March 31, 1883: in the Cox Papers, Brown.
4. Letter to W. C. Ford from Cox, Washington, March 24, 1883: in the Cox Papers, NYPL.
5. Letters to Cox from T. A. Hendricks, Indianapolis, July 22, 1883; and

from W. S. Holman, Aurora, Ind., September 15, 1883: in the Cox Papers, Brown.

6. Letters to Cox from John G. Carlisle, Covington, Ky., August 11, 1883; White Sulphur Springs, W. Va., August 28, 1883: in the Cox Papers, Brown.

7. Letter to Cox from A. S. Hewitt, Bohemia, August 30, 1883: in the Cox Papers, Brown.

8. Letters to Cox from I. R. Hill, Newark, O., September 17, 1883; and from W. D. Hill, VanWert, O., September 18, 1883: in the Cox Papers, Brown.

9. Letters to W. C. Ford from Cox, Washington, October 6, 14, New York, October 29, 30, November 8, 1883: in the Cox Papers, NYPL; Eugene H. Roseboom and Francis P. Weisenberger, *A History of Ohio* (New York, 1934), p. 351.

10. Letters to Cox from A. G. Comstock, Detroit, November 3, 1883; and from H. S. Greenleaf, Rochester, N. Y., October 26, 1883: in the Cox Papers, Brown.

11. Letters to W. C. Ford from Cox, Washington 24, 1883, January 27, 1884: in the Cox Papers, NYPL; Barnes, *John G. Carlisle*, pp. 67-71.

12. Letters to Cox from W. W. Warden, Washington, January 6, 1884; from W. R. Myers, Indianapolis, December 29, 1883; and from W. J. McCord, Washington, May 28, 1884: in the Cox Papers, Brown.

13. Letter to Cox from Amos J. Cummings, New York, December 7, 1883: in the Cox Papers, Brown.

14. Message to J. G. Carlisle from Cox, headed "House of Representatives," n. d.: in the Cox Papers, Brown.

15. Letters to W. C. Ford from Cox, Washington, March 21, April 13, 1884: in the Cox Papers, NYPL; *Cong. Rec.*, 48 Cong., 1 sess., App., pp. 3-11.

16. *Cong. Rec.*, 48 Cong., 1 sess., pp. 231, 240, App., pp. 403-410; letter to W. C. Ford from Cox, Washington, April 18, 1884: in the Cox Papers, NYPL; Nevins, *Hewitt*, pp. 425-429; Taussig, *Tariff*, p. 251; Tarbell, *The Tariff in Our Times*, pp. 137-139.

17. Letters to Cox from L. J. Velasquez, New York, January 15, 1884; from J. J. Ferris, New York, May 9, 1884: in the Cox Papers, Brown; letters to W. C. Ford from Cox, Washington, January 27, 1884, April 27, 28, May 3, June 18, July 17, 1884: in the Cox Papers, NYPL; New York *Tribune*, February 18, 1884; *Cong. Rec.*, 48 Cong., 1 sess., pp. 98, 270, 394, 3431-34, 3450.

18. *Cong. Rec.*, 48 Cong., 1 sess., pp. 409, 1503, 5308-14; Cox and Northrup, *Cox*, p. 183; Allan Nevins, *Grover Cleveland* (New York, 1933), pp. 217-220.

19. *Cong. Rec.*, 48 Cong., 2 sess., pp. 403, 665, 833, 1917; letter to Cox

from W. S. Hancock, Governor's Island, N. Y., June 2, 1884: in the Cox Papers, U of C.

20. *Cong. Rec.*, 48 Cong., 1 sess., pp. 98, 391, 551-554, 1420; Cox, *Three Decades*, pp. 597-601; Russ, *Disfranchisement*, pp. 232-233.

21. *Cong. Rec.*, 48 Cong., 1 sess., pp. 3936, 4174, 98, 1412, 1473, 1360; letters to W. C. Ford from Cox, Washington, January 25, July 17, 1884: in the Cox Papers, NYPL; New York *Tribune*, January 25, 1884.

22. Oberholtzer, *History*, IV, 405-406.

23. *Cong. Rec.*, 48 Cong., 1 sess., pp. 5338-41.

24. *Ibid.*, 2 sess., p. 814; 1 sess., pp. 97, 98, 279; 2 sess., pp. 57, 82, 707.

25. Ford, *Adams Letters*, p. 358.

26. Letter to W. C. Ford from Cox, Washington, June 11, 1884: in the Cox Papers, NYPL.

27. Alexander, *Political History*, II, 6-13; McGurrin, *Cockran*, pp. 53-54.

28. New York *World*, June 8, 1884; New York *Tribune*, July 12, 1884; Oberholtzer, *History*, IV, 178-179, 199-200.

29. Alexander, *Political History*, IV, 32-35.

30. *Cong. Rec.*, 48 Cong., 1 sess., App., 403-410; Cox, *Three Decades*, p. 125.

31. H. C. Thomas, *Return of the Democratic Party to Power* (New York, 1919), pp. 136-137, 200, 204, 215, 220-226 (hereafter cited as Thomas, *Return to Power*); New York *World*, June 15, September 30, 1884.

32. Letter to Cox from W. C. Ford, New York, October 7, 1884: in the Cox Papers, Brown.

33. Ford, *Adams Letters*, p. 360.

34. Alexander, *Political History*, IV, 37.

35. Letters to Cox from W. P. Bell, Washington, September 1, 1884; and from W. H. Ludlow, Oakdale, N. Y., October 1, 1884.

36. New York *Herald*, October 5, 7, 1884.

37. Letter to Cox from W. H. Ludlow, Oakdale, N. Y., October 1, 1884: in the Cox Papers, Brown.

38. Letter to Cox from W. C. Ford, New York, October 7, 1884: in the Cox Papers, Brown; letter to Ford from Cox, New York, October 8, 1884: in the Cox Papers, NYPL.

39. Letter to W. C. Ford from Cox, October 13, 19, 1884: in the Cox Papers NYPL; New York *Herald*, October 16, 23, 28, November 1, 1884.

40. Weitenkampf, *Kaleidoscope*, p. 16.

41. Letter to G. Cleveland from Cox, New York, November 8, 1884: in the Cleveland Papers, LC; Thomas, *Return to Power*, pp. 227-228.

42. Letters to Cox from Edwin C. Grosvenor, Constantinople, November 11, 1884; and from W. C. Boggs, New York, November 28, 1884: in the Cox Papers, Brown.

43. New York *Tribune*, November 5, 19, 1884; letter to W. C. Ford from Cox, New York, November 11, 1884: in the Cox Papers, NYPL.

44. Letter to Cox from W. S. Hancock, Governor's Island, November 25, 1884: in the Cox Papers, U of C; Nevins, *Grover Cleveland*, p. 108.

45. Cox and Northrup, *Cox*, p. 127; Cox, *Three Decades*, pp. 683-684.

46. Letter to R. Atkinson from Cox, Washington, February 27, 1885: in the Cox Papers, New York Hist. Soc. Lib.

47. Letter to W. F. Vilas from Cox, Washington, May 28, 1885: in the Vilas Papers, Wisconsin State Hist. Soc. Lib.

48. Letters to G. Cleveland from Cox, Washington, December 6, 15, 25, 1884; January 11, February 24, March 24, 1885; letters to D. S. Lamont from Cox, Washington, March 25, April 11, 1885: in the Cleveland Papers, LC.

49. Letters to Cox from E. J. Anderson, San Francisco, April 3, May 12, 1885; from Thomas Ewing, Jr., April 8, 1885; from W. F. Meany, Washington, April 16, 1885; from J. J. Ferris, New York April 16, 1885; from W. S. Yard, New York, April 20, 1885; from E. Cowles, Cleveland, April 2, 1885; and from J. M. Ball, New York, April 26, 1885: in the Cox Papers, Brown.

50. Nevins, *Grover Cleveland*, pp. 203-204.

51. Letter to Cox from G. Jones, New York, February 5, 1885: in the Cox Papers, Brown.

52. New York *Tribune*, March 5, 1885; *Cong. Rec.*, 48 Cong., 2 sess., p. 2503.

53. Cox, *Three Decades*, pp. 124-125, 680, 684.

54. Letter to G. Cleveland from Cox, Zanesville, O., April 3, 1885: in the Cleveland Papers, LC; *Zanesville Courier*, April 3, 6, 1885.

55. Cox and Northrup, *Cox*, pp. 128-129.

56. Letters to Cox from S. B. Sturgis, Brooklyn, April 1, 1885; from L. H. Anderson, Trenton, N. J., April 16, 1885; and from J. Hood, Baltimore, May 31, 1885: in the Cox Papers, Brown.

57. Letter to Cox from J. T. Agnew, March 30, April 30, 1885: in the Cox Papers, Brown.

58. Letter to Cox from E. K. Apgar, Albany, June 4, 1885: in the Cox Papers, Brown.

59. New York *Tribune*, May 26, June 10, 1885.

60. Letter to W. F. Vilas from Cox, at sea, June 28, 1885: in the Vilas Papers, Wisconsin State Hist. Soc. Lib.

61. Letter to D. S. Lamont from Cox, Constantinople, October 20, 1885: in the Cleveland Papers, LC.

62. Letters to G. Cleveland from Cox, Constantinople, October 6, 1885, January 1, 1886: in the Cleveland Papers, LC.

63. Letter to Cox from W. H. English, Indianapolis, March 7, 1886: in the English Papers, Indiana State Hist. Soc. Lib.
64. Letter to Cox from J. N. Barnes, Washington, December 16, 1885: in the Cox Papers, Brown.
65. Letter to Cox from Joseph E. Brown, Washington, December 31, 1885: in the Cox Papers, Brown.
66. New York *World*, April 11, May 8, 1886; New York *Tribune*, January 31, April 11, May 13, 1886; Nevins, *Grover Cleveland*, p. 294.
67. Information gathered by the author during an interview with Mrs. James Bailey, niece of Mrs. Cox, who remembers the servants.
68. Letter to G. Cleveland from Cox, New York, October 22, 1886: in the Cleveland Papers, LC.
69. Dept. of State, Dispatches to the Field, dispatch to Cox from the Secretary, October 29, 1886: in the U. S. National Archives; New York *World*, October 26, 1886.
70. Barrows, *William M. Evarts*, pp. 469-472.
71. Alexander, *Political History*, p. 149.
72. Cox and Northrup, *Cox*, p. 149; Nevins, *Hewitt*, pp. 460-464.
73. Wheeler, *Sixty Years*, pp. 165, 175.
74. Nevins, *Hewitt*, p. 468; Alexander, *Political History*, IV, 77-82; Myers, *The History of Tammany Hall*, p. 270; letter to G. Cleveland from Cox, New York, October 29, 1886: in the Cleveland Papers, LC.
75. Letters to G. Cleveland from Cox, New York, November 24, 1886; Washington, December 6, 1886: in the Cleveland Papers, LC; Richardson, *Messages*, VIII, 504-511; *Cong. Rec.*, 48 Cong., 2 sess., p. 14.
76. *Cong. Rec.*, 48 Cong., 2 sess., pp. 150-154.
77. *Ibid.*, pp. 288, 580; New York *Herald*, January 3, 1887.
78. Letter to D. S. Lamont from Cox, Washington, February 18, 1887; letters to G. Cleveland from Cox, Washington, March 17, April 25, New York, May 10, July 5, August 23, November 6, 14, 1887: in the Cleveland Papers, LC.
79. Letter to Cox from Mark Twain, Elmira, N. Y., July 9, 1887: copy of this Ms letter is in the author's possession; letter to J. W. Green from Cox, New York, November 22, 1887: in the Cox Papers, NYPL; New York *Tribune*, November 23, 1887; letter to Fred Hall from Mark Twain, Elmira, N. Y., quoted in S. C. Webster, *Mark Twain, Businessman*, p. 384.
80. *Cong. Rec.*, 50 Cong., 1 sess., pp. 8, 279-280, 519, 1225, 4990, 5972, 6319, 9657.
81. Letter to G. Cleveland from Cox, Washington, March 9, 1888: in the Cleveland Papers, LC.
82. *Cong. Rec.*, 50 Cong., 1 sess., pp. 6695, 7434, 7997, 8258.

83. Wheeler, *Sixty Years*, pp. 181-191

84. Richardson, *Messages*, VIII, 580-591; Nevins, *Grover Cleveland*, pp. 379-381.

85. Letter to G. Cleveland from Cox, March 9, 1888: in the Cleveland Papers, LC.

86. Letter to A. S. Hewitt from Cox, Washington, May 22, 1888: in the Cooper-Hewitt Papers, Cooper Union Lib.

87. *Cong. Rec.*, 50 Cong., 1 sess., p. 4336.

88. *Ibid.*, pp. 4330-46.

89. Letter to David A. Wells from Cox, Washington, June 2, 1888: in the Wells Papers, NYPL.

90. *Cong. Rec.*, 50 Cong., 1 sess., pp. 4862, 4917, 5028, 5992, 6434.

91. Nevins, *Grover Cleveland*, pp. 432-433; Josephson, *The Politicos, 1865-1896*, p. 403.

92. *Cong. Rec.*, 50 Cong., 1 sess., pp. 2779, 6158-72, App., pp. 288-302; letter to A. R. Spofford from Cox, Washington, January 16, 1888: in the Spofford Papers, LC.

93. Letters to T. F. Bayard from Cox, Washington, August 6, 9, 1888; letter to Cox from Bayard, August 7, 1888: in the Bayard Papers, LC; Wright, *Census*, pp. 68-76.

94. *Cong. Rec.*, 50 Cong., 1 sess., pp. 3291-97.

95. *Ibid.*, pp. 223, 635, 1759, 2192, 2278-80, 4494, 6193, 6538.

96. Letter to G. Cleveland from Cox, Washington, June 15, 1888: in the Cleveland Papers, LC.

97. Letter to Cox from R. W. Raymond (Hewitt's secretary), New York, September, 24, 1888: in the Cooper-Hewitt Papers, Cooper Union Lib.

98. Alexander, *Political History*, IV, 111-113; Nevins, *Grover Cleveland*, p. 427.

99. Letter to D. S. Lamont from Cox, Washington, October 17, 1888: in the Cleveland Papers, LC.

100. Letter to G. Cleveland from Cox, New York, November 5, 1888: in the Cleveland Papers, LC.

101. Alexander, *Political History*, IV, 129-131; Nevins, *Grover Cleveland*, pp. 437-439; Cox and Northrup, *Cox*, p. 150.

102. *Cong. Rec.*, 50 Cong., 2 sess., pp. 406-408, 1108, 1301.

103. *Ibid.*, pp. 83-84, 261, 1938.

104. *Ibid.*, p. 513; letter to Cox from Mark Twain, Hartford, Conn., February 8, 1888: copy in the author's possession; Arthur M. Schlesinger, *The Rise of the City, 1877-1898* (New York, 1933), pp. 251-255.

105. *Cong. Rec.*, 50 Cong., 2 sess., pp. 800-812, 939, 1908-39; Cox and Northrup, *Cox*, p. 150, 218.

106. S. S. Cox, *Address . . . on the Parliamentary Heroes of Ireland* (New York, 1889).

107. Quoted in Cox and Northrup, *Cox*, p. 151.

108. Quoted in *ibid.*, pp. 220-222; New York *Tribune*, July 5, 1889.

109. Cox and Northrup, *Cox*, pp. 151-152; New York *Times*, September 11, 1889; Philadelphia *Public Ledger*, September 11, 1889; *Harper's Weekly*, September 21, 1889.

110. Letter to Mrs. S. S. Cox from John Hay, Washington, Saturday, n. d. 1889: in the Cox Papers, Brown.

111. Cox and Northrup, *Cox*, pp. 265-6; New York *Times*, September 11, 14, 1889; New York *Tribune*, September 11, 14, 1889.

112. New York *Times*, September 11, 1889; *Harper's Weekly*, September 21, 1889.

113. New York *Tribune*, October 11, 1889; *Cong. Rec.*, 51 Cong., 1 sess., pp. 3588-90.

114. Certified copy of Cox's will obtained from the clerk, Surrogate's Court, County of New York; letter to the author from William H. Timbers (formerly of law firm, Cummings & Lockwood), Stamford, Conn., November 10, 1949.

115. *Cong. Rec.*, 51 Cong., 1 sess., pp. 3558-87; *Memorial Addresses on the Life and Character of Samuel Sullivan Cox* (Washington, 1890), *passim*.

116. Zanesville *Signal*, January 2, 1891; Zanesville *Times-Recorder*, July 9, 1891; New York *Tribune*, July 5, 1891; Cox and Northrup, *Cox*, pp. 197-199.

117. Letter to the author from Henry Vail (superintendent, Greenwood Cemetery), January 24, 1950.

118. Cox and Northrup, *Cox*, pp. 210-216.

Chapter X

SUNDOWN

1. David S. Barry, *Forty Years in Washington* (Boston, 1924), pp. 85-86; Carl Schurz, *The Reminiscences of Carl Schurz* (3 vols.; New York, 1906-1909), II, 215.

2. Ford, *Adams Letters*, p .231.

3. *Cong. Rec.*, 45 Cong., 2 sess., p. 279.

4. Josiah B. Grinnell, *Men and Events of Forty Years* (Boston, 1891), p. 142.

5. New York *Times*, September 11, 1889.

6. Samuel W. McCall, *The Life of Thomas B. Reed* (Boston, 1914), p. 116.

7. *Memorial Addresses on . . . Cox*, pp. 261-262.

PUBLISHED WRITINGS AND SPEECHES OF
SAMUEL S. COX

Address on the Parliamentary Heroes of Ireland. New York: Metropolitan Job Print Co., 1889.

Arctic Sunbeams: or from Broadway to the Bosphorus by Way of the North Cape. New York: G. P. Putnam's Sons, 1882.

Before the New Granadian Claims Commission. Washington: Towers, Printers, 1861.

A Buckeye Abroad: or Wanderings in Europe and the Orient. New York: G. P. Putnam's Sons, 1852.

Decay of Integrity. New York: no publisher, 1884.

De Jure and De Facto. New York: National Printing Co., 1877.

Diversions of a Diplomat in Turkey. New York: C. L. Webster Publishing Co., 1887.

Eight Years in Congress, from 1857 to 1865. New York: D. Appleton Co., 1865.

Eulogy of Hon. Stephen A. Douglas. Washington: The Smithsonian Institution, 1862.

Free Land and Free Trade. New York: G. P. Putnam's Sons, 1880.

Grant or Greeley? New York: S. W. Green, 1872.

The Isle of the Princes: or the Pleasures of Prinkipo. New York: G. P. Putnam's Sons, 1888.

Memorial Eulogies Delivered in the House of Representatives, 1861-1883. Washington: Government Printing Office, 1883.

The Monmouth Centennial. Freehold, N. J.: no publisher, 1878.

"The Moravian and Gnattenhutten Massacre," *Knickerbocker Magazine*, XVII (1846), 204-214.

Orient Sunbeams. New York: D. Appleton Co., 1882.

Puritanism in Politics. New York: Van Evire, Herton & Co., 1863.

The Scholar as the True Progressive and Conservative. Columbus: Scott and Bascom, 1852.

Search For Winter Sunbeams. New York: D. Appleton Co., 1869.

Speech at a Meeting of the Hickory Club. New York: no publisher, 1872.

Speech Before Johnson Union Club of the 6th Congressional District of New York. New York: no publisher, 1866.

Three Decades of Federal Legislation. Providence: J. A. and R. A. Reid, 1885.

United States and Colombian Commission: Claim of Pacific Steamship Company. Washington: Gibson, 1868.

Why We Laugh. New York: Harper & Brothers, 1876.

MANUSCRIPTS

Thomas F. Bayard, Library of Congress.

James Buchanan, Library of Congress; Historical Society of Pennsylvania Library.

Salmon P. Chase, Historical Society of Pennsylvania Library.

Grover Cleveland, Library of Congress.

James M. Comly, Ohio Historical Society Library.

Peter Cooper—Abram S. Hewitt, Cooper Union Library.

Samuel S. Cox, Brown University Library; Library of Congress; New York Historical Society Library; New York Public Library; Ohio Historical Society Library; University of Chicago Library.

John J. Crittenden, Library of Congress.

Stephen A. Douglas, University of Chicago Library.

William H. English, Indiana State Historical Society Library.

Charles S. Fairchild, New York Historical Society Library.

Worthington C. Ford, New York Public Library.

Parke Godwin—William C. Bryant, New York Public Library.

Andrew Johnson, Library of Congress.

Charles Lannan, Library of Congress.

Emma Lazarus, New York Public Library.

Robert T. Lincoln Collection of Abraham Lincoln, Library of Congress.

Madigan Collection of George B. McClellan—S. S. Cox Correspondence, New York Public Library.

Daniel Manning, Library of Congress.

Manton Marble, Library of Congress.

Hugh McCulloch, Library of Congress.

John G. Nicolay, Library of Congress.

Franklin Pierce, Library of Congress.

Bibliography

Carl Schurz, Library of Congress.

Ainsworth R. Spofford, Library of Congress.

Samuel J. Tilden, New York Public Library.

William F. Vilas, Wisconsin State Historical Society Library.

Elihu B. Washburne, Library of Congress.

David A. Wells, New York Public Library.

Records of the Athenian Literary Society, Ohio University Library.

Minutes of Board of Deacons of Market Street Baptist Church, Zanesville, Ohio.

Minutes of Board of Trustees of Market Street Baptist Church, Zanesville, Ohio.

GOVERNMENT DOCUMENTS

Manual of the Corporation of the City of New York. New York: E. Jones and Company, 1869.

New York State Legislative Manual. Albany: Weed, Parsons, 1870.

Ohio, General Assembly. *Executive Documents.* Columbus: no publisher, 1861.

Ohio, General Assembly. *House of Representatives Journal.* Columbus: no publisher, 1858-65.

Ohio, General Assembly. *Senate Journal.* Columbus: no publisher, 1858-1865.

Ohio, *Laws of Ohio.* Cincinnati: Robert Clarke and Company, 1865.

U. S. *Congressional Directory.* 41st to 50th Congress. Washington: Government Printing Office, 1869-1889.

U. S. *Congressional Globe.* 35th to 38th Congress and 41st and 42nd Congress. Washington: Rives, 1857-1873.

U. S. *Congressional Record.* 42nd to 50th Congress. Washington: Government Printing Office, 1873-1889.

U. S. Congress. *House Report* No. 648. 36th Congress, 1st sess., Washington: Rives: 1860.

———. *House Report* No. 31. 40th Congress, 3d sess. Washington: Government Printing Office, 1871.

———. *House Report* No. 31. 41st Congress, 2d sess. Washington: Government Printing Office, 1870.

————. *House Report* No. 22. 42d Congress, 2d sess. Washington: Government Printing Office, 1872.

————. *House Report* No. 1121, 46th Congress, 2d sess. Washington: Government Printing Office, 1880.

————. *House Report* No. 1827. 47th Congress, 2d sess. Washington: Government Printing Office, 1883.

————. *House Report* No. 1499. 50th Congress, 1st sess. Washington: Government Printing Office, 1889.

————. *House Report* No. 2810. 50th Congress, 1st sess. Washington: Government Printing Office, 1889.

————. *Memorial Addresses on the Life and Character of Samuel Sullivan Cox.* 51st Congress, 1st sess. Washington: Government Printing Office, 1890.

————. *Ninth Census of the United States.* Washington: Government Printing Office, 1870.

U. S. *The War of the Rebellion: A Compilation of the Official Records of the Union and Confederate Armies.* 4 series, 128 volumes; Washington: Government Printing Office, 1880-1901.

The United States Coast Guard: Its History, Vessels and Doctrine. Washington: Government Printing Office, n. d.

PARTY DOCUMENTS

Official Proceedings of the National Democratic Convention. Chicago: Democratic National Committee, 1864.

Official Proceedings of the National Democratic Convention. New York: Democratic National Committee, 1868.

Official Proceedings of the National Democratic Convention. Baltimore: Democratic National Committee, 1872.

Official Proceedings of the Democratic National Convention. St. Louis: Democratic National Committee, 1876.

NEWSPAPERS AND PERIODICALS

Chillicothe, *Scioto Gazette.*
Cincinnati, *Commercial.*
          Enquirer.

Bibliography

Columbus, *The Crisis.*
         Dispatch.
         Ohio State Journal.
         Ohio Statesman.
New York, *Herald.*
         Times.
         Tribune.
         World.
Zanesville, *City Times.*
         Signal.
         Times-Recorder.
Appleton's Annual Cyclopedia, 1873-1878.
Harper's Weekly, 1861-1889.
The Nation, 1875-1889.

BOOKS

Alexander, DeAlva S. *The History and Procedure of the House of Representatives.* Boston: Houghton Mifflin, Co., 1916.
————. *A Political History of the State of New York.* 3 vols. New York: Henry Holt and Co., Inc., 1906-1923.

Barnes, James A. *John G. Carlisle.* New York: Dodd Mead & Co., 1931.

Barrows, Chester L. *William M. Evarts.* Chapel Hill: University of North Carolina Press, 1941.

Barry, David S. *Forty Years in Washington.* Boston: Little Brown & Co., 1924.

Beale, Howard K. *The Critical Year.* New York: Harcourt Brace and Co., 1930.

Benton, Elbert J. *The Movement for Peace Without a Victory during the Civil War.* " Western Reserve Historical Collections," No. 99, Cleveland: Western Reserve Historical Society, 1918.

Blaine, James G. *Twenty Years of Congress, From Lincoln to Garfield.* 2 vols. Norwich, Conn.: Henry Bill Publishing Co., 1884-1886.

Boutwell, George S. *Reminiscences of Sixty Years of Public Affairs.* 2 vols. New York: McClure, Phillips, 1902.

Bowers, Claude G. *The Tragic Era.* Cambridge: Houghton Mifflin Co., 1929.

Breen, Matthew J. *Thirty Years of New York Politics.* New York: Polhemus Co., 1899.

Buckingham, James, compiler. *The Ancestors of Ebenezer Buckingham and His Descendents.* Chicago: Donnelley and Co., 1892.

Bryce, James. *The American Commonwealth.* 2 vols. New York: Macmillan Company, 1891.

Caldwell, Robert G. *James A. Garfield.* New York: Dodd Mead & Co., 1939.

Chapman, F. W. *The Buckingham Family.* Hartford, Connecticut: no publisher, 1872.

Clark, Champ. *My Quarter Century of American Politics.* 2 vols. New York: Harper & Brothers, 1920.

Coleman, Charles H. *The Election of 1868.* "Columbia University Studies in History, Economics and Public Law," No. 392, New York: Columbia University Press, 1933.

Cox, Jacob D. *Military Reminiscences of the Civil War.* 2 vols. Columbus: Follett Publishing Co., 1900.

Cox, William Van Z. and Northrup, Milton H. *Life of Samuel Sullivan Cox.* Syracuse, N. Y.: M. H. Northrup, 1899.

Craven, Avery. *The Coming of the Civil War.* New York: Charles Scribner's Sons, 1942.

Cullom, Shelby M. *Fifty Years of Public Service.* Chicago: McClurg & Co., 1911.

Dennett, Tyler. *John Hay.* New York: Dodd Mead & Co., 1934.

DuBois, William E. B. *Black Reconstruction.* New York: Harcourt Brace and Co., 1935.

Dunning, William A. *Reconstruction, Political and Economic.* New York: Harper & Brothers, 1907.

Eckenrode, H. J. *Rutherford B. Hayes.* New York: Dodd Mead & Co., 1930.

Ewing, Thomas, Jr. *Samuel S. Cox.* New York (no publisher), 1891.

Fielde, A. M. *A Political Primer of New York State and City.* New York: Macmillan Company, 1897.

Flick, Alexander. *Samuel Jones Tilden.* New York: Dodd Mead & Co., 1939.

Ford, Worthington C., ed. *Letters of Henry Adams, 1858-1891.* Boston: Houghton Mifflin Company, 1930.

Forney, John W. *Anecdotes of Public Men.* 2 vols. New York: Harper & Brothers, 1873-1881.

Gabriel, Ralph H. *The Course of American Democratic Thought.* New York: Ronald Press, 1940.

General Catalog of the Ohio University, 1804-1857. Athens, Ohio: VanVorhes, 1857.

Gordon, L. J. *American Relations with Turkey, 1830-1930.* Philadelphia: University of Pennsylvania Press, 1932.

Gosnell, Harold F. *Boss Platt and His New York Machine.* Chicago: University of Chicago Press, 1924.

Gray, Wood. *The Hidden Civil War.* New York: Viking Press, 1942.

Grinnell, Josiah B. *Men and Events of Forty Years.* Boston: Lothrop, 1891.

Harrington, Fred H. *Fighting Politician: Major General N. P. Banks.* Philadelphia, 1948.

Haworth, Paul L. *The Hayes-Tilden Disputed Election of 1876.* Cleveland: Burrows, 1906.

Hooper, Osman C. *The Crisis and the Man.* "Ohio State University Contributions in Journalism," No. 5, Columbus: Ohio State University Press, 1929.

————. *Samuel Sullivan Cox.* Columbus: Ohio State University Press, 1929.

Hubbart, Henry C. *The Older Middle West, 1840-1880.* New York, Appleton-Century, 1936.

Johnson, Allen. *Stephen A. Douglas.* New York: Macmillan Co., 1908.

Josephson, Matthew. *The Politicos, 1865-1896.* New York: Harcourt Brace and Co., 1938.

Kenworthy, Leonard S. *The Tall Sycamore of the Wabash, Daniel Wolsey Voorhees.* Boston: Humphries Co., 1939.

Kirkland, Edward C. *The Peacemakers of 1864.* New York: Macmillan Company, 1927.

Kohlmeier, Albert L. *The Old Northwest as the Keystone of the Arch of the American Federal Union.* Bloomington, Indiana: Principia Press, 1939.

Lynch, Denis T. *The Wild Seventies.* New York: Appleton-Century, 1941.

McCall, Samuel W. *The Life of Thomas B. Reed.* Boston: Houghton Mifflin Co., 1914.

McGurrin, James. *Bourke Cockran, A Free Lance in American Politics.* New York: Charles Scribner's Sons, 1948.

McPherson, Edward. *A Handbook of Politics* (annually for years from 1868 to 1894). Washington: Philp and Solomon, 1868-1894.

————. *The Political History of the United States During the Rebellion.* Washington: Philp and Solomon, 1865.

————. *The Political History of the United States During the Period of Reconstruction.* Washington: Philp and Solomon, 1871.

Merrill, Horace S. *Bourbon Democracy of the Middle West, 1865-1896.* Baton Rouge: Louisiana State University Press, 1953.

Milton, George F. *The Eve of Conflict.* Boston: Houghton Mifflin Co., 1934.

Moore, Frank. *Rebellion Record.* 3 vols. New York: Macmillan Co., 1861-63.

Muzzey, David S. *James G. Blaine.* New York: Dodd Mead & Co., 1934.

Myers, Gustavus. *History of Tammany Hall.* New York: Boni Liveright, 1916.

Nevins, Allan. *Abram S. Hewitt, with Some Account of Peter Cooper.* New York: Harper & Brothers, 1935.

————. *Grover Cleveland.* New York: Dodd Mead & Co., 1933.

————. *Ordeal of the Union.* 2 vols. New York: Charles Scribner's Sons, 1947.

Nichols, Roy F. *The Disruption of American Democracy.* New York: Macmillan Co., 1948.

Nicolay, John G. and Hay, John. *Abraham Lincoln: A History.* 10 vols. New York: Century Co., 1890.

————. *Complete Works of Abraham Lincoln.* 2 vols. New York: Tandy, 1905.

Oberholtzer, Ellis P. *A History of the United States since the Civil War.* 5 vols. New York: Macmillan Co., 1917-1930.

Pleasants, Samuel A. *Fernando Wood of New York.* "Columbia

University Studies in History, Economics and Public Law,"
No. 536. New York: Columbia University Press, 1948.

Poore, Ben Perley. *Reminiscences of Sixty Years of the National Metropolis.* 2 vols. Philadelphia: Hubbard, 1886.

Porter, George H. *Ohio Politics During the Civil War Period.* " Columbia University Studies in History, Economics and Public Law," No. 40. New York: Columbia University Press, 1911.

Randall, James G. *The Civil War and Reconstruction.* Boston: D. C. Heath and Co., 1937.

Reid, Whitelaw. *Ohio in the Civil War.* 2 vols. Cincinnati: Moore, 1868.

Rhees, W. J. *The Smithsonian Institution: Documents Relative to Its Origin and History, 1835-1899.* 2 vols. Washington: Government Printing Office, 1901.

Rhodes, James F. *History of the United States from the Compromise of 1850.* 9 vols. New York: Macmillan Company, 1906.

Richardson, James D., compiler. *Messages and Papers of the Presidents.* 10 vols. Washington: Government Printing Office, 1898.

Rippy, J. Fred. *America and the Strife of Europe.* Chicago: University of Chicago Press, 1938.

Roseboom, Eugene H. *The Civil War Era.* Vol. IV, *History of the State of Ohio,* ed., Carl Wittke. Columbus: Ohio State Archaeological and Historical Society, 1944.

Roseboom, Eugene H. and Weisburger, Francis P. *A History of Ohio.* New York: Prentice-Hall Inc., 1934.

Sandburg, Carl. *Abraham Lincoln: The War Years.* 4 vols. New York: Harcourt Brace & Co., 1936.

Schlesinger, Arthur M. *The Rise of the City, 1877-1898.* New York: Macmillan Company, 1933.

Schuckers, John W. *Life and Public Services of Salmon Portland Chase.* New York: Macmillan, 1874.

Schneider, Norris F. *Y Bridge City.* Cleveland: World Publishing Co., 1950.

Schurz, Carl. *The Reminiscences of Carl Schurz.* 3 vols. New York: McClure, 1906-9.

Scrugham, Mary. *The Peaceable Americans,* 1860-1861. " Columbia

University Studies in History, Economics and Public Law," No. 96. New York: Columbia University Press, 1925.

Seitz, Don C. *The Dreadful Decade*. Indianapolis: Bobbs-Merrill, 1926.

Sherman, John. *Recollections of Forty Years*. 2 vols. New York: Werner, 1895.

Smith, Theodore C. *The Life and Letters of James Abram Garfield*. 2 vols. New Haven: Yale University Press, 1925.

Stampp, Kenneth M. *And the War Came: The North and the Secession Crisis, 1860-1861*. Baton Rouge: Louisiana State University Press, 1950.

Stanwood, Edward. *American Tariff Controversies of the Nineteenth Century*. Boston: Houghton Mifflin Co., 1903.

Tarbell, Ida M. *The Tariff in Our Times*. New York: Macmillan Co., 1911.

Taussig, Frederick W. *The Tariff History of the United States*. New York: G. P. Putnam's Sons, 1923.

Taylor, William A. *Ohio Statesmen and Annals of Progress, 1788-1900*. Columbus, no publisher, 1899.

Thomas, H. C. *Return of the Democratic Party to Power*. New York: Columbia University Press, 1919.

Trimble, Bruce R. *Chief Justice Waite*. Princeton: Princeton University Press, 1938

Turner, Frederick J. *The United States, 1830-1850*, ed., Avery Craven. New York: Henry Holt, 1935.

Utter, William T. *The Frontier State, 1805-1825*. Columbus: Ohio State Archaeological and Historical Society, 1942.

Vallandigham, Clement L. *Speeches, Arguments, Addresses and Letters of Clement L. Vallandigham*. New York: no publisher, 1864.

Vallandigham, James L. *A Life of Clement L. Vallandigham*. Baltimore: Turnbull, 1872.

Webster, Samuel C. *Mark Twain, Business Man*. Boston: Little Brown & Co., 1946.

Werner, M. R. *Tammany Hall*. New York: Doubleday Doran, 1928.

Weisenberger, Francis P. *The Passing of the Frontier, 1825-1850*.

Vol. III in series, *History of the State of Ohio*, ed., Carl Wittke. Columbus: Ohio State Archaeological and Historical Society, 1941.

Weitenkampf, Frank. *Manhattan Kaleidoscope.* New York: Charles Scribner's Sons, 1947.

Wheeler, Everett P. *Sixty Years of American Life.* New York: E. P. Dutton & Co., Inc., 1917.

Williams, Charles R. *Diary and Letters of Rutherford Birchard Hayes.* 5 vols. Columbus: Ohio State Archaeological and Historical Society, 1922-26.

Woodward, C. Van. *Reunion and Reaction.* Boston: Little Brown & Co., 1951.

Wright, Carroll D. *History and Growth of the United States Census.* Washington: Government Printing Office, 1900.

PERIODICAL ARTICLES

Beale, Howard K. " On Rewriting Reconstruction History," *American Historical Review*, XLV (1940), 807-827.

————. " The Tariff and Reconstruction," *American Historical Review*, XXXV (1930), 276-294.

Birdsall, D. C. " McClellan and the Peace Party," *Century Magazine*, XIX (1890), 638-639.

Crenshaw, Ollinger. " The Speakership Contest of 1859-1860," *Mississippi Valley Historical Review*, XXIX (1942), 323-339.

Dorris, J. T. " Pardoning the Leaders of the Confederacy," *Mississippi Valley Historical Review*, XV (1928), 3-21.

DuBois, William E. B. " Reconstruction and Its Benefits," *American Historical Review*, XV (1910), 781-799.

Fesler, Mayo. " Secret Societies in the North During the Civil War," *Indiana Magazine of History*, XIV (1918), 183-186.

Gladden, Washington. " Samuel Galloway," *Ohio State Archaeological and Historical Society Publications*, IV (1890), 263-278.

Hesseltine, William B. " Economic Factors in the Abandonment of Reconstruction," *Mississippi Valley Historical Review*, XXII (1935), 191-210.

Northrup, Milton H. " A Grave Crisis in American History," *Century Magazine*, LXII (1901), 23-24.

Rhodes, James F. " Samuel S. Cox's ' Three Decades of Federal Legislation '," *Magazine of Western History*, III (1886), 356-366.

Simkins, Francis B. " New Viewpoints of Southern Reconstruction," *Journal of Southern History*, V (1939), 49-61.

Volwiler, A. T., ed. " Tariff Strategy and Propaganda, 1887-1888," *American Historical Review*, XXXVI (1930), 76-96.

Wilson, Charles R. " McClellan's Changing Views on the Peace Plank of 1864," *American Historical Review*, XXXVIII (1933), 498-505.

UNPUBLISHED MATERIAL

Bradford, David. " The Background and Formation of the Republican Party in Ohio, 1844-1861." Ph. D. dissertation, University of Chicago, 1947.

Gray, Wood. " The Peace Movement in the Old Northwest, 1860-1865." Ph. D. dissertation, University of Chicago, 1933.

Iles, Mayo B. " Samuel Sullivan Cox and His Opposition to the Lincoln Administration." Master's thesis, Ohio University, 1942.

Russ, William A., Jr. " Congressional Disfranchisement, 1866-1898." Ph. D. dissertation, University of Chicago, 1933.

Tingley, Ralph R. " American Cobden Clubs." Master's thesis, University of Chicago, 1947.

Wells, Edward S. " The Political Career of Samuel Sullivan Cox during the Ohio Phase." Master's thesis, Ohio State University, 1935.

INDEX

Manuscript edited by Esther Ellen Jacoby

Designed by S. R. Tenenbaum
Set in Garamond and Comstock type faces
Printed on Warren's Olde Style Antique Wove Paper
Bound in Columbia Mills Bayside Linen
Manufactured in the United States of America